Macroeconomics
for Business and Society

A Developed/Developing Country
Perspective on the "New Economy"

Macroeconomics
for Business and Society

A Developed/Developing Country
Perspective on the "New Economy"

F. Gerard Adams

Northeastern University, USA and
Sasin Graduate Institute of Business Administration, Thailand

World Scientific
New Jersey • London • Singapore • Hong Kong

9-5-02

Published by

World Scientific Publishing Co. Pte. Ltd.

P O Box 128, Farrer Road, Singapore 912805

USA office: Suite 1B, 1060 Main Street, River Edge, NJ 07661

UK office: 57 Shelton Street, Covent Garden, London WC2H 9HE

Library of Congress Cataloging-in-Publication Data
Adams, F. Gerard (Francis Gerard), 1929–
    Macroeconomics for business and society : a developed/developing country perspective
on the "new economy" / F. Gerard Adams.
        p. cm.
    Includes index.
    ISBN 9810243243 : alk. paper -- ISBN 9810243251 (pbk. : alk. paper)
    1. Macroeconomics. 2. Economic policy. 3. Economic development. I. Title.

HB172.5 .A325 2002
339--dc21   2001056894

British Library Cataloguing-in-Publication Data
A catalogue record for this book is available from the British Library.

Printed in Singapore by World Scientific Printers

Preface

Economics is an integral part of the business curriculum in mature countries and developing countries, alike. And, well it should be! The economy, the setting in which business firms operate, is a dominant factor influencing business performance. It affects decisions by investors, manufacturers, distributors, importers and exporters, etc. in all parts of the world. Often, it is the difference between growth and profitability, on one hand, and stagnation or failure, on the other. Yet, understanding what is going on in the local economy and "out there in the world" has become a particular challenge to managers in recent years as the world economy has undergone overwhelming changes:

In many dimensions, today's economic environment represents a "new economy:"

* New information technologies have created a knowledge-based economy where brain power is more important than muscle power. Networked computers are the basis for new systems of information and control being introduced by businesses worldwide. New technologies are producing rapid increases in productivity, creating a "second wind" of economic progress, even in the most advanced mature economies.
* The result has been a broad restructuring of the nature and location of production. Manufactures are being increasingly assembled in the developing nations, while the advanced developed countries are turning to high technology and high income services like computer programming and consulting, technology development, financial and insurance services, communications and entertainment.
* The global economy is far more interrelated than in the past. Barriers to international trade and finance have been greatly reduced. Trade flows have become the engine of growth in many developing countries. Capital flows have turned out to be a mixed blessing, providing finance for development

and increasing the volatility of world capital markets, perhaps even destabilizing them. A country's economic performance is increasingly influenced not only by the local economic environment and policy but also by external shocks through trade and capital flows.

* The relative rankings of the world's regions with respect to output, welfare and competitiveness are shifting drastically. While some of the mature industrial countries were showing signs of stagnation and rising unemployment, until the recent crisis, East Asia was undergoing a headlong rush to development. Huge consumer markets were created in areas that once offered households little more than chickens and coconuts. In the past decade, even the very poor countries have had a far better record of growth than at earlier periods. Most, but not all, of the transition economies of Eastern Europe are also showing signs of economic resurgence.

* Economic priorities are changing worldwide: from stability to growth, from planning to free markets, from state-owned enterprise to private businesses.

* Even economic theory has changed: the new theories of growth, international development and economic geography have greatly influenced economic thinking and policy prescription. On the other hand, most of the traditional elements of economic theory still apply even in the "new economy."

Macroeconomics is no longer just for economics specialists. A knowledge of the mechanisms that influence the economy's growth, income, employment, prices, interest rates and international trade is essential background for business and financial decision makers.

Macroeconomics is no longer simply for a domestic audience concerned with the ups and downs of the American economy. The focus of concern is shifting geographically outside the United States and toward the developing countries. With the emergence of rapidly growing economies in Asia — some of which have achieved high income status — and with renewed growth in many other parts of the world, business managers see opportunities in faraway places. The globalization of business calls for managers with perspectives over a world that stretches far beyond our national boundaries, from developed countries to developing ones. The growth spurt of the developed countries is a result of the "new economy" of IT networks and sophisticated high technology. Macroeconomics is no longer primarily concerned with the business cycle and fiscal and monetary stabilization policy. The macro course must encompass questions of growth and development, technical change and international economic linkages.

There is need, consequently, for a new perspective to macroeconomics. This book seeks to provide a new, more up-to-date, view relevant to the issues encountered by business in developed and developing countries. It is a challenge to deviate from the approach focused on the business cycle and stabilization policy of the typical macro course, to a more global, development and business-oriented perspective. We pose questions that prospective international business people ask and seek to provide answers that they will find useful.

Our primary concerns have been as follows:

* to recognize the significant changes in the world economic environment associated with the "new economy;"
* to cover questions of growth and development in the world economy, as well as the traditional issues of stabilization theory and policy;
* to view the issues from an international perspective: as seen in developing countries as well as in developed countries;
* to discuss the aspects of macroeconomics that are relevant to business, showing the linkages from the national economic situation to the variables directly influencing the performance of enterprises;
* to present the subject, insofar as it is possible, in realistic terms, recognizing the underlying theories and illustrating them with examples and case studies from contemporary policy-making and business practice; and
* to consider the implications of the economic setting for business strategy.

A central theme of this volume is the startling contrast between the growth and stabilization experience of the industrial world and of the developing countries of East Asia. This contrast in economic performance serves as a focus for discussions of growth and development. Economic stabilization plays an important role in both the developed and developing countries. The advent of financial crisis in East Asia and the impact of the "new economy" also inform our evaluation of policy for the advanced and the developing world. This analysis serves as a framework for appraising opportunities and risks from the perspective of business.

This volume was written initially to meet the needs of a business curriculum based on the programs sponsored by the Wharton and Kellogg business schools at the Sasin Graduate Institute of Business Administration of Chulalongkorn University in Bangkok. For this reason, many of the country examples cover East Asian experience. Draft versions have also been used in courses at other universities, for example, at the University of Pennsylvania and Northeastern University in the US and at the International University of Japan. The book is intended for a broad audience, domestically and internationally, one that includes mature business students, intermediate level undergraduates, and informed laypersons.

Contents

PART I

Macro for Developed and Developing Economies

This part introduces macroeconomics from the perspective of developed and developing economies. The common concerns of advanced and developing countries with growth and stabilization are considered. Do we need a "new" macroeconomics to deal with the "new" economy? We conclude that many new challenges confront policy makers and business managers in this new environment. But the fundamental framework of economic theory still serves. Next, we consider: "What is macroeconomics?" and "How does the macroeconomic environment — domestic and international — relate to the industry and the firm?" The objectives of policy makers are an important aspect of evaluating the economic environment since these aims are often contradictory and must be prioritized. Finally, we study measurement of economic performance, the quantitative dimensions of how the economy is operating. The important measures include the GDP and the national income and product accounts, the rate of inflation, financial statistics and interest rates, and import and export data and the balance of payments.

Chapter 1

Macroeconomics and the "New" Economy: A Developed and Developing Country View

This chapter introduces macroeconomics and the "new" economy. What is macroeconomics? How is macroeconomic perspective different in developed and developing countries? How is it changed by the advent of the "new" economy? What is the relationship between stabilization over the business cycle and growth? What is the distinction between growth and development? How does the macroeconomy relate to business decision-making?

Introduction

At the beginning of the 21st century, we are confronted with a paradigm shift in economic growth, the "new" economy. In the 1970 to 1995 years, we had become accustomed to the contrast between the headlong rush to development in East Asia and the laggard growth and employment of the mature economies of the United States, Japan and Europe. In the mid-1990s, the rapid expansion or "economic miracle" in East Asia turned into a "meltdown." The "tigers" became "sick cats." Europe and Japan were finding it difficult to shake off their extended stagnation. The United States, on the other hand, was in a spectacular growth spurt — the "new economy." Rapid technical change and globalization was spreading worldwide, to developed and developing countries alike. East Asia was again showing significant growth and there was hope that Europe and Japan would join the world economic recovery.

But conditions changed rapidly in 2000 and 2001. North America's industrial growth was fading and there were quickly indications that the stock market "bubble" would burst. The European economies were showing signs of slowing expansion and Japan was again mired in its extended recession. Optimism about the vast potentials of information technology (IT) was tempered by the realities of the business cycle. This record of economic change, which we consider in greater detail below, informs our introduction to macroeconomics.

We begin this chapter by describing the rapid fire changes that are sweeping across the world economy today. The term "the new economy" may mean different things to different observers. But certain ingredients are common to the new developments taking place in individual countries and in the relationships between them during the first decade of the new century.

This book looks at these developments from a macroeconomic perspective. In contrast to *microeconomics*, that is focused on the interaction of individual participants in the economy, *macroeconomics* views the economy as an aggregate. It is the study of the performance and operation of the economy as a whole: the nation's gross domestic product (GDP), consumption, saving and investment, employment and unemployment, price level, interest rates, imports and exports, exchange rate, capital flows, etc. The aggregate statistics of economic performance reflect the fundamental changes taking place in the world economy.

Traditionally, macroeconomic analysis was a concern of developed mature economies dealing with problems of recession and inflation: stabilization over the business cycle. Increasingly, macroeconomics has been refocused toward longer term equilibrium, and particularly, the questions of growth and development that originally appeared to be of importance primarily to developing economies. In turn, the developing countries have recognized that they must place greater emphasis on macroeconomic stability, since it affects their ability to compete and to attract capital inflows. All countries are increasingly linked by the global economy. Today, we know that the concern about questions of domestic and international stability and of growth is common, though perhaps in somewhat different ways, to developed economies and to developing countries. Macroeconomics has been integrated into the theoretical and policy models of industrial and developing economies alike. Our presentation of macroeconomics for developed and developing countries recognizes that modern macroeconomics draws on the traditions of business cycle stabilization, growth and development economics, the economics of technical change and information, and international trade and finance. We explain how these approaches are linked together, complementing rather than replacing one another.

Since macroeconomics deals with the economy as a whole, one might well ask how economic performance at the aggregate level is relevant to individual enterprises. Why is the study of macroeconomics a part of the business curriculum? As we outline in greater detail below, business enterprises operate in the setting of the economy. The market for products, supplies and the costs of raw materials and labor, interest rates and financing, and international competitiveness, all influence the performance of the business. Managers need not only react to current conditions, but to understand and, if possible, to forecast them. Business people must be "on top of" the economy, making forward-looking strategy in a precarious world. We conclude this chapter by showing the links between the macroeconomy and the business enterprise as a "cascade," from the national economy to the industry and the firm.

Case 1.1
Distinguishing Between Developed and Developing Countries

How do we distinguish between developed and developing countries? We may use the terms: *rich* and *poor*, *advanced* and *backward*, *high income* and *low income*, *industrial* and *agricultural*, etc. The literature is full of euphemisms, particularly for the lower income countries, for example, *emerging economies, countries on the way to development*. The point is not so much in the name as in the meaning.

Countries range across a broad spectrum of economic development. Map 1.1 provides a geographic perspective. A detailed, statistical discussion of these differences is presented in Chapter 2.

At the upper end are the high income countries, with per capita incomes ranging in the $10,000 to $30,000 range (dark colored on the map). These are countries with extensive infrastructure, a largely urban population, an

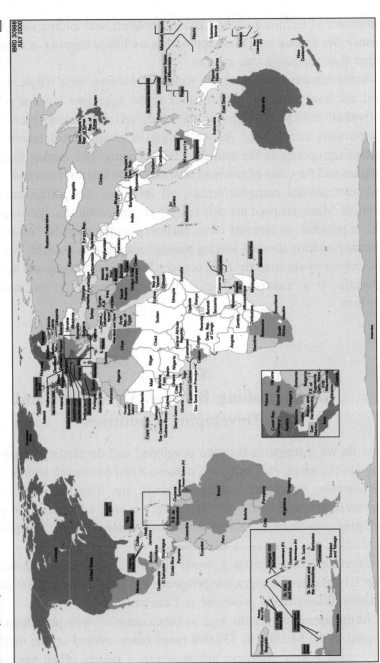

The World by Income

This map presents economies classified according to World Bank estimates of 1999 GNP per capita. Not shown on the map because of space constraints are French Polynesia (high income); American Samoa (upper middle income); Fiji, Kiribati, Samoa, and Tonga (lower middle income); and Tuvalu (no data).

Low $755 or less
Lower middle $756–2,995
Upper middle $2,996–9,265
High $9,266 or more
No data

IBRD 30988
JULY 2000

Map 1.1

educated labor force, and, frequently, competence in high tech and science. Many of these countries are mature, and consequently, are growing only slowly. Interestingly, where we once could call them industrial countries, increasingly the center of gravity of economic activity in these countries has shifted toward service activities. Included in this category are: in North America, the United States and Canada; in Europe, the countries of the European Union including the United Kingdom, France, Germany, and others; in the Pacific, Japan, Australia and New Zealand. These advanced countries work together in the Organization for Economic Cooperation and Development (OECD).

In the middle is a wide range of developing countries, in terms of the World Bank's terminology, "lower middle and upper middle income" countries. These countries have per capita incomes ranging from almost $10,000 at the upper end to less than $1000 per year at the bottom (medium colored). Some of these countries have been growing rapidly for many years, and are approaching maturity. Others are only at the beginning of the development process. East Asia is a good example of the great differences among these countries, ranging from Singapore, Korea and Taiwan at the top, to Indonesia and Vietnam at the lower end. Latin America belongs to this category, as do many countries of North Africa. Many of these countries still lack sufficient infrastructure and education. They are increasingly becoming industrialized, indeed, some of them are now centers of the world's labor-intensive mass production industries. These countries are also rapidly becoming urbanized, creating some of the world's largest cities, like Lagos, Bangkok and Mexico City. On the other hand, many of them still have large rural populations engaged in agriculture. In these countries, development is clearly a primary concern.

Finally, there are the very poor countries, with per capita incomes of less than $755 (light colored). These countries, for example in Sub-Saharan Africa, are still largely dependent on primitive subsistence agriculture. Many of then lack the infrastructure, education and stable political organizations necessary to begin the development process.

Often, we also refer to the *transition* economies. These are the countries of Eastern Europe and the former Soviet Union that have been in the process of transition from Soviet-style command economies to the free market.

(China is also a transition economy in this sense though it is often dealt with separately.) Many of these countries have substantial industry and had attained a middle income living standard. But many of them have found the transition process difficult and have seen substantial decline in income in the past decade.

In this text, we will distinguish between *developed* and *developing* countries and use these terms as consistently as possible. The *developed* economies comprise the advanced countries. The term *developing economies* will be used to refer to the others.

The Facts of Economic Growth, Development and the Business Cycle

The record of economic statistics over the past two decades illustrates the interplay between economic development and the business cycle.

Until very recently, economic growth in the developed world was relatively slow (Table 1.1). In the United States, during the period from 1980 to 1997, annual GDP growth was only 2.7%, about in line with the long term trend. Only in the late 1990s, was there an acceleration of growth to 4% per year or more. Today many economists are suggesting, perhaps with excessive optimism, that we are in a "new" economy that will grow more rapidly in the future. Europe and Japan also saw sluggish growth, with marked slowing in the 1990s. Allowing for the fact that population was increasing, growth rates of GDP per person averaged only 1 to 2% per year. Consequently, in many countries of the advanced world, living standards had been barely increasing, often not rapidly enough to offset social problems like urban poverty. There is hope now that in Europe the period of low growth and high unemployment, what has been termed "Eurosclerosis," is over and that increasing internationalization and rapid technical progress will advance these economies more rapidly in the 21st century.

In sharp contrast, the developing countries of East Asia had been in a headlong rush to economic development for several decades. Starting out as very poor countries in the 1960s, they have more than doubled per capita GDPs every ten years. Some of them — Singapore, Hong Kong, Taiwan and

Table 1.1   GDP Growth in Developed and Developing Countries (% per year).

	1980–90	1990–97	1998	1999 (Est.)	2000 (Est.)
Developed Economies					
US	2.9%	2.5%	4.3%	4.2%	4.9%
Germany	2.2%	3.1%	2.5%	1.3%	2.8%
UK	3.2%	1.9%	2.6%	2.1%	2.9%
France	2.4%	1.3%	3.2%	2.9%	3.5%
Japan	4.0%	1.4%	−2.5%	0.3%	1.9%
East Asian Economies					
South Korea	9.5%	7.2%	−6.7%	10.7%	8.2%
China	10.2%	11.9%	7.8%	7.1%	7.7%
Hong Kong	6.9%	5.3%	−5.1%	3.0%	7.8%
Malaysia	5.2%	8.7%	−7.4%	5.6%	6.5%
Thailand	7.6%	7.5%	−10.2%	4.2%	4.2%
Indonesia	6.1%	7.5%	−13.4%	0.2%	3.4%
Singapore	6.6%	8.5%	1.5%	4.9%	6.3%
Philippines	1.0%	3.3%	−0.5%	3.2%	4.1%
Rest of the World					
South Asia	5.7%	5.7%	5.6%	5.7%	5.9%
Latin America	1.8%	3.3%	0.9%	2.6%	5.9%
Middle East	0.4%	2.6%	−0.9%	2.6%	5.9%
Sub-Saharan Africa	1.8%	2.1%	2.2%	2.0%	2.5%

Source: WEFA Group, various publications.

Korea — are close to achieving advanced country status. Even huge countries like China and India are joining the "development ladder." Other parts of the developing world have not done as well as East Asia, however. Latin America, which looked just as promising as East Asia in the 1960s, has been hobbled by the debt crisis, resulting in a "lost decade" throughout the 1980s and has, in recent years, again been hit by contagion from the East Asian financial crisis. In Africa, there are still countries ravaged by wars and internal conflicts, where people are dirt poor and where little progress is being made. The so-called *transition economies* of the former Soviet Union and Eastern Europe have gone through a wrenching downward shift. Some, like Poland and the Czech Republic have made good progress, but others, like Russia and the Ukraine, are still trying to find their way.

In the 1970s and early 1980s, sharp recessions following the "oil shocks," buffeted the world economy, industrial and developing economies alike (Fig. 1.1). The ups and downs of year-to-year growth of GDP are a reminder that economists and policy makers have not learned fully to control the business cycle, after all. That particular events in the developing world, like the rise of petroleum prices, could so sharply affect the economic situation of advanced industrial countries is an example of the complex and increasingly close inter-relationships of the world economy. The late 1980s and early 1990s were a period of upsurge in many parts of the developing world, leading to the hope that many countries would sustain the process of rapid economic advancement. But, the 1997 crisis experience interrupted rapid growth in East Asia. Now, that the situation in East Asia has stabilized, there is hope the East Asian development process is back on track. Before one can make optimistic statements about a resumption of rapid growth — and we are inclined to be optimistic — one must know why the growth trend occurred and why it was interrupted. We discuss these developments in Chapter 5.

The inflationary experience of various parts of the world differs greatly (Fig. 1.2). In the industrial world, inflation was moderate except in the 1970s and early 1980s, a consequence of economic overheating and of the upsurge of oil prices. In the developing countries, inflation has been much higher. Today, even the hyperinflation countries in Latin America, have managed to slay their inflationary dragons. Price increase is once again at moderate rates in the industrial world and in many of developing countries.

In the United States, productivity gains attributed to the "new" economy are widely thought to be offsetting wage increases and therefore easing inflation. Nevertheless, the US Federal Reserve raised interest rates to ward off early signs of inflationary price increases and reduced interest rates again quickly when inflationary pressures faded during the 2001 recession. Central banks in other countries are ever watchful against a resurgence of inflation.

The expansion of trade, fostered by reductions in trade barriers under the World Trade Organization (WTO), has permitted readjustment of world production and exchange patterns (Fig. 1.3). The advanced countries vastly

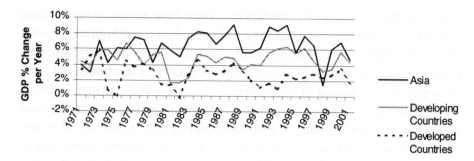

Fig. 1.1   Real GDP Growth (1971–2001).

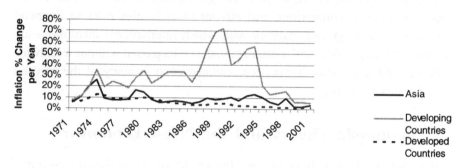

Fig. 1.2   Inflation Rate (1971–2001).

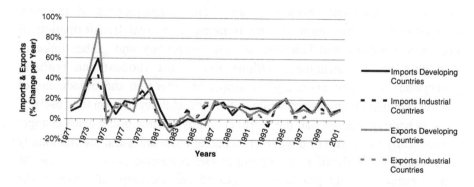

Fig. 1.3   Imports and Exports (1971–2001).

increased their imports of manufactures. They have turned their activities from mass production manufacturing to the production of high-tech capital goods, especially Japan, and high value-added services like entertainment, finance and communications, particularly the US. Trade has turned out to be an engine of growth in East Asia where much of the world's labor-intensive manufacturing is being concentrated. Trade and capital movements have linked the world's economies ever more tightly into a unified trade and financial system. On some occasions, in 1997, for example, these capital flows swung sharply from positive to negative causing financial panic, exchange devaluation, and depression in many parts of the developing world. Some people began to fear that globalization, much touted for its encouragement of competition and efficiency, embodies risks to financial market and exchange rate stability with which international institutions are not yet fully prepared to deal. Fortunately, the crisis passed without worldwide collapse, and rapid growth has been resumed even in many of the hard hit East Asian economies.

Economic Theory and the "New Economy?"

Today, we find ourselves on the threshold of a profound economic transformation to a "new economy" (Case 1.2). The data do not yet provide an unequivocal confirmation of the changes that are taking place. There is not yet agreement about the nature and consequences of the new developments. Some observers are thinking of a total transformation of economic structure and behavior as new technology and global linkages dominate present structures. Others have more modest and realistic perceptions: the "new economy" is simply an extension and broadening of the old. Though the precise meaning of the term still depends on the observer, there is wide consensus that the world economy is undergoing a sea change; domestically as a result of a wave of technical innovation and internationally as a result of globalization. Assuming proper economic policies, we can be quite optimistic about prospects for growth and development even in the face of temporary cyclical ups and downs.

We will conclude: "Yes, there is a 'new economy'." The "new economy" has important implications that we must take into account. But the reader should be warned that, the "new economy" does not replace the macroeconomic structures and behaviors that have existed until now and that will be considered in this book.

Case 1.2
A "New Economy?"

Beginning in the mid-1970s and until quite recently, the advanced economies of Europe and North America grew very slowly. After an initial post-war spurt, output per worker increased at little more than 1% per year. Consequently, living standards showed little improvement. This slow pattern of growth was widely attributed to maturity. The mature economies were losing competitiveness in mass production goods, now increasingly being supplied from East Asia. They were becoming service economies. Most economists thought that because services are labor-intensive, there was little opportunity for improving services productivity and/or for introducing new technology.

The events of the past five years have called this view into question. Suddenly, the US, seen by many as the most mature economy of them all, was growing rapidly. Between 1999 and 2000, GDP grew by almost 5% per year, and output per worker increased at a spectacular 3.5% annual rate. Moreover, this growth record was achieved with very low unemployment, close to 4%, and with modest rates of inflation, between 2 and 3%. Past experience would have suggested slower growth, more unemployment, and much greater inflation at this stage of the business cycle. Have traditional macroeconomic "laws" been suspended? Do we have a "new economy?"

The record of growth on which "new economy" theories are based is very brief. One powerful business recovery does not make a historical trend! Consequently, much effort is going into providing some microeconomic underpinnings to the idea that the observed changes in the economy are real and that they will persist. There has, of course, been a spectacular boom in the use of computers. But, in the mid-1980s, Nobel Laureate Robert Solow said pointedly: "You can see the computer everywhere, but in the productivity statistics." Since then, Solow has reconsidered this view, but the fact remains that computers have been around for some time and big productivity gains are very recent. Economic historians like Paul David point out that earlier technological revolutions, like the introduction of electric motors, took many years to produce significant gains in productivity. In that case, the argument goes, electric motors were a flexible power source replacing large centrally located steam engines or water wheels that were linked by belts to individual machines. The electric motor made a difference in overall productivity only after the entire factory had been restructured. Gains in productivity took many years to show up though introduction of the electrical motor was the harbinger of a long period of growth.

This time the new development consists of the information technology (IT) and network capabilities of modern computers. Today's "new economy" theorist hails not just the computer but the importance of the networking of computers, the internet and all of the related e-business possibilities. The computer has been around for some time, but the internet adds a new dimension. It enables computers to communicate with one another, worldwide, regardless of the programming system, regardless of the origin or destination. A central element of the notion of the "new economy" is that the interaction of many computers, tied together into a vast interconnected system, offers positive externalities and vastly increasing returns to scale. It is all about networks and interactions. To illustrate with a related case: one free standing fax machine is worth very little; many fax machines linked together are a way to vastly increase the speed of communication.

As the computer stretches beyond the individual office, it creates new ways to carry on business. Airline reservation networks are an example that has been operational for many years. Now, they are accessible to individual travelers. The internet has made possible connections between separate company systems. It has facilitated business to business (B2B) and business to consumer (B2C) transactions. Many aspects of business can be run electronically — orders, supplies, inventory management, transmission of information, electronic marketplaces and exchanges, etc. Businesses are setting up their entire supply chain systems on computer networks. As communication and order processing speed up, "just in time" inventories are becoming a reality. While in many cases physical delivery of product is still required, in some cases the entire transaction including the delivery of the book, CD, movie or financial security can be done over the web. For many products, exchanges are being developed in electronic space, allowing transactions to be carried out instantaneously. In 2000, approximately 40% of stock market transactions in the US are already being done on the internet. Banks have also used computers for a long time, but now individuals and businesses are beginning to do their banking on the web, so called e-banking. The point here is that the opportunities for cutting out human intervention and automating transactions on the internet are practically without limit.

Some of the advantages are measured and some are not. Production costs are being reduced and productivity improved as entire layers of clerical workers are eliminated. For many business dealings, the paperless office is arriving at long last The IT revolution is also producing cost reductions as a result of greater competition. Whereas previously, firms dealt with a small number of suppliers, web-based purchasing has opened the market to many more potential suppliers, often competing with lower costs. In some cases, like writing software for business systems, firms located as far away as India are able to compete. When these gains affect costs, they account for measurable increases in productivity. But there are also important gains that remain unmeasured. The increased availability of information — news, stock market quotes, search facilities, for example — represents an enormous gain. Similarly, web-based ordering of books, records and many other products offers convenience gains that are not measured in GDP.

The IT revolution also means that markets are being expanded on an international scale. The new technologies are likely to accelerate the process of globalization of business, finance and communications. The extension of enterprises across national boundaries will pay off in terms of reduced costs: better use of resources and greater scale of production These developments promise huge gains in the next few years.

It is clear from the above discussion that great changes are underway. In many cases, only the first phases of these developments have taken place. The revolution is much further along in some countries — in the US based on PCs, in Europe and Japan based on cellular phones — than in others where internet connectivity has only begun to spread. As the penetration of IT proceeds, there will be significant gains in productivity for many years to come.

What is Macroeconomics?

Instead of dealing with the behavior and interaction of the individual units making up the economy, as we do in microeconomics, macroeconomics looks at the economy as an aggregate. The analogy of the forest and the trees is appropriate. The aggregate economy considered in macroeconomics is like the forest, a macro issue — the total timber being grown, the total absorption of moisture, the total quantity of finished lumber being produced, etc. The behavior of the individual trees and the forces influencing their growth, competition for light and moisture in the forest environment, and the management of the lumbering operation are micro questions. Obviously, there are links between the micro and the macro aspects. The aggregate result depends in many ways on what is happening at the micro level. We will also describe how the individual business enterprise is linked to the aggregate economic setting in which it operates.

Macroeconomics is structural

Macroeconomic theory identifies the structural relations of the complex system that makes up the economy. What are the forces that influence demand, income, growth, inflation, interest rates, foreign trade, exchange rates etc. How do these factors interact? What causes boom or recession? What accounts for the very different growth and inflation performance of different parts of the world? As we note above, a "new" economy may involve broad changes in the performance of the economy without undermining its basic bahavioral and structural relations.

Macroeconomics is concerned with economic performance

How well is the aggregate economy achieving its objectives? In the US, one task of the Council of Economic Advisers (CEA) in its annual *Economic Report* is to evaluate how well the economy has performed and how it is likely to do in the future. Such evaluation and forecasting, in some countries "planning," are the job of central banks, ministries of finance, and economic planning agencies.

Macroeconomics is often quantitative

Economic policy managers are concerned with aggregate measures of GDP, employment and unemployment, inflation, imports and exports, trade balance, interest rates, exchange rate, etc. Their analyses will also make use of more detailed statistics on specific industries and regions, on prices of important products like fuel oil and electricity, on sectoral productivity, income and profits, on advance indicators of the business cycle like new orders and shipments, inventories, stock market indexes, money supply and credit extensions. The economic data from national accounts and other sources are the basis for building models of the economy to be used to forecast or to simulate the effects of alternative policies.

Macroeconomics is concerned with policy

What policies are required to achieve the economy's objectives? How can we achieve faster economic development? How can we stabilize the economy, avoiding inflation or balance of payments disequilibrium? What will be the impact of fiscal and monetary and exchange rate policies? What should be the responses of policy makers to threatened domestic or international crisis? Some economists are asking whether there is a need for new international economic policy institutions supplementing or replacing the International Monetary Fund or the World Bank.

Macroeconomics has important implications for business

Managers are concerned with how the economic outlook will affect their businesses. This is not so much a concern for the aggregate statistics of the economy, but rather for how these figures break down to reveal information on very detailed aspects of the economy relevant to a particular business.

What will happen to a particular market and the sales of specific products? What is the outlook for wages, for production workers or managers? How much will prices of petroleum go up? What are prospects for financial markets and interest rates? How will the balance of payments deficit affect the exchange rate and international competitiveness of the firm in particular markets? Note, for example, that the answer to the last question depends on information on the exchange rate between the dollar and specific currencies, and on costs in the US and costs in the competing country. The answers to questions like these have their basis in macroeconomics.

Macroeconomics for Developed Countries

For more than two generations, macroeconomics was primarily an economics for developed industrial countries, focused on issues of short-run economic stabilization and full employment. Keynesian macroeconomics, based on the theories of the great British economist John Maynard Keynes, was a response to the problems of the Great Depression. The primary concern was with unemployment. The means was fiscal policy: government spending to stimulate economic activity. The setting was primarily domestic, though international considerations were not disregarded altogether.

Over the years, particularly since the 1960s and 1970s, the scope of the macro approach in the industrial countries has widened. The vogue for demand stabilization using on public spending was already past in 1971, when Richard Nixon was quoted as saying, probably without fully realizing the implications: "We are all Keynesians now." This approach is still valid and operational in many settings, even today. (Note the emphasis on public works spending to stimulate the economy in Japan, and lately, in China.)

First, was the recognition that macro theory and policy were useful not only to deal with recession and unemployment, but also to deal with problems of inflation. During most of the post-war period, inflation has been as much, if not more, a concern for monetary and fiscal policy than recession.

During the 1960s, came the increased emphasis on monetary policy. "Money matters!" The extreme monetarist view that simple monetary rules can control the entire economy, waxed and then waned. In the early 1990s, the Federal Reserve recognized that stable relationships between money supply and GDP no longer held. Nevertheless, economists agree that aggregate monetary management is an important dimension of economic policy.

Beginning in the mid-1970s, the increasingly dismal productivity performance of the developed economies began to direct interest toward questions of long-term growth and productivity. In 1976, Nobel Laureate Lawrence Klein's presidential address to the American Economic Association was entitled: "The Supply Side." He spoke about the limits of the economy's capacity and about policies to improve the economy's productive potential. "Supply Side" policies, which were the backbone of President Reagan's politics and took the form of massive tax cuts, will be discussed in greater length below. Regardless of one's political position, there is no denying that greater emphasis on technical change, entrepreneurial effort and privatization have had large benefits toward international economic growth.

The 1980s and 1990s have seen a huge change in macroeconomic theory. Recognition that consumers, workers and business managers are likely to embody expectations about the future in their decision-making has altered the thinking of many economists. Many have returned to the fold of classical economics, arguing that, with flexible prices and wages, things will work out in the long run. Recessions and unemployment are temporary phenomena. In the long run, labor markets may tend toward equilibrium, to full employment. In this context, if consumers take expected public policies into account, only unanticipated macroeconomic policy actions are unlikely to make a real difference. In the eyes of some economists, these notions have undermined traditional Keynesian economics calling into question the effectiveness of macroeconomic policy as a stabilization instrument.

As a consequence, many macroeconomic theorists in the industrial world have swung from the Keynesian consensus in the direction of neoclassical ideas. Modern economic theorists, thus, lack consensus on the business cycle and focus on long-run adjustment. Politicians, business managers and economic policy makers in the industrial world are, of necessity, concerned with stabilization over a relatively short-run horizon to achieve and maintain full employment and to prevent inflation. In this context, the Keynesian approach still appears to have substantial validity.

More recently, economists are augmenting traditional ideas of the theory of production to recognize the contribution to technical change and growth of accumulation of knowledge (technology) and human capital (skills) and their interactions with the traditional production factors: labor and capital. These views, closely tied to the concept of the "new economy," are leading to very different perspectives on policies for economic development in industrial and developing countries alike.

Finally, in recent years, the internationalization of the economic system led to greater emphasis on international questions: the trade and capital flow linkages between countries, the exchange rate and the policies for international adjustment. Reconciling balance of payments equilibrium and/or exchange rate stability with the other stabilization or growth objectives is an important but difficult challenge, particularly as world trade and capital flows have become more open. Indeed, some economists are beginning to question whether a fully open international regime is consistent with stability.

Macroeconomics for Developing Countries

In the developing world, primary emphasis has always been on economic growth and development. But the thinking about paths toward development and the appropriate policy strategies have undergone considerable change since the early post-World War II years.

At that time, developing countries were generally very poor. Their economies were based largely on subsistence agriculture or the production of primary commodities. Their populations were increasing rapidly while health and education remained at abysmally low levels; a Malthusian vicious circle of rapid population growth was a barrier to development. They also faced well-nigh insurmountable problems with respect to shortages of saving and investment and technology.

Traditional development economics, consequently, had a very different focus from mainstream macroeconomics. The emphasis was on duality and structural disequilibrium. As we will see, developing economies have a dual nature, a large low income rural subsistence economy and a small higher income urban sector. The development process represents a gradual shift from one of these worlds to the other. While this process is going on, there will be substantial disequilibria, ones that are not easily surmounted by market forces.

With respect to development strategy, the early post-war view was that the world economic system favored the rich industrial countries producing manufactures to the detriment of less developed countries dependent on exporting primary commodities that sold at low prices and had little prospect for market expansion. This accounted for the so-called "dependence" of the developing countries. Third World development, it was widely thought, required stabilization of commodity prices, presumably at high levels, and contributions of aid, sometimes called *Overseas Development Assistance* (ODA), from the industrial world.

Early economic development thinkers shared the belief that industrialization would be the means for achieving rapid growth, in most cases, through a series of centrally coordinated industrial investments. Others emphasized shortfalls of saving, domestically and internationally, as the constraint on developing country growth.

These views led quite naturally in the developing countries to policies of import substitution. Shortages of foreign exchange represented a constraint on the purchase of foreign raw materials, fuels and capital goods. Substituting domestic products for imports was a way of saving foreign exchange and helping to develop domestic industries. But often, these industries were not able to stand on their own two feet. Newly created protected industries did not advance quickly to world technology levels. On the contrary, they tended to remain inefficient, requiring continued protection, and frequently, producing low quality products of static old fashioned design. Professor Anne Krueger, an eminent development economist says: "Little wonder that exports of manufactures and primary commodities grew slowly, if at all, in most countries pursuing import substitution policies."

Beginning in the 1960s, Japan and the four Asian "Tigers," Korea, Hong Kong, Taiwan and Singapore, began to achieve striking success with export-oriented development policy. It would be an over-simplification to say that these countries simply encouraged exports by providing favorable exchange rates and other fiscal incentives to locally based exporters and to foreign direct investors. Development strategies in East Asia were holistic; they included agricultural land reform, industrial policies favoring specific industries such as shipping and steel in Korea and chemicals in Taiwan, vast infrastructure projects, and emphasis on education and technology transfer. They involved a great deal of planning and interaction between the government and business. They included important macro policy considerations, dealing with fiscal, monetary and exchange rate policy.

While the overwhelming emphasis in the developing world is on growth, stabilization is a *sine qua non* for the success of the development effort. Again and again, failures to maintain price stability and exchange rate stability have driven developing countries into crisis and depression. The East Asian crisis in 1997–8 is only the latest example. The difficulty is that the continued growth of developing countries depends greatly on their continued international competitiveness and on foreign capital inflows. In these respects, developing countries operate with smaller margins than many advanced economies, and are frequently victims of their inability to achieve a stable non-inflationary growth path and to maintain, at the same time, a stable competitive exchange rate.

Stabilization and Growth

The distinction between *stabilization* and *growth* is at the heart of the difference between traditional macroeconomics in developed and developing countries.

We have already noted the importance of booms and recession in the industrial world and the consequent pressures for stabilization policy. Figure 1.4, which shows the movement of real GDP in the US from 1966 to 2000, illustrates our point. The line marked "Actual GDP," shows the actual values of GDP attained. The smooth line marked "Potential GDP" shows the long-term trend of the output potential of the economy. Actual GDP touches potential GDP only at the peaks of the business cycle. After the peak, the economy drops off into a trough at the bottom of the cycle, and then resumes its growth. The periods of recession, for example in 1973–5, in 1981–3, and in 1991–3, are the times when the economy is operating below its full capacity. Profit margins are squeezed. Production activity is depressed.

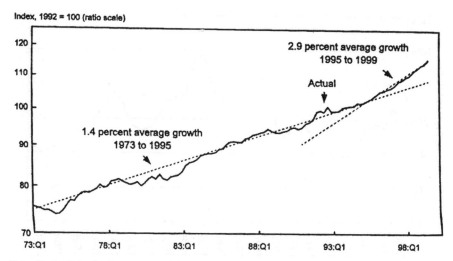

Index, 1992 = 100 (ratio scale)

Note: Productivity is the average of income- and product-side measures. Productivity for 1999 is inferred from the first three-quarters.

Sources: Department of Commerce (Bureau of Economic Analysis) and Department of Labor (Bureau of Labor Statistics).

Fig. 1.4   Trends of US Economic Growth.

There is unemployment, as shown in Fig. 1.5. At peak of the cycle, for example in 1973 and 1979, inflationary pressure builds. The two horns of inflation evident in Fig. 1.6 also reflect the additional pressure from the oil price shocks. The closer the economy is to full employment, i.e: the lower the unemployment rate, the greater the buildup of inflationary pressures. Excessive demand on the available capacity and labor supply leads to increases in wages and prices, rises in interest rates, and balance of payments disequilibrium. As the US economy has become more open to foreign trade, and as it has switched from traditional manufacturing to high-tech and services, some of the regularities of the business cycle may have eased. That accounts for the long period of growth without inflationary pressure that was observed in the 1990s. But it would be hazardous to assume that inflation no longer poses a risk as the economy approaches its full capacity rate of operation.

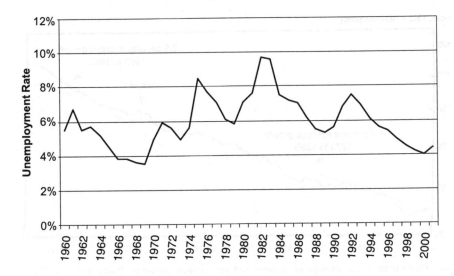

Fig. 1.5   US Unemployment Rate (% of labor force).

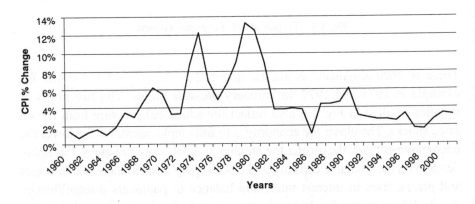

Fig. 1.6   US Inflation Rate (1960–2001).

There is much debate in the economics profession about the sources of business fluctuations. In some cases, the origin is clear, as we have noted above with regard to the recessions of 1974–5 and 1981–2, which were linked to the Middle Eastern "oil shocks." Other recessions reflect policy — for example, monetary tightening by the Federal Reserve in an effort to contain inflationary pressures in 1979–82 and in 1990–1. But business cycles may also have their origin in the natural dynamics of the economy. The business cycle is not so much a regularly spaced rhythm, as a tendency for booms to create an environment of inflation and excess inventories that leads to a downturn, and for recessions eventually to fade out as inventories are drawn down and as new industrial and housing capacity is needed. That process seems to have been one of the elements that lies behind the beginning of the East Asian crisis in 1997, unsustainable buildups of investment in real estate and industry, in Thailand and Korea, respectively, funded by unrealistic inflows of foreign capital.

The long boom in the US, from 1991 into 2000, is an example of what might be termed a positive supply shock. The gains in productivity that are part of the "new" economy, have made possible faster growth and a lower unemployment rate without inflation than had earlier been anticipated. At the time, some optimists proclaimed that the business cycle is dead. If so, more recent evidence suggests that it has revived.

Stabilization policy consists of the policy measures used to try to stimulate a weak economy, or alternatively, to slow an economy that has too much inflationary pressure. Public policy makers want to avoid the recession periods on one hand and the excessive demand pressure at the peak of the cycle on the other. The aim is to prevent the adverse economic and social consequences of recession. On the other hand, the peak of the expansion phase, poses dangers of inflation and balance of payments disequilibrium.

Once upon a time, we thought that the economy could be "fine tuned" to a non-inflationary full employment output path, but we have long since learned that macro policy control is difficult. Far from achieving stability, the most we can do is to moderate the cyclical extremes. Public authorities are sometimes said to be "leaning against the wind."

In a developed country, an example of such a policy was the Federal Reserve's effort to slow the US economy in 1994–5. Fearing a buildup of inflation — the economy was expanding briskly and prices of primary materials were rising sharply — the Fed raised short-term interest rates from 3% in February 1994 to 6% one year later. The aim was to produce a "soft landing." There were fears among some economists that tighter monetary policy actions would drive the country into recession, on the eve of the 1996 election. In retrospect, the Fed's strategy appears to have been successful. Higher interest rates slowed residential construction and consumer durable spending. The growth of GDP slowed and inflationary pressures eased. Fortunately, economic fundamentals like business fixed investment and exports remained strong and growth resumed in 1996 giving the economy a second wind. As we note above, in the late 1990s, economists were surprised by the vigor of the expansion and rapid productivity growth. The Fed, again fearful of inflation, began to intervene forcefully, raising interest rates to ease prospective inflationary pressures. Then, with the prospect of recession in 2001, the Fed cut interest rates vigorously.

The international linkages between countries are an important consideration. It is often said that when the US economy catches cold, neighboring Canada suffers from pneumonia. Developing countries are affected not only through the volume of their exports to the developed world but also through the prices they can get for their products which are often sensitive to market conditions.

The business cycle looks somewhat different in the developing world than in the industrial economies. In some countries, like the rapidly growing economies of Southeast Asia, cyclical fluctuations in the rate of growth are apparent, but until recently there have been few true recessions with negative GDP growth. In the upswing of the cycle, growth is very rapid; in the downswing, growth continues but at a somewhat slower pace. Would that developed countries only had "growth recessions!" In other developing countries, in Argentina or Nigeria, for example, cyclical swings are much wider. Many of these countries have the so-called stop-go economies, often as a result of unsteady economic policies.

Developing economies lack foreign exchange reserves, and thus, are greatly dependent on their foreign markets. Stable exports require competitively low wages, stable domestic prices, and undervalued exchange rates to make products competitive in world markets. Unfortunately, many developing countries have been unable to assure domestic economic stability. Budget deficits, rapidly increasing money supplies, and upward pressures on wages have frequently undermined domestic stability. Speculative excesses in real estate have threatened the solvency of the banking system and caused financial crises. Balance of payments deficits with vain attempts to maintain overvalued exchange rates have undermined international payments stability as well. Again and again, developing countries face foreign exchange crises, causing massive devaluation. The resulting financial crash leads to severe recession. Such crises call for IMF financial aid and for structural adjustment programs, with tight money and fiscal discipline and much industrial and financial system reorganization. As the cases of Latin America in the 1980s and East Asia in the 1990s demonstrate, the social burdens like unemployment are very high. The business cycle in these countries is, in large part, a financial and balance of payments crisis phenomenon.

Until the early 1990s, the striking contrast between growth in East Asia and in Latin America, that we have noted above, reflects, at least in part, differences between the two regions with respect to economic stabilization. The East Asian countries had been able to avoid runaway budget deficits. They had managed to prevent hyperinflation. Generally they had maintained stability in their balance of payments In contrast, Latin America's wild swings of inflation, and trade and capital flow disequilibrium resulted in the "lost decade" following the 1982 debt crisis. Macroeconomic stability represents a principal explanation for the contrast between continued progress in East Asia and financial failure and recession in Latin America during the 1980s. The East Asian crisis may be the exception that proves the rule.

Growth and Development

We turn next to the question of growth. A growing GDP, on a per capita basis, means improvement in welfare; the average citizen has increased purchasing power. In Fig. 1.1, growth is shown by the slope of the trend line marked "Potential GDP." This represents the long-run trend of production capacity.

As we discuss in Chapter 4, potential output depends on inputs, usually summarized in terms of the available capital and labor, and on gains in productivity. In the early post-war years, per capita growth in GDP in the US was at rates of 3% per year. This implies a doubling of purchasing power every 20 to 25 years.[1] Young couples could raise their children with the expectation that the kids would enjoy purchasing power about twice that of the parents. But in more recent years in the industrial countries (with the striking exception of the US in the late 1990s), the growth of productivity has slowed. With growth of per capita GDP of 1% per year, it would take 70 years for incomes to double! Not surprisingly, questions of how to accelerate growth gained priority in the industrial world.

In the developing countries of East Asia, growth of GDP was extremely rapid until 1997, between 7 and 9% annually. Even allowing for more rapid population growth than in the industrial world, this translates into per capita growth of GDP of some 5 to 7% per year. Living standards have doubled in as short a period as ten years in some countries.

It would be good if such a growth pattern applied in all the developing countries. Today, a record of successful development is considerably more widespread than we had once anticipated. Rapid growth is taking place in big countries like China and India and globalization is extending to many peripheral countries as well. However, some of the poor countries in Africa have had very low GDP growth rates, lower than the growth of their populations. This means that this region is sinking further into poverty, per capita income and living standards in these countries have actually been falling.

Questions of growth call for very different theoretical approaches than questions of stabilization. A concern with growth will lead us to the theory of the production function and the concept of total factor productivity (TFP). This has been an area of economics where extraordinary progress is currently being made. Economists are developing new theories that introduce development of human resources, and new technology, increasing returns and externalities, into the growth process. At this juncture, we must also consider the field of economic development theory which has been undergoing change in its own right.

---

[1]The rule of 70 is a convenient way to gauge the effect of a constant geometric growth rate. Suppose you expect GDP to grow at an annual percentage rate of 10%. Divide 70 by 10, to find that GDP will double in approximately seven years. On the other hand, suppose GDP grows only 2% annually, then 70 divided by 2 indicates that income will double only every 35 years.

Growth also calls for very different views of policy. The issues here are those of providing the appropriate infrastructure, public services, education and support for science and technology. Many countries have also sought to promote growth by providing incentives for investment and for the inflow of foreign capital and transfer of technology. Traditionally most countries, developed and developing alike, have assigned major responsibility for growth policy to the public sector. In recent years, however, the trend has been away from government intervention.

There is an ongoing debate among economists concerning the role of government in economic development. Some see East Asian development as the result of concerted government industrial policies while others give priority to the operation of the market unfettered by government intervention. While this argument remains unsettled, outward-oriented policy has gradually been adopted by nearly all developing countries seeking to advance their economic growth. Promotion of exports has included tax incentives to favor exporting industries and to attract foreign investment, favorable treatment under tariff regulations, undervalued exchange rates, creation of special economic zones, and provision for communication and transportation infrastructure. The promotion of more advanced technology has been a key ingredient of the development strategy of many countries.

Should a country have an industrial policy, promoting selected industries or technologies that are thought to be crucial to a modern economy? In most countries, this question goes without asking. The need for an industrial policy is simply accepted. The US has been a striking exception, in this regard, though increasingly other countries as well — the United Kingdom, Germany, New Zealand, Chile and Argentina — have been relying primarily on free market forces, minimizing government intervention. The "new economy" represents an interesting paradox in this regard. On one hand, entrepreneurial private enterprise is undoubtedly the backbone of the IT and dot.com firms that make up the "new economy." On the other hand, a look back in history will show that many of the technological antecedents of today's entrepreneurial developments were financed by government research grants.

In the developing world, government policy continues to play an important role in promoting industrial development. Students of economic development speak of the *developmental state* that collaborates with private sector interests in advancing economic development. Such a strategy appears to have been most successful in the dynamic economies of East Asia. But even in these countries, liberalization and privatization are today the watchwords of development policy.

The Global Environment

Globalization has become a way to describe the broadening of development across the world landscape and the linkages between businesses in the mature developed countries and in the newly developing ones. Globalization is responsible for much of the progress that has been made in recent generations. The developing countries have acquired capital and advanced technology, accelerating some of them along the road to high incomes, as we have noted above. The industrial countries have gained, as well, through low costs for manufactures and through profitable outlets for their capital.

Where, not so long ago, globalization was primarily about manufacturing in low cost countries, today it involves a far broader range of activities. Financial flows have become transnational, feeding money from the surplus countries, like Japan, to East Asia and Latin America. Foreign direct investment (FDI) is a welcome contributor since it represents funds that go into long-term investments, businesses and joint ventures, and is often accompanied by contributions of management skill and technology by the investing enterprise. Multinational corporations have made large contributions to technical and management skills in the host countries.

Globalization also encompasses service flows, trademark and technology licensing, entertainment, and most recently, software programming and data processing. Services provided by international financial institutions and insurance companies are sweeping the world, competing with, and often, supplying skills to domestic partners in many countries. International trademarks like Coca Cola or Mercedes have become global icons. Many disputes still surround the illegal distribution and use of intellectual property and copyrighted entertainment. (Rock music is a surprisingly important element.)

We are learning that globalization does not come without pain or risk. Globalization has meant huge adjustments. We have seen a "hollowing out" of manufacturing industries in the old industrial countries as their old high cost industries, the US *rustbelt*, for example, have not been able to compete successfully against their younger competitors in the developing world. In turn, we have seen the growth of environmentally damaging industries — steel plants emitting smoke, paper operations denuding the forests and polluting the water — in the developing countries.

Recent developments have raised a further concern, that the financial linkages between the world's economies might not be stable. We have long known that business cycle phenomena transcend national boundaries. The experience of financial crises in Latin America in 1982, in Mexico in 1994, and in East Asia in 1997 is causing some experts, in addition, to question the natural stability of financial flows in the world economy. Is it just a coincidence that some apparently healthy countries were drawn into financial crisis at about the same time? Or does this reflect an innate instability of international short-term capital flows? In recent years, an increasing part of the capital flow has been in the form of "hot money." This is short-term lending, often for six months at a time, offered at favorable interest rates. These funds have often gone into longer term investments on the assumption that they will always be rolled over. That represents a mismatch: short to long. When the creditors want to withdraw their funds, the debtors do not have the liquidity to meet their obligations. This was a familiar situation in East Asia, precipitating the 1997 crisis. There is not yet consensus on how to deal with this issue, nor is there yet agreement on the underlying causes. But it is clear that businesses operating in a global economic environment must be aware of the realities — the world economy remains a very uncertain setting in which modern business managers must find their way.

Nation, Industry and Firm

How does the picture look from the "trenches?" How does the aggregate economy impact on the typical business enterprise? The business firm operates in a broad business environment, the global economy, the nation and the industry. To see more clearly the position of the business in this wider setting, we turn to a "cascade" shown in Fig. 1.7.

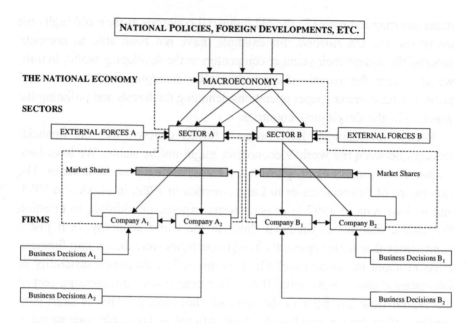

Fig. 1.7   Relations between the Nation, Industries and Firms: A Cascade.

On top of the diagram, we show the national economy. There are many such economies, linked together by trade and financial flows. We concentrate our detailed presentation here on only one country, but we recognize in Chapters 11 to 13 that the interactions between various countries are likely to be important.[2] Each national economy is affected by numerous external forces. We have noted the effects of other countries on the domestic economy through trade, export markets, the prices of imported materials, and flows of capital.

The national level is also the level where aggregate economic policy applies. For stabilization, government officials make fiscal, monetary and balance of payments policy. For growth, they provide investment incentives, export promotion, infrastructure development, educational programs, etc. Note that the

---

[2]We would complicate the figure greatly by showing many interacting countries at the top of our diagram, but that is, in fact, the way in which the real world operates.

objectives of policy are national objectives. In principle, government officials seek to advance the welfare of the nation as a whole, though, realistically in a political world, politicians may want to favor their constituencies or, in some unfortunate cases, may seek personal financial gain.

As we learned again from the effects of weather change, *el nino*, and more recently, *la nina*, accidents of nature — monsoons, droughts or earthquakes — and unfortunately, also wars affect national economic performance, often in serious ways.

The economic performance of each nation is best described by statistics like the GDP, the price indexes, interest rates and balance of payments data. These represent aggregates or averages for the nation as a whole, though in many cases regional breakdowns of this information may be available.

At the next level of the cascade (Fig. 1.7) are the sectors of the economy, traditionally called "industries" even though they include non-industrial activities like agriculture and services. We can break the economy down into many different sectors; sometimes as few as five or six but occasionally as many as the 435 industry breakdown of the US input-output table (only two sectors are shown here). The industries are linked to the national economic scene, in a satellite relationship. Note that the arrows point from the national economy to the industries. This is not meant to imply that there is no backward relation from industries to the nation. In fact, we show dashed arrows leading in the upward direction. But each industry, making up only a relatively small part of the total national economy, can take the national environment largely as given.

There is also an arrow from Industry A to Industry B, a two-headed arrow. This signifies that many industries are linked to other industries, as suppliers. Steel industry output is greatly influenced by the requirements for steel in the auto industry, for example, and in turn, the steel industry draws on the producers of iron ore, scrap and fuel, etc. The relationships between the national demands by industry and among the industries themselves are usually described by economists in terms of the "input-output" system. There are also external forces at the industry level. These include industry-specific regulations such as industrial policies, environmental restrictions, tariffs, foreign competition, technological change, etc.

The third level of the cascade represents the level of the firm. In Fig. 1.7, we show only two firms for each industry though there could obviously be many more. Firms are linked to the market through their market shares. Again the principal relationship is from the industry (market) down to the firm. There are two-headed arrows recognizing that firms have impact on one another.

The picture at the firm level is quite different from that at higher levels of the cascade. By and large, business managers must take the economic environment as given, though the largest or the most technologically advanced firms, like Microsoft or GE, may have substantial market power and may influence the industry or the economy as a whole.

At the firm level, the objectives are different. The business enterprise is seeking to maximize the performance of the firm, usually measured in terms of profits or the value of the owners' equity. In other words, firms seek private rather than social gain. The approach is strategic and entrepreneurial, involving not only questions of managing existing enterprises, but also of promoting new businesses and/or of developing and introducing new technologies.

The actions of one business affect its competitors and the response of competing businesses must be taken into account. A promotional program, advertising or price reductions, for example, by Firm A will have impacts on Firm B, which in turn, may devise a strategy response. At the firm level, the short-run perspective may indeed be from the market to the firm as shown by the downward pointing arrows, but in many ways initiatives at the firm level, the introduction of new products or new production technology, the development of a new marketing system, new pricing policies, for example, are likely to have impact on all the firms in the industry.

The nexus of the "new" economy lies at this level of the cascade. This is where entrepreneurs introduce new technologies. This is where the internet links businesses to consumers and businesses to their suppliers. This is where mergers and acquisitions expand the scale of operations in the home market, and most recently in world markets. The interrelationship of the firm and the industry is a close one. After all, the industry is the sum of the firms that make it up.

The cascade serves as a framework for discussion. We can talk about the nation and the industry. In many respects, they are the setting in which the firm operates. But ultimately, the basic decisions that affect the profitability and prospects of an enterprise are made at the firm level. A managers' strategy must take the economic setting into account, but managers must also recognize the opportunities for action at the level of the enterprise.

Information for Business

What does this mean for business? During one of my presentations on the macroeconomic outlook, a concerned businessman from a paper company once said to me: "How is this material actionable?" He simply wanted to know how he, as a business executive, could use the material about the growth of GDP, prices and interest rates I had presented. A legitimate question!

For many businesses, a general overview of the economy is only of limited interest. Like the paper company man, business managers want to know what is the outlook for specific variables that directly influence their business. Consumption of paper products fortunately is closely related to economic activity, indeed sales of paper packaging materials are one of the most accurate short-term indicators. So I could tell my questioner to look not only at GDP but to look closely particularly at the markets where orders for paper originate among the industries that use paper for packaging, among printers, in newsprint and magazines, and in consumer products. I could also tell him that the prices of cellulose and newsprint are quite variable, sensitive to the demand and supply balance for these products. These prices would greatly affect his costs and profit margins. I could suggest that he look at the tightness of labor markets to gauge pressures for higher wages and labor costs. Finally, I could direct him toward financial market information to determine the cost and availability of funds.

Macroeconomists do tend to talk in terms of broad economic aggregates and their values. Does it make a difference to business whether the GDP is increasing at 2.5% or at 3.5%? Probably not from one quarter to the next, because from quarter to quarter the figures are very variable. But the growth of GDP as a measure of business conditions does affect financial markets and the outlook for business. Macroeconomics, deals first of all, with the business climate, the environment in which business operates. This environment is described by the measures of economic activity we have noted.

An important consideration is the timeliness of the information. The importance of up-to-date evaluations and forecasts cannot be underestimated. Often, business executives need to know "before it happens." A turndown in business activity, an unanticipated slack in consumer spending, a rise in interest rates, or depreciation of the exchange rate can turn what seemed like a profitable business opportunity into a disaster.

On the other hand, managers should not take every forecast too seriously. Sometimes forecasts reflect the wishful thinking of an optimist or the fears of a pessimist. This may be particularly true if there are political reasons for projecting the outlook with one way or the other. Sometimes, there is a tendency simply to project the past. If the economy has been growing rapidly, why should it not continue to grow? Could it slow down next year? There may be good reasons. They need to be studied. For the business manager, the best motto is, as for the Boy Scout, "Be Prepared!"

Firms operating internationally require a broad range of international market and country risk information. The problems of obtaining appropriate international information are considerably greater than for the domestic economy since understanding of the investment climate abroad depends not only on evaluation of the economy itself but also on political matters, issues that are often poorly understood by foreign investors. Imagine, for example, the effect of the Thai devaluation crisis in July 1997 on firms that had begun to build plants there. Or visualize the risks of making joint venture agreements in China where property rights and legal procedures are still very badly defined.

Firms operating in international markets need specific information on their markets relevant to proposed business ventures. That may involve data on local costs for materials, for electric power, for office and factory space, or of wages for managerial and production personnel. Promotional privileges, allowing foreign investors tax concessions, are a consideration in international investment decisions in many countries. These may take a specific form depending on the project proposed, how much of the product is intended for export markets, for example. It is wise to call on local expertise or an embassy's commercial officer to provide the specific information required.

Questions for Discussion

* Does the contrast in economic performance between developed and developing countries persist? Why? Why do some developing countries lag behind?
* How can we think about the recent surge of productivity growth? Is there really a "new" economy?
* How are business cycle forces affecting the industrial countries and the developing countries currently? Are there big differences between various countries? Why?
* Is monetary and fiscal policy having big impacts on the world economy? Which way?
* How are various industries and firms affected by the economic situation? Is the business cycle more important for some kinds of business activity than others?
* What is the impact of the "new" economy at the firm level? How can firms take advantage of the opportunities created by the advent of the "new" economy?
* How can individual business managers protect their firms against the vagaries of the world business cycle?

Chapter 2

Economic Policy Objectives and Measurement

In this chapter, we discuss the aims of economic policy, the performance of the economy and the environment for business. What are the objectives of macroeconomic policy? We consider the tradeoffs between achievement of different aims. Are rapid growth and full employment consistent with price stability and balance of payments equilibrium? Can a fair income distribution be maintained while an economy is undergoing structural change? Is environmental preservation compatible with rapid growth of industry? Are the priorities of economic policy makers and business leaders in the advanced countries different from those of their counterparts in the developing world? We contrast the differences between rich and poor countries, between developed and developing countries. Finally, we are concerned with the implications for business.

The Economy's Objectives

What are an economy's objectives? Ultimately, as a society, we seek the highest possible standard of living, given the economy's limited resources and technology. This represents the fundamental economic problem — making the most of our limited resources. Since various dimensions of economic performance can define how well off we are, we must specify the economy's fundamental aims and how they are measured. We may find it difficult to distinguish between *basic* objectives — those that directly determine our well-being — and *intermediate* objectives — those that are a means to achieving more basic targets. The aims of the economy are summarized in brief in Table 2.1. We are also concerned here with how the performance of the economy with respect to these objectives can be measured?

Rapid growth

A matter of increasing citizen purchasing power and well-being; the objective is to achieve as fast as possible high real gross domestic product (GDP) per

Table 2.1   Economic Objectives and Their Measurement.

Macroeconomic Objective	Explanation	Measurement
Rapid Growth	Maximizing the rate of economic growth	Growth of per capita GDP in real terms
Price Stability	Stable or gently increasing price level	Growth of GDP deflator, CPI and PPI
Full Employment	Minimizing unemployment, maximizing jobs	Unemployment as fraction of labor force
Balance of Payments Equilibrium	International payments stability	Current account deficit, foreign exchange reserves and exchange rate
Fair Income Distribution	Minimizing inequality, protecting the poor	Number below the poverty line, and measures of inequality
Environmental Quality	Good air and water quality, and climate	Measures of particulates and gases in the atmosphere and water

capita. GDP is the broadest measure of the economy's output of goods and services. It is measured at market prices. Adjustment is made for inflation to produce a measure of the growth of real output. From a welfare perspective, we want to know what happens not only to total output but rather to productivity, i.e. output per capita. People's real purchasing power increases as output per capita grows. The "new" economy is seeing a resurgence of productivity growth and a rising standard of living in the US and promises similar gains in other countries as well.

Full employment

A matter of jobs, renumerative employment opportunities for as many people as possible; the aim is to minimize unemployment. Ideally, all people in the labor force should be able to find jobs that will enable them to make productive use of their skills and experience. The unemployed are defined as people who are out of a job but are actively seeking employment. In practice, large segments of the population are not working but are not, technically speaking, unemployed. Young people, retired people and women who are not gainfully employed outside the home are not considered to be in the labor force. Most of these people are not working by choice, but some of them would like to work if they could find jobs. Some of the people outside the labor force have quit looking, because there are no suitable jobs available, while others may be underemployed, working at jobs for which they are overqualified.

At any time, even when there are abundant work opportunities, some people will be between jobs. Consequently, full employment in the industrial world represents a situation where there remains a certain amount of "frictional" unemployment. How large a fraction of unemployment is frictional has been a subject of heated debate in the US. We used to think that frictional unemployment could account for as much as 5 to 6% of the labor force. At lower unemployment rates, labor markets were said to be "tight," meaning that businesses have difficulty finding workers. Tight labor markets are often associated with rapid wage increase and inflation. In recent years, the unemployment rate has dropped to 4% in the US. We do not know whether this change is a real change in the nature of labor markets or whether it reflects the aging of the labor force — older workers simply do not change jobs as much as young people. Some economists would argue that a lower unemployment rate is a feature of the "new" economy, where labor markets are more flexible and more competitive. In any case, there are always some workers between jobs, so that, even in the best of all possible worlds, full employment means low but not zero unemployment.

In developing countries, formally reported unemployment rates may not be high, but underemployment is pervasive. The unemployment rate is often measured badly, reflecting labor market conditions only in organized labor markets in the big cities. In developing countries, many people are in subsistence agriculture or low productivity service jobs. Many are part of a vast "informal" sector, the people who run the market stalls that are widely prevalent on the streets of Bangkok or Bangalore, for example. Some economists have argued that this "informal" sector represents the most vibrant part of developing economies. That may well be, but the incomes of the people working "off the books" are likely to be very low. In the Third World, full employment may not mean so much finding more jobs, but finding more *productive* jobs.

Price stability

Deals with avoiding inflation; prices are usually measured by a consumer price index (CPI), measuring today's cost of a market basket of commodities purchased by the typical (lower middle income) consumer relative to its cost in a base year. Broader measures of inflation are also used, such as the GDP deflator, which is a measure of price movement for all goods and services included in GDP, or the producer price index (PPI) which measures prices of goods at the wholesale level.

There is no doubt that hyperinflation (for example, more than 50% per year) like that seen until recently in many Latin American countries and in the former Soviet Union, is undesirable. Indeed, most experts would look for inflation rates below 5 or 10%. Inflation distorts the economy, causing business to be motivated by financial considerations related to rising prices rather than improvement of productivity. Inflation erodes the purchasing power of pensions and assets denominated in nominal terms. An important question then is whether the target of economic policy should be to achieve a "zero" inflation rate. That may be an extreme target. On the other hand, moderate inflation, say 2 or 3% per year, seems quite normal, particularly when it is reasonably predictable. Most businesses and individuals can deal with moderate inflation.

Why then is there concern when the inflation rate begins to rise to somewhat higher figures? The problem is that inflation tends to accelerate. Higher prices call for higher wages and in turn that calls for still higher prices, the so-called *wage-price spiral*. Only in recent years, have Latin American countries been able to overcome their hyperinflations, and then, only at high cost in terms of recession. East Asian central bankers were notably conservative with regard to inflation, aiming for lower rather than higher rates of price increase. Such a policy stance appears to have paid off for many years in the stable growth performance of the East Asian countries. But, in some cases — Indonesia in East Asia and Brazil in Latin America — exchange rate depreciation in the late 1990s has been a source of renewed inflationary pressure.

Balance of payments equilibrium

This is somewhat more difficult to discuss. Some people argue that exports should be maximized. That may well be a good short-run goal. Exports provide foreign exchange that may be used to import essential commodities. Competing in export markets has been a way to bring many countries' industrial base into the 20th century. Exports have been the stimulus to growth in many East Asian economies, allowing them to build their capital stocks and modernize their industries. But, in the long-run, we don't "eat" exports, we consume imports. A balance of payments surplus is not an advantage in its own right. Indeed, for a low income country, a modest deficit offset by inflows of foreign capital may be advantageous.

The important thing is that a country cannot live beyond its means over an extended period. A balance of payments deficit of moderate proportions is all right as long as capital inflows go into productive investment. Growth and competitiveness, financed by foreign capital and supported by modern technology, enable the borrowing country to meet its debt obligations and encourage lenders to provide additional funding. On the other hand, excessive international deficits, often funded by short-term money used for speculation, are an invitation to disaster. This is what happened in Mexico (Case 2.1) and East Asia (Case 11.1), where foreign capital inflows fueled a speculative investment boom that ultimately became unsustainable. Once foreign lenders lose confidence and seek to withdraw their funds, we have the makings of exchange rate depreciation, financial crisis and depression.

Case 2.1
The Mexican Balance of Payments Crisis of 1994

The year 1994 was the last year of President Salinas' six-year term. Throughout the year, the overvaluation of the Mexican peso was becoming increasingly clear as was the growing balance of current account deficit. Wise economists advised the government to put on fiscal and monetary policy brakes and to allow the Mexican peso to depreciate with respect to the US dollar. But President Salinas opted to maintain an artificially strong peso using the nation's gold and foreign exchange reserves to support the peso and raising domestic interest rates. For a while, the Mexican deficit was financed by inflows of "hot money" attracted by high rates of interest and assurance by the government that the peso would not be devalued. But in December, 1994, as the new presidential term began, investors lost confidence and the capital flows ceased. Mexico was on the brink of running out of foreign exchange reserves, when a modest devaluation was announced. It was not sufficient. The result was abrupt depreciation of the peso of some 50%. The Mexican economy went into crisis. Mexican firms that had borrowed in dollars in US financial markets, taking advantage of comparatively low interest rates there, found themselves paying back twice what they had borrowed in terms of pesos. To stabilize the situation, the government cut spending, raised interest rates and engineered a sharp recession. The US government in collaboration with international financial organizations, the World Bank and the IMF, provided an emergency lending facility. The situation was stabilized, but not without serious losses by Mexican business firms and significant deterioration in the living standard of the middle class.

The crisis had implications for many other countries, though the consequences were not as serious as for Mexico. Brazil, Argentina, and other Latin American countries felt what has since been called the "tequila effect" raising interest rates and putting severe pressure on their currencies. But, perhaps because of the prompt and effective policy response by the US and the international financial organizations, most of Latin America was able to deal with the crisis.

Two years later, the trade balance was positive and the emergency loans had been repaid. Mexico was resuming its growth — particularly since US foreign direct investment had continued — but living standards were still substantially lower than before the crisis.

Fair income distribution

Fair income distribution can have a number of interpretations. One approach is to have income distributed more evenly. (Only an extreme radical view would have income distributed equally.) A more realistic approach is simply to be concerned with eliminating poverty.

Market forces normally produce some spread between earnings of highly skilled workers and those who are less skilled. The frequency distribution of income typically takes a bell shape skewed to the right with a long tail, the few very high income recipients. An equal distribution would see all people concentrated around the mean.

In the US, rapid economic growth with low unemployment rates has helped less advantaged groups to participate in the benefits of the economy. More minority workers are finding employment and their wages have gone up relative to the rest of the population. That is the positive side. On the other hand, the "new" economy has also produced some increase in inequality at the upper end of the distribution where scarce technological workers and computer entrepreneurs have made huge windfall gains.

In the poorest developing countries, much of the population is at low incomes, at or below subsistence. It has been argued that the inequality of income increases in the early stages of development as some people move ahead into urban and professional activities, while others remain behind in primitive agriculture. As an economy matures, the inequality of income again tends to moderate. Much of the population is urban, and most workers earn a living wage though there remain pockets of poverty. There is also an important group of high income professionals and property owners.

In most countries, a progressive tax system and social welfare provisions are designed to reduce the inequality of income. Most people would prefer to see less inequality but are not prepared to try to wipe it out altogether. In any case, it is not practical in a market economy to assign equal incomes to everybody because that would interfere with incentives and with operation of market forces.

A more practical view of inequality is concerned with absolute poverty. Suppose a government sets a minimum income standard necessary to provide adequate nutrition and health care, a *poverty line*. Then it may want to supplement the incomes of people below the poverty line in order to prevent extreme hardship. Such an approach is quite widespread, applied to a greater or lesser degree in many countries. The striking thing about it is that the definition of poverty varies widely. What is called poverty in the advanced industrial countries is often a good lower middle class income in the developing world. In the developing countries, the poverty line is sometimes set in terms of a minimum of calories needed to maintain health. In other cases, it has been defined as an income of one US dollar per capita per day. In the industrial world, the costs of providing a safety net — welfare and health care for the unemployed, the needy and the aged — are much higher and have imposed increasing burdens on the public budget. In the developing world, there is little if any safety net; the poor must fend for themselves on the streets or in subsistence agriculture. This makes the economic crises in developing countries all the more damaging since urban people, newly arrived in the middle class, are driven back into poverty.

Environment and quality of life

These are an important, though sometimes forgotten, objective. Most observers recognize that rapid growth has often come at the cost of considerable environmental degradation in the form of smog, polluted water, urban crowding and deforestation. The difficulty is that, in most cases, pollution represents an *externality*. It affects the society but it is not a cost to the specific firm producing it. A firm operating with narrow margins in a highly competitive market is likely to disregard the social cost externalities, e.g. smoke, effluents, etc., associated with its production activity. More noxious fumes will be produced and less done about them than is socially desirable. The society bears the cost in the form of environmental degradation.

In the mature developed countries, where the problem might be most serious, costly environmental regulations have been imposed. Air and water quality have actually improved, during the past few decades. though we know that emissions of carbon dioxide (CO_2), the greenhouse gas, are still increasing rapidly. In East Asia, the problem is apparent with increasing smog, declining water quality and other evidence of environmental degradation. In the transition countries of Eastern Europe, years of environmental neglect during the communist period have created massive threats to health and safety. The problem has an international dimension. As China industrializes, largely on the basis of burning coal, sulfur dioxide (SO_2) and particulates are spewed into the atmosphere and carried by the prevailing westerly winds toward Japan where they cause acid rain. A still broader perspective involves international efforts to deal with global warming which appears to be affecting climate worldwide. That poses several additional complexities. First, empirical evidence points strongly in the direction that greenhouse gases are causing a gradual warming, and perhaps, more violent storms. But we cannot be sure. It is difficult to distinguish the greenhouse effect from natural cycles in the weather. Second, the increase in ambient temperature will be very slow, mainly apparent toward the second half of the 21st century. Discounting to the present with a reasonable rate of interest leaves little impact. Finally, from an economist's perspective, it is difficult to evaluate the economic impact of global warming. Some regions will lose, but others will gain — Canada and Siberia may become warm enough for intensive agriculture. Much depends on the how economies adapt to gradual change in the weather.

The traditional way to deal with environmental degradation has been by imposing regulation on how much particulate can be emitted and what must be done to prevent emissions of SO_2 or CO_2. Alternatively, incentives in the form of emissions taxes or marketable emission permits represent ways of discouraging emissions. Such measures have been quite successful in the industrial world where air and water quality have improved in recent decades even in highly industrialized locations. Poor countries have frequently tolerated pollution, arguing that they are poor and that it would be costly to worry about the environment. As a result, the degradation of the environment in these countries has been severe, creating incalculable costs in health and comfort. The Kyoto meetings on the environment in 1997 produced an agreement among the developed countries to hold environmental deterioration in check. While the developing countries were not signatories, many of them are taking environmental issues more seriously. The advanced countries are helping the poorer countries to meet emission standards. Sometimes this can be accomplished by emissions permit trading. A poor country would be paid by a richer country to reduce its emissions, which would cost more to reduce if equivalent environmental improvements were sought in the more advanced country.

There are significant problems of measurement. One approach is to think simply in terms of the physical measurement: the number of units of particulate in a cubic meter of air, the percent of CO_2 in the atmosphere, etc. But this approach says little about the impact of the environment on the living standard.

Other aspects of the quality of life are also relevant but even more difficult to measure. Social statistics, like life expectancy and data on educational attainment and real purchasing power, have been combined by the United Nations Development Programme (UNDP) to produce a Human Development Index (HDI). Such a measure is pretty arbitrary, and it does not as yet include environmental considerations. There is no objective way, moreover, to weight the importance of the various statistical ingredients in the index. There is consensus on the fact that social and cultural dimensions as well as environmental and economic attainment go into determining the quality of life but the difficulty is one of measurement.

We have tried to summarize the objectives of the economy succinctly into broad categories. Are there also other objectives? Certainly, we can think of numerous other aims: regional development, social welfare and educational attainment, for example. Some, like child health, are aims in their own right although they may be included in broader categories such as Fair Income Distribution. Others like export promotion, budget balance, or the encouragement of saving may be seen as means to an end rather than as fundamental objectives. Some are better achieved through microeconomic policies than through the aggregate fiscal and monetary policies that we will emphasize here.

An important question for a business audience is how much businesses should be involved in achieving the economy's objectives. Social aims are for all members of the society and they have substantial political content. Businesses are stakeholders, of course. The operations of business, for instance, production costs, are significantly affected by environmental regulations. It is understandable, therefore, that business is sometimes on the "wrong" side of the environmental debate, hoping to keep production costs as low as possible, lest they impair competitiveness. Yet, many business executives are profoundly concerned about the environment. They see good environmental practice as good business. Meeting the objectives of a country's citizens is the ultimate purpose of political and economic activity.

Case 2.2
The Ford Motor Company and the Environment

Environmental activists do not like sports utility vehicles (SUVs). These vehicles guzzle much more gasoline and produce lots more air pollution than ordinary passenger cars. So it is with some surprise that the *Economist* (20 May 2000) reports that William Clay Ford, boss of the Ford Motor Company and greatgrandson of Henry Ford, seems to care about the environment. In his company's "corporate citizenship" report, Ford admits that "the gas guzzling SUV is a rolling monument to environmental destruction." The company will continue to make SUVs, since they are very profitable, but they will devote some of the profits to look for new technologies to make them cleaner.

Tradeoffs and Priorities

Can the various aims of economic policy be achieved consistently? This question would be relatively easy to answer if economists and politicians had only one simple target such as rapid growth. But the preferences of a society with regard to a number of different aims must be taken into account simultaneously. The objectives may not be mutually consistent; achievement of one aim usually comes at some cost to another.

The most apparent tradeoffs are between growth and employment, in one direction, and price stability, balance of payments equilibrium, fair income distribution and quality of life, in the other. Pushing an economy to faster growth and employment may produce inflation and deterioration of the balance of payments. Faster growth may also widen the disparities of incomes, though some have argued that rapid growth trickles down to the poor.

Certainly, rapid growth is likely to produce environmental degradation, unless resources are set aside to protect the environment.

Economic history in the developed and developing world provides numerous illustrations of the contradictions between the economy's objectives. In the industrial world, the relationship between the rate of wage and price increase and the level of unemployment is a good example of the tradeoffs. As the economy approaches closer to full employment, pressures for higher wages and prices build. We will discuss the mechanics underlying the Phillips curve that links unemployment and inflation at greater length below (Chapter 9). Environmental pollution represents another classic case of the contradictions between the economy's objectives. It takes only a brief visit to Bangkok, Mexico City, or other developing country capitals to see that a high price is being paid for rapid economic growth in undrinkable water, urban crowding, traffic jams, noise and air pollution — in some countries, traffic cops on the street wear surgical masks to protect against the lead and other pollutants in the atmosphere. But we know, from looking at the advanced industrial countries that environmental degradation can be controlled. In Pittsburgh, Pennsylvania or Kitakyushu, Japan, both once polluted by steel industry smoke, the atmosphere today is clear and the water supply potable — but at considerable cost!

If the objective is heavily one-sided — suppose, for example, that the growth objective overrides all other considerations — all the policy tools can be used to achieve the primary objective, though the costs in other dimensions of economic performance, such as inflation or balance of payments difficulties, may ultimately become apparent. But, in most cases, all the objectives must be taken into account at the same time, though some may be more important than others. Policy makers must, consequently, attach weights to the various objectives. We may combine performance in various desired directions as a weighted average, sometimes called a *welfare function*, that policy makers seek to maximize. It is a challenge to control an economy on a path that will maximize welfare. To do so, we must use our policy instruments to come as close to full employment and/or rapid growth as possible without causing too much damage along other dimensions of economic performance like inflation.

Case 2.3
Surveys of Economic Priorities

An interesting perspective on the differences between the objectives of developing and developed countries is provided by the following experiment. For several years, I asked my students at the University of Pennsylvania in Philadelphia, at the International University of Japan, and at the Sasin Graduate Institute of Business Administration in Bangkok to list their perceptions of the principal objectives of the economy.

It is not difficult for any of these groups to come up with a set of aims. With a little coaching and interpretation, the aims are always substantially the same, as shown on the left of Table 2.2.

The last objective in Table 2.2, Quality of Life/Environment, is bracketed. In fact, very few groups volunteer the Quality of Life objective. After the first five objectives have been listed on the blackboard, I usually question the group about whether they have omitted something. Eventually, I ask what about the environment? I am invariably greeted with a chorus of "Ah."

Then, we proceed to establish some priorities among the objectives. I have done so by polling my classes about their preferences. We vote, first asking how many favor each objective as "number 1," and then going to

Table 2.2   Typical Responses to Objectives Survey.

	Rankings		
	Philadelphia Wharton	Japan IUJ	Bangkok Sasin
Rapid Growth	3	4	1
Full Employment	1	3	3
Price Stability	2	1	4
Balance of Payments Stability	4	2	2
Fair Income Distribution	5	5	5
(Quality of Life/Environment)	(6)	(6)	(6)

"number 2," and so on. The results for groups at well-known business schools, Wharton in Philadelphia, at IUJ in Japan, and at Sasin in Thailand, are summarized in Table 2.2.

There is no surprise about the most important objective. In a developing country, growth must be the primary aim. For an advanced economy, particularly one that was in recession at the time the survey was taken, employment is most important. Paradoxically, full employment is often considered less important in the developing economy, though the underutilization of labor is a serious problem in most developing countries where a large fraction of the labor force is underemployed, if not formally unemployed. Price stability and balance of payments equilibrium are important aims particularly when people are aware of threatening inflation or balance of payments problems. It is noteworthy that fair income distribution is low on the scale of importance in both types of countries. Similarly there is not much emphasis on the environment. The quality of life concern is much more of a problem in developing countries where environmental degradation is proceeding apace, than in the industrial world. In the latter, people are aware of environmental questions and much has been done in the last 20 years to improve the environment. Only the most dedicated "greens" make the environment a priority issue.

It is interesting to note that the results of the surveys are quite variable over time. I had originally thought that fundamental economic objectives might vary between countries reflecting differences in culture, and that they would remain relatively stable over time. In fact, the objectives reported vary greatly even in the short term. Apparently, the respondents are concerned with what is currently going on in the society, so that recent economic experiences and political campaigns weigh heavily. When the economy is in a recession, they put high priority on employment; when there is inflation they emphasize price stability. In fairness, I should add that recent surveys show considerably greater interest in fair income distribution, particularly in Thailand. The objectives of a society are not cast in stone. As the politics of a society change, particularly in the direction of popular democracy, considerations like income distribution and quality of life gain in importance.

Differences Between Rich and Poor Countries

Are developing economies fundamentally different from the industrial countries? Do they require a different economics?

As the saying goes: "The rich are different from you and me. They have more money!"[1] If this comment were applied to countries, it would greatly oversimplify the differences between rich and poor, between developed and developing. The contrasts are not just a matter of wealth. They involve differences in economic and social structure and in objectives. In this section, we contrast the basic economic statistics for developing countries and industrial countries. Table 2.3 summarizes data from the World Bank's *World Development Report* according to the stage of development of different parts of the world economy. As we have already noted in Chapter 1, the principal country categories are the low income countries, with 1999 per capita incomes of $755 or less, the lower middle income developing countries with incomes between $756 and $2995, the upper middle income developing countries with incomes from $2996 to $9266, and the high income countries with incomes above $9266. Statistics are also shown in Table 2.4 separately for the major East Asian countries, and for comparison, for the US and Japan. (The discussion below follows the content of the tables. Please compare the verbal discussion with the statistics shown in the tables as you go along.)

The reported differences *in per capita GDP* translated to US dollars on the basis of exchange rates are very large. In East Asia, Singapore is a high income country ($29,610), at developed country level, and others like Indonesia and the Philippines are much lower ($580 and $1020). Differences between the rapidly developing Asian countries and the mature economies are also large. For example, per capita income for Thailand is reported at $1960 compared to figures for Japan of $32,230 and the United States of $30,600.

---

[1]The saying has its origin with Hemingway. He used to make fun of what he took to be F. Scott Fitzgerald's awe of the very wealthy. According to Hemingway, Fitzgerald said that the rich were very different from you and me. Hemingway claims to have replied, "Yes, they have more money!" Spencer Carr, to whom I owe this story, added, "So far as history goes, I wouldn't trust anything Hemingway said about Fitzgerald."

Table 2.3   Economic and Social Characteristics of Countries at Various States of Development.

	Low Income	Low Middle Income	Upper Middle Income	High Income
Gross National Product				
GNP per capita $ 1999	410	1,200	4,900	25,730
GNP measured at PPP $ 1999	1,790	3,960	8,320	24,430
Change in GNP per capita (1998–1999)	2.5%	2.3%	2.7%	2.1%
GDP Growth				
1980–1990 (% p.a.)	4.4%	4.0%	2.5%	3.1%
1990–1999 (% p.a.)	2.4%	3.4%	3.6%	2.4%
Export Growth				
1980–1990 (% p.a.)	3.3%	7.6%	7.0%	5.0%
1990–1999 (% p.a.)	5.3%	6.7%	10.8%	6.5%
Structure of GDP (value added as a % of GDP)				
Agriculture 1999	27%	15%	7%	2%
Industry 1999	30%	40%	32%	30%
Manufacturing 1999	18%	23%	24%	21%
Services 1999	43%	46%	61%	64%
Commercial Energy Use				
Energy consumption growth per capita (% p.a.) 1980–1997	−1.2	−1.2	2.2	1.1
Energy use per capita 1997 (kg of oil eq.)	563	1,178	2,068	5,369
Energy use per $ of GDP (1997–1999) (kg of oil eq.)				
Nominal terms	1.37	0.98	0.42	0.21
PPP terms	0.31	0.30	0.25	0.22
Electric Power				
Consumption per capita (Kwh 1997)	357	1,042	2,434	8,238
Pollutant Emissions				
Carbon dioxide tons per capita 1996	1.1	3.3	5.1	12.3

Table 2.3 (Continued)   Economic and Social Characteristics of Countries at Various States of Development.

	Low Income	Low Middle Income	Upper Middle Income	High Income
Quality of Life				
Life expectancy at birth in years				
Males	59	67	67	75
Females	61	72	74	81
Adult illiteracy rate (% of people 15 and above in 1997)				
Males	30%	10%	9%	NA
Females	49%	23%	11%	NA
Urban population (% of total)				
1980	24%	31%	64%	75%
1999	31%	43%	76%	77%
Population growth (ave annual growth rate %)				
1980–1990	2.3%	1.6%	1.8%	0.6%
1990–1999	2.2%	1.1%	1.4%	0.6%
Fertility rate (births per woman)				
1980	4.3	3.7	3.7	1.8
1998	3.1	2.5	2.4	1.7
Modernization				
Television sets 1998	76	250	285	661
Telephone main lines 1998	23	90	176	567
Mobile telephones 1998	2	18	76	265
Personal computers 1998	3.2	13.6	53.1	311.2
Internet hosts per 10,000 people January 2000	0.37	2.83	35.88	777.22
Scientists and Engineers in R&D Per million people 1987–1997	NA	763	660	3,166

Note: The economies are divided among income groups according to 1999 GNP per capita, calculated using the World Bank Atlas method. Low Income = $755 or less, lower middle income = $756–$2995, upper middle income = $2996–$9265, and high income = $9266 or more.
Source: World Development Report 2000–2001.

Table 2.4   Economic and Social Characteristics of East Asian Countries and USA.

	China	South Korea	Singapore	Malaysia	Philippines	Indonesia	Thailand	Vietnam	Japan	USA
Gross National Product										
GNP per capita $ 1999	780	8,490	29,610	3,400	1,020	580	1,960	370	32,230	30,600
GNP measured at PPP $ 1999	3,291	14,637	27,024	7,963	3,815	2,439	5,599	1,755	24,041	30,600
Growth										
Real GDP 1980–1990 (% p.a.)	10.1%	9.4%	6.7%	5.3%	1.0%	6.1%	7.6%	4.6%	4.0%	3.0%
Real GDP 1990–1999 (% p.a.)	11.7%	5.7%	8.0%	6.3%	3.2%	4.7%	4.7%	8.1%	1.4%	3.4%
GNP per capita (% change 1997–1998)	6.5%	−7.1%	−0.4%	−8.4%	−2.1%	−16.2%	−8.5%	2.8%	−2.8%	2.8%
GNP per capita (% change 1998–1999)	6.3%	10.1%	3.6%	1.9%	1.4%	0.3%	4.1%	2.9%	0.8%	3.1%
Export Growth										
1980–1990 (% p.a.)	19.3%	12%	10.8%	10.9%	3.5%	2.9%	14.1%	NA	4.5%	4.7%
1990–1999 (% p.a.)	13.0%	15.6%	13.3%	11.0%	9.6%	9.2%	9.4%	27.7%	5.1%	9.3%
Structure of Output (Value added % of GDP)										
Agriculture 1999	17%	5%	0%	14%	17%	20%	13%	26%	2% (1980)	2%
Industry 1999	50%	44%	36%	44%	31%	45%	40%	33%	37% (1980)	26%
Manufacturing 1999	24%	32%	26%	35%	21%	25%	32%	NA	24% (1980)	18%
Services 1999	33%	54%	64%	43%	52%	35%	49%	42%	61% (1980)	72%
Agricultural Productivity (per worker) $ 1995										
1979–1981	161	3,800	13,937	3,725	1,347	610	634	NA	15,698	NA
1996–1998	307	11,657	41,673	6,061	1,352	749	932	230	31,094	39,001

Table 2.4 (Continued)   Economic and Social Characteristics of East Asian Countries and USA.

	China	South Korea	Singapore	Malaysia	Philippines	Indonesia	Thailand	Vietnam	Japan	USA
Energy Use										
Energy consumption (% growth p.a.) 1980–1997	2.90%	8.90%	8.40%	6%	2.30%	3.10%	8.50%	4.90%	2.20%	0.80%
Energy consumption per capita (% p.a.) (kg oil eq.)										
1990	763	2,132	4,938	1,317	452	555	786	369	3,552	7,720
1997	907	3,834	8,661	2,237	520	693	1,319	521	4,084	8,076
Energy use per $ of GNP (1997–1999) (kg oil eq.)										
Nominal basis	1.16	0.45	0.29	0.66	0.51	1.19	0.67	1.41	0.13	0.26
PPP basis	0.28	0.26	0.32	0.28	0.14	0.28	0.24	0.30	0.17	0.26
Electric Power										
Consumption per capita 1997 (Kwh)	714	4,847	7,944	2,352	432	329	1,360	203	7,241	11,822
Pollutant Emissions										
Carbon dioxide tons per capita 1996	2.8	9.0	21.6	5.6	0.9	1.2	3.4	0.5	9.3	20.0
Quality of Life										
Life expectancy at birth in years										
Males	68	69	75	70	67	64	70	66	77	74
Females	72	76	79	75	71	67	75	71	84	80
Adult illiteracy rate (% of people over 14, 1997)										
Males	9%	1%	4%	9%	5%	9%	3%	5%	NA	NA
Females	25%	4%	12%	18%	5%	20%	7%	9%	NA	NA
Urban population (% of total)										
1980	20%	57%	100%	42%	38%	22%	17%	19%	76%	74%
1999	32%	81%	100%	57%	58%	40%	21%	20%	79%	77%

Table 2.4 (Continued) Economic and Social Characteristics of East Asian Countries and USA.

	China	South Korea	Singapore	Malaysia	Philippines	Indonesia	Thailand	Vietnam	Japan	USA
Population growth (ave annual growth rate %)										
1980–1990	1.5%	1.2%	1.7%	2.8%	2.6%	1.8%	1.7%	2.1%	0.6%	0.9%
1990–1999	1.1%	1.0%	1.9%	2.5%	2.3%	1.7%	1.2%	1.8%	0.3%	1.0%
Total fertility rate (births per woman)										
1980	2.5	2.6	1.7	4.2	4.8	4.3	3.5	5	1.8	1.8
1998	1.9	1.6	1.5	3.1	3.6	2.7	1.9	2.3	1.4	2
Modernization										
Television sets (per 1000 people) 1998	272	346	348	166	108	136	236	47	707	847
Telephone main lines (per 1000 people) 1998	70	433	562	198	37	27	84	26	503	661
Mobile telephones (per 1000 people) 1998	19	302	346	99	22	5	32	2	374	256
Personal computers (per 1000 people) 1998	8.9	156.8	458.4	58.6	15.1	8.2	21.6	6.4	237.2	458.6
Internet hosts (per 10,000 people) 2000	0.57	60.03	452.25	25.43	1.58	1	6.46	0.02	208.06	1,939.97
Scientists and engineers in R&D (per million people) 1987–1997	454	2,193	2,318	93	157	182	103	NA	4,909	3,676

Source: World Development Report 2000–2001.

Is the living standard in Japan and the US really more than ten times what it is in lower middle income countries like Thailand? The comparison shown exaggerates the difference, since the exchange rates used to make the conversion understate real purchasing power in developing currencies (Case 2.4). In the case of Thailand, the undervaluation is by about one-half, meaning that in terms of PPP dollars, Thai purchasing power is about twice the exchange rate basis figure shown. Professors Heston and Summers at the University of Pennsylvania have made elaborate statistical studies. They show that differences between PPP and exchange rates vary systematically between the poor and the rich countries: the lower the GDP per capita, the greater the undervaluation.

Case 2.4
PPP Comparisons

A simple story provides a good illustration. Going to a Thai restaurant along the Chao Phaya river in Bangkok, I asked for an English language menu. I was handed the menu of the restaurant's branch in New York. For every item, the US dollar price had been crossed out and the corresponding price in Thai baht had been written in. When the New York price for a dish was US$10, the Thai price was 200 baht. On that basis, the translation of baht to dollars was 20 baht to the dollar as compared to an exchange rate then of 40 baht to the dollar.

I could have taken my US$10 that would have bought one dish of food in the New York restaurant, exchanged them at the going exchange rate for 400 baht and bought two dishes of food in Bangkok. On the basis of local prices, a purchasing power parity (PPP) basis, the baht bought twice as much as on an exchange rate basis. GDPs per capita are usually translated into dollar values on the basis of the exchange rate. But if we allow for the fact that the domestic purchasing power of the baht was at that time twice its exchange rate value, Thai GDP per capita is worth about two times as much as the exchange rate-based dollar figures suggest. Moreover, this calculation suggests why Thai goods have been very competitive in world trade. Even if real production costs in Thailand were the same as in the US, at the prevailing exchange rate, dollars would buy much more in Thailand than at home. Statistics on per capita income in terms of purchasing power adjusted currency (PPP $) bear out these differences. For the lowest income countries, PPP-based per capita income is about four times the exchange rate-based figure. For the middle income countries, the comparison is about two to one. For the high income countries, PPP based income is a little less than exchange rate-based income.

Similar calculations can be made from the *Economist* magazine annual comparison of Big Mac hamburger prices in various countries. Hamburger prices are all over the map, very high in Switzerland and Israel and very cheap in East Asia and Russia. Of course, hamburgers are not a good basis for comparing competitiveness since hamburgers are not a product that is traded internationally. For traded goods, international trade would tend to wipe out such price differentials. They would be bought where they are cheap and shipped to where they are expensive. It turns out that hamburger prices are determined on the basis of local marketing strategy, and since there is no international market for hamburgers, their prices can be relatively higher or lower than in the US. Obviously, my story about restaurant meals in Bangkok suffers from the same problem.

This makes prices in many developing countries cheap to travelers and importers from the industrial countries and systematically understates their real GDPs. Turning now to growth (Tables 2.3 and 2.4), the high rates of growth, observed in East Asia until 1997, represent the success story of economic development. In recent decades, the rate of growth of the middle income developing countries has been considerably greater than that of the high income countries (and of the poor countries). As we discuss in more detail in Chapter 5, this is particularly true of the East Asian countries that have been participants in an almost miraculous development process. On the other hand, the period from the early 1980s to the early 1990s was difficult for lower middle income countries, especially those in Latin America as a result of the 1982 debt crisis.

The East Asian crisis, which first became apparent in Thailand in 1997, and subsequently engulfed most of East Asia, interrupted the rapid growth path (see the declines in GNP in 1998). Fortunately, many of these countries, but not all, are back on a path of renewed growth.

Trade patterns are also revealing. To begin with, exports have been growing much more rapidly in the middle income developing countries than elsewhere. This reflects the fact the most successful countries have based their development on a strategy of export promotion. Not surprisingly, as their export earnings have grown so have their imports. Trade in primary products is still important, but it is noteworthy that the exports of the middle income countries consist increasingly of manufactures.

Even after we allow for PPP exchange rates, per capita output in the developing countries remains much lower than in the advanced world. Behind this difference lies a fundamental duality which we have noted in Chapter 1. In the developing world, two societies exist side by side; a modern world typically with large urban centers, with modern industry and technology; and a traditional sector, usually rural where primitive methods such as the wooden plow drawn by oxen, are still being used. The statistics, Table 2.3, show that the traditional sector is still very important in the lower middle income countries. In these countries, a substantial part of output still originates in agriculture and agricultural workers in these economies are not very productive. As we look across from "low income" to "upper middle income" countries, the share of agriculture in GDP declines.

Industrial growth has been a feature of "middle income" country development, and accordingly, the share of industry increases as we move from poorer to more advanced countries. The path toward industrialization is particularly apparent if we focus on production of transportation equipment, machinery and electronics. The more advanced the economy, the more it produces high-tech products.

Expansion of the service sectors is a feature, particularly, of advanced economic development. We used to refer to the high income countries as industrial economies. Today, the most advanced countries like the US are becoming increasingly service economies, albeit not in the sense of low wage, low productivity services. Services are not, at some argue, just "taking in each others' washing." Some desperately poor countries like Cambodia also rely heavily on tourist services for growth and development, but these tend to be low value added activities. In contrast, modern service activities in finance, communication and technology represent high-tech high value added sectors. This is the essence of the "new economy."

In the developing economies, capital intensity is low. While we cannot easily compare measures of capital internationally, the statistics on per capita energy consumption, closely related to capital intensity, show how much less capital is used in the developing than in the industrial countries. Energy consumption per capita is only 563 kg (oil equivalent) in the low income countries as compared to 5369 kg in the high income countries, and 8076 kg in the US. Of course, differences in motorization also affect energy consumption, and the US has more cars and trucks per capita than poorer countries. Similar comparisons can be made in terms of electric power consumption. Energy use per $ of GDP indicates the intensity of heavy industry, which is a large energy consumer. We might also note that energy use produces pollutants. In that regard, China, a country with a relatively low capital intensity, nevertheless uses energy inefficiently and causes much atmospheric pollution.

Social statistics are a reflection of the duality of the developing economy. In the lower middle income countries, less than half of the population as yet live in urban centers. Surprisingly, this figure is much lower in some countries like Thailand, the Philippines and Indonesia. But that is changing as urbanization takes place at a rapid rate. One needs only to observe the crowds of people and the construction cranes to be aware of the burgeoning growth of Shanghai or Bangkok. Movement from the impoverished countryside to the city, which offers opportunities, though sometimes little better living conditions, is a basic ingredient of the development process.

Life expectancy, another measure of social conditions, has been improving in the middle income countries, but remains some ten years lower in the developing countries than in the advanced world. This is not because the life span tends to be significantly different. Rather, it is because infant mortality in the poor countries is still high and fewer babies survive their first two years. These figures have a parallel in the birth and death rate statistics: high birth rates and declining death rates in the poorest countries. As a result, population is growing rapidly in the poor countries, calling for still more rapid growth of GDP to raise per capita living standards. In this respect, the middle income developing countries have made much progress: a low death rate with improved health conditions and a birth rate which, though still high, is dropping rapidly. Thailand has been a leader in efforts to reduce the birth rate. Strategies developed there are paying off in neighboring countries, as well.

Education is a critical input into development. Primary education is now almost universal though the statistics still show substantial illiteracy in the low income countries, especially among women. Unfortunately, secondary and tertiary education are still far behind in most developing countries. This accounts for the fact that shortages of specialized labor — managers and engineers, and frequently, even skilled and semi-skilled blue collar workers — are being encountered in some of the rapidly growing East Asian economies long before the total labor pool approaches exhaustion.

Finally, Tables 2.3 and 2.4 provide some approximate figures on modernization, how far along the path toward the electronic information technology these countries have gone. There are still remarkable differences between the poor countries and the high income ones on the number of TVs, telephones, personal computers, etc. However, as is apparent in Table 2.4, some countries in East Asia have made remarkable progress — Singapore and South Korea almost match the US in some of the attributes of the IT economy.

There are also important institutional differences between the developing countries and the industrial economies. These involve the structure of business and the role of government.

The market economy has increasingly become the system of choice in developed and developing countries alike. But the structure of business remains quite different. Most developing economies do not have the extensive system of shareholder-owned large corporations that we observe in the mature economies. Nor do they have the same degree of competition. This may simply be a matter of scale and maturity. While there are very large firms, many of them are still family owned or controlled. Many rely heavily on personal connections as a basis for business dealings. Most of them do not follow systematic objective business practices that are typical of large corporations in Europe and North America. Many of them lack large competitors in their home countries though they encounter healthy competition once they venture into outside markets.

Another difference is that in the developing world, the public sector accepts a far larger role — some observers would say too large a role. In many countries, government agencies engage in extensive development planning. In the past, infrastructure investment, fundamental to transportation, power distribution and communication, has typically been under government auspices. Corporatization and privatization of national enterprises, that promise to instill private sector efficiency into these operations, is now spreading widely. Private sector build-operate-transfer (BOT) projects are drawing entrepreneurial capital even to building expressways and mass transportation in China. There is, nevertheless, much government intervention in the private sector with capital allocation and special financing institutions and numerous specific product and price regulations. In Thailand, for example, new industrial projects can seek tax incentives with the approval of the Board of Investment (BoI) which grants seven-year tax holidays and other tax concessions, and which can provide tariff protection for industries that would not otherwise survive foreign competition. (In recent years, the BoI has used its incentives to steer industries away from the crowded area around Bangkok and the Eastern Seaboard to the northeast and the south of Thailand.) In many less developed countries, the role of government extends to extreme efforts that favor domestic industries and protect them from foreign competition. Developing countries complain vigorously about US and European protectionism, but in order to promote *import substitution*, their own inefficient and backward industries were long protected by high tariff and import restriction walls. That is why the turn to *export promotion* made such a difference. To compete in the wide world, industries must produce products of international quality and design at competitive costs. Exporting industries have made important improvements in production efficiency. Domestically oriented industries have been forced to keep up, leading to a general improvement in production efficiency and quality.

The differences between developing and developed economies suggest that there is a different, probably broader, scope for government policy in the developing world than in the developed countries. In the latter, many traditional social problems are being met, though many new ones have cropped up. But the market mechanism serves fairly well to guide economic decisions, and increasingly there is a swing toward privatizing those few industries which are still in state hands. In the developing world, problems seem to be more pressing. The market is frequently not well organized and government accepts (perhaps the word *takes* is more appropriate here) responsibility for accelerating growth.

Whether government policy making has been the reason for the rapid growth of the East Asian countries is subject to intense debate among development economists. The role of the government sector and of export promotion in economic development is discussed in greater detail in Chapter 6.

Finally, we turn to the question: "Do developing countries require a different economics?" Our answer to that question must remain equivocal: "yes and no." The differences in objectives and structure we discussed above, suggest that a mature economy approach is not always appropriate in the developing economies. Recent controversies about the policies of the International Monetary Fund (IMF) illustrate this well. The IMF provided financial assistance to many countries during the 1997 financial crisis. This aid has been conditional on reforms in the fiscal and financial regimes of the recipients. The IMF is dominated by the big industrial countries, the US, UK, Germany, etc. And it has followed, what might be termed conservative "Western" policies. These tight credit and budget balancing policies appeared to the recipient countries and to some economists as policies more appropriate to advanced countries than to developing countries. Obviously, the special characteristics of the developing countries must be taken into account.

But there is also a substantial case for the "no" response to the question about a "different economics." The nature of economics, as a discipline, is not different between countries. The understanding of how growth and stability are achieved calls for the same analytical tools. The approach to macroeconomic policy is based on the same principles. Many of the principles of modern macroeconomics can be demonstrated in a developing country framework.

The "New Economy" and Developed/Developing Countries

Is the "new economy" as important to developing countries as developed economies? Sophisticated information technology (IT) has had its origin in the advanced countries, particularly in the US, where high level scientific expertise and venture capital are readily available. The new techniques, which are uniquely suited for international distribution since they are linked to communication and the Internet, are spreading rapidly in Europe and Japan and making inroads in the developing countries as well. Generally, the level of scientific sophistication in the newer economies is not yet high enough to lead in these fields, though there are exceptions, like Taiwan, Korea, Israel and even Bangalore in India, where high-tech centers are growing rapidly. Some policy makers have held out the hope that technological "leapfrogging" will enable poorer countries to move to the forefront of the IT fields. But this is unlikely since most lack the requisite education and networks of trained workers and suppliers. On the other hand, as the developing countries make progress, they shift into more advanced industries that require higher technical expertise. As industry becomes more sophisticated, insufficient technical education and inadequate communication infrastructure in many developing countries stand in the way of quick participation in the "new economy."

Implications for Business

As we have noted, the nature of business is likely to be quite different in the advanced world than in the developing countries. Economic, sociological and cultural factors account for these differences.

From an economic perspective, many product markets in the industrial world are large and competitive reflecting high consumer incomes. The variety of products is large and there are many competitors. In sharp contrast, markets for manufactures in developing economies are generally smaller and less competitive. The duality of the developing economy means that there is a chasm of difference between well-to-do city dwellers and subsistence farmers who still make up a large part of the population. Where many developing countries have a small upper class and some are creating a growing middle class, the market for luxury products, durables and housing is likely to be much smaller than in developed countries, though growing rapidly. Many high grade products are still being imported as are most capital goods. On the other hand, the proliferation of new shopping centers in some of the metropolitan centers of East Asia is astonishing. The rapid progress in East Asia is creating a middle class who offer vast opportunities for business development. Its markets are rapidly becoming similar to those in the industrial world.

From a sociological perspective, there are also substantial differences. Obviously markets are different as we note above. But there are also big differences in terms of social organization. The big cities of Asia and Latin America are a relatively recent phenomenon. Much of the population is still scattered in rural villages. Modern means of communication like the cell phone and television have tended to reduce the disparities, but there remain enormous differences between life in the countryside and in the city. Tradition and the family are still more important in Asia than in Europe or North America. This has implications for business, in that much Asian business is in the hands of families and is based on mutual trust, in contrast to more formal organizational forms, accounting controls and structured management in Western corporations. The consequences for the ability of businesses to expand in terms of size and scope and across national boundaries are the subject of considerable debate.

Cultural considerations have often been advanced as an explanation for the differences between advanced and developing economies. In recent years, cultural considerations have often been raised as an explanation for the rapid growth of East Asia. Undoubtedly, there are big differences between cultures, as many businesspersons have found out, often too late. There is no question that East Asian countries are linked by an entrepreneurial class of "overseas" Chinese. Entrepreneurs from Hong Kong and Taiwan have been influential in developing industries in China, in Vietnam and in other East Asian countries. On the other hand, it is difficult to link specific cultural characteristics to the developments in Asia just as it is not always possible, except through the historian's rose-colored glasses, to use culture to explain the success of the

US. While cultural differences as a basis for economic phenomena are better left to courses in history and sociology, international business managers must take such differences very seriously.

Questions for Discussion

* How would you weight the different dimensions of economic performance?
* Why might poor countries place less priority on environmental considerations than rich countries?
* What lies behind the tradeoffs between growth and a fair income distribution? Between full employment and balance of payments equilibrium?
* If priorities change over time, can we take them seriously?
* In what ways do the economies of developed and developing countries differ? What are the most important aspects of these differences?
* How might the "new" economy affect a country's economic growth and stability?
* From the perspective of economic structure, what are the principal differences between developed and developing countries?
* How does success or failure to achieve an economy's objectives affect business?

Chapter 3

Measuring Economic Performance

In this chapter, we consider the principal measures of economic performance. Whereas in the previous chapter, we have looked at economies from a comparative perspective, comparing the developing and the developed countries, here we will see how economic variables move over time. First, we consider aggregate output and prices. Then we turn to the components of demand and the basic accounting framework that provides consistency between the flows of product and income. Financial data and trade will also be presented. We comment on the process of obtaining the statistics and on their likely reliability. Does the "new economy" call for a new approach to economic data?

Introduction

In the "new economy," a quantitative view of the world is just as important as in the "old economy." But rapid technological change and the increasing role of services rather than physical manufactured products are making the data difficult to establish and to interpret.

Government officials and business managers in the mature economies have long been accustomed to reviewing economic statistics — the budget, the national accounts, the trade balance, etc. In some developing countries, such statistics are unreliable or not up-to-date so that decision makers are still "flying by the seat of their pants." Increasingly, though, even in less developed countries, businesspeople rely on economic data to evaluate the current situation of the economic environment and to project the future. It makes a difference to business operations whether the economy is bumping against capacity ceilings with the threat of supply shortages and inflation or whether it faces recession. It makes a difference whether the currency has become overvalued, as in Thailand in 1997, or is subject to political uncertainties, as in Indonesia, with the risk of currency depreciation and financial crisis. On the other hand, it is important to keep in mind that aggregate economic statistics, though useful for business, are no substitute for detailed data about orders, product sales, occupancy rates, costs, etc. that must be taken into account for business decision making.

The Gross Domestic Product Concept

The Gross Domestic Product (GDP) is the broadest measure of the nation's production activity. In nominal terms, GDP represents the total value of the nation's production of goods and services at current market prices. Changes in GDP from one year or quarter to the next reflect both changes in output and changes in prices. It is useful, consequently, to disentangle the GDP into a component consisting of real output (GDP_{real}), which represents the value of the nation's production of goods and services measured in the prices of a base year, and a price deflator (PGDP) which accounts for the level of prices.

$$GDP = GDP_{real} \times PGDP \qquad (3.1)$$

or

$$GDP_{real} = GDP/PGDP. \qquad (3.2)$$

GDP is a measure of production activity. The GDP represents production of goods and services. As we have noted in the previous chapter, the share of GDP originating in agriculture, industry and services changes as countries mature. At the earliest stages, output is largely from agriculture. As countries move up the development ladder, the output of industry tends to become more important. In advanced economies, high-value added services like finance, medical care and technology become most important.

For most goods and services, the criterion for inclusion in GDP is whether production is marketed — *marketed production*. For these products, there is a market value that can be summed up to GDP. But important parts of the nation's product are not sold on the market and have no measured market value. They must be included in GDP nevertheless. Specifically:

1. Inventory accumulation. To the extent that some of the current product of the economy is not sold, it piles up in inventories. If we base our estimate

of GDP on marketed product, in other words, the product that is sold, we must also add goods that have been produced but accumulated in inventories rather than sold. Inventory change is the result of production activity and must be included in GDP. Sometimes, inventories build up inadvertently, as sales fall short of expectations. This is often a sign of imminent recession.

2. The production activity of the government sector. Everyone will agree that we must count as output, the services of teachers, police officers and public service doctors. There may be less agreement on the contribution to output, at least to useful product, of the work of bureaucrats and military personnel. Some economists have referred to military spending as *regrettables*, but this activity too, must be included in GDP. As there is no market price for these services, the work of government employees is valued at *factor cost*, i.e. what they are paid.

3. The product produced and directly consumed by farmers. In the advanced countries, this accounts only for a very small part of GDP. But in less developed countries, with significant subsistence agriculture, a fairly important part of the nation's product never reaches the market. It is consumed right where it is produced, on the farm. It is a challenge to put a value on the product of subsistence agriculture. Usually a rough calculation is made on the basis of agricultural surveys. The typical small holder family produces: "so many" chickens, "so much" corn, "so many" coconuts, etc. We put a price on these products, usually a very low one since much of the value of the goods we buy is in their transportation to market, and wholesale and retail distribution. We multiply the value of the product of the typical subsistence farm family by the estimated number of such families in subsistence agriculture. The figures can be quite large in poor populous countries like those of Africa, but the statistic is not likely to be very accurate. Note that the figure for output of subsistence farmers also represents the estimate for their consumption.

4. The services of owner occupied homes is, conceptually, a somewhat similar case. The services of houses that are rented are clearly part of GDP, since rental services are part of the product of the economy. What to do about the services of houses that are lived in by their owners? A fundamental principle of national income and product accounting is that the figures

should be invariant to the institutional arrangement: it should make no difference whether the home is lived in by its owner or whether it is rented. To deal with this problem, we pretend that owner-occupied homes are rented by their owners to themselves! We estimate the value of the service provided by the home to its owner as equivalent to the rental on a similar home. We include the imputed rental in the product of the economy and we include the imputed income in the income receipts of the owner.

5. The underground economy. In principle, if not always in practice, the product of what we call the informal or underground economy is a part of GDP. There is obviously a problem of measurement. But, the critical question here is not only measurement but also what should be included. The underground economy includes illegal activities like drugs. We cannot expect government accountants to include these activities in the national accounts. Unfortunately, in some countries, they are very large. The official national accounts statistics do not include illegal activities in GDP. Could it be that some of the Latin American countries look more prosperous than the statistics suggest because of the large amount of illegal activities?

6. What about the services of homemakers? Women's groups like the National Association of Women (NOW) have long argued that it is only right to include the services of housewives or househusbands in GDP. One must agree in principle. This is not only a matter of justice. If these services were performed for pay, by a housekeeper, for example, they would certainly be included in GDP. The problem is one of measurement. How do we value the work of homemakers? We could argue that they perform services like a professional housekeeper and value their services accordingly. This would not make anyone happy. Since there are many millions of homemakers, even a modest wage would yield a very large and very imprecise figure. It is better to leave well enough alone, leaving these services unmeasured.

Does the "new economy" pose any problems for measuring GDP? In nominal terms, where we are simply measuring the flow of product in terms of its market value, there is no overwhelming difference. The products of the "new economy" are sold at market prices. So long as we are simply concerned with the total market value of goods and services, dollar value figures will accurately reflect output even if the products themselves are changing.

Products in the "new economy" are likely to be very different from those in the "old." Many goods come with technologically advanced features — faster chips, video cards, flat monitors, etc. In place of manufactured goods, the output of the mass production economy, more and more "new economy" output consists of services, some of them very high-tech like Internet services, financial transactions, consulting, medical care, etc. While we can measure them in nominal terms, it is difficult to measure them in real terms. The difficulty arises when we want to measure real GDP. As we note above, real GDP represents current output at base year prices. But what do we do when product specifications change or when new goods and services are introduced for which there are no base year prices? Computers have been doubling in speed and capacity every couple of years. The Internet as a source of information or as a means of buying goods or trading stocks was unknown less than a decade ago. New medicines are being introduced that bear high prices but that are also highly effective in dealing with common diseases. Statisticians are developing techniques, called hedonic indexes, to deal with some of the difficulties posed by the "new economy." We will discuss some of these methods below. In the "new economy," there is a good deal more uncertainty with regard to measures like real GDP and the price deflator than there was in the past.

Three approaches to GDP

National accountants take three approaches to evaluating the nation's GDP (Table 3.1):

1. The Demand Approach
2. The Income Approach
3. The Value Added Approach

All three approaches should produce the same result, except for statistical discrepancies, since we are simply computing the same total, GDP, in three different ways.

Table 3.1   Three Approaches to GDP.

Value Added Approach	Income Approach	Demand Approach
Value Added, Agriculture	Wages and Salaries	Consumption
Value Added, Mining	Rental Income	Investment
Value Added, Manufacturing	Proprietors' Income	Equipment and Software
Value Added, Construction	Interest Income of Persons	Business Structures
Value Added, Services	Corporate Profits	Residential Construction
	Indirect Business Taxes	Change in Inventories
	Allowances for Depreciation	Government Consumption
	Net Income from Abroad	Government Investment
		Exports less than Imports
Gross Domestic Product	Gross Domestic Product	Gross Domestic Product

The fundamental idea is the equality between product and income. If a thousand dollars of product has been produced (and sold), then a thousand dollars of income has been generated. On the right side of Table 3.1, we sum up total sales (adjusted for inventory change):

to Consumers (C)
to Investors (I) (including inventory accumulation)
to Government (G)
plus Exports (X) (sold to abroad)
minus Imports (M) (bought abroad).

$$GDP = C + I + G + X - M. \qquad (3.3)$$

We get a figure for GDP which corresponds to the income generated plus adjustments for indirect business taxes (IBT), capital consumption allowances (CCA), and net income from abroad (NIA), shown in the middle of Table 3.1.

Wages, a return to labor (W)
Interest, a return on capital (Int)
Profit (Pr)
Indirect Business Taxes, excises, gasoline taxes, sales taxes (IBT)

Capital Consumption Allowances, adjustments for depreciation (CCA), accounting for the difference between net and gross, and

Net Income from Abroad (NIA), the difference between international income inflows and outflows, which accounts for the difference between GNP and GDP.

$$\text{GDP} = W + \text{Int} + \text{Pr} + \text{IBT} + \text{CCA} - \text{NIA}. \tag{3.4}$$

Finally, there is also a third way, to sum up GDP, shown on the left of Table 3.1. This is by looking at all the producing sectors of the economy, and by summing up their separate contributions to GDP. Each sector produces some "Value Added," one of the few self-explanatory terms in economics.

$$\text{VA}_j = \text{Sales}_j - \text{Purchases of Materials and Supplies}_j. \tag{3.5}$$

Value Added is the value of sales (adjusted for inventory accumulation as above) of sector j less what sector j has purchased from other sectors. Note that we would not want to double-count what was produced in one sector in another sector where it is utilized. That's why we compute Value Added, which equals the gross income flows generated in each sector. Adding across all the sectors j, we get a measure of total output.

$$\text{GDP} = \Sigma_j \, \text{VA}_j. \tag{3.6}$$

The fact that GDP can be computed from these three approaches has important implications for theory as we see below. It also assures some consistency since the GDP statistic can be computed from a variety of statistical sources. Hopefully, the results from various approaches will be approximately the same.

How to measure real GDP

Real GDP cannot be measured directly. We simply cannot add together apples and oranges. We can think of real GDP as a concept:

$$\text{GDP}_{\text{real}} = \Sigma_i (Q_{it} \times P_{i0}) \tag{3.7}$$

where the summation sign sums over all types of goods and services i. Quantities Q_{it} represent different product categories in year t and P_{i0} represents prices in the base year 0. The common sense interpretation is the output of the current year t in the prices of the base year 0. Note that we can also write approximately

$$\%\text{Change GDP}_{real} = \%\text{Change GDP} - \%\text{Change P}. \qquad (3.8)$$

If we begin our calculation with a figure for change in nominal GDP, the measurement of the change in the price index is critical to accurate measurement of change in real GDP.

Measuring Inflation

Inflation has been less of a problem in the 1990s than in the previous two decades. After the inflationary shocks related to oil prices in the 1970s and early 1980s (the two "horns" apparent in Fig. 1.6), it has been a pleasant surprise that inflationary pressures have abated. Low inflation has prevailed recently in the United States even though labor markets have been tight with record low unemployment rates, an indication that we are perhaps in a "new economy." Even in the developing countries, which had a spotty inflationary record often related to high rates of money growth, inflation rates have come down. Particularly notable is the improvement in Latin America where Brazil has been able to bring inflation from sky high "triple digit" rates, that impeded the development process, to single digit inflation rates that are compatible with stable economic growth.

To measure inflation, the movement of many different prices, one must define an average, one presumably which will weight prices of various goods and services according to the importance. Prices are usually measured in relation to a base year value. It is standard practice to multiply the index by 100. Suppose we define a price relative (RP_i) as the ratio of price of a particular product in the current year I, P_{it}, to its base year (year 0) price, P_{i0}. A price index can be defined as a weighted average of price relatives:

$$I_t = \Sigma_i w_i (P_{it}/P_{i0}) \times 100 \qquad (3.9)$$

where w_i represents a set of weights adding up to one. The issue, then, is what weights to use. An easy way is to simply weight the various products according to their importance in consumer purchasing, i.e. the amount spent on the particular product ($P_{i0} \times Q_{i0}$) divided by total purchasing ($\Sigma_i(P_{i0} \times Q_{i0})$) in a base year 0.

An index using base year weights, called a Laspeyres index, is

$$I_{Lt} = \Sigma((P_{i0} \times Q_{i0})/(\Sigma_i(P_{i0} \times Q_{i0}))) \times (P_{it}/P_{i0}) \times 100$$
$$= \Sigma_i(P_{it} \times Q_{i0})/\Sigma_i(P_{i0} \times Q_{i0}) \times 100. \tag{3.10}$$

This index has a common sense interpretation, the cost of buying a given market basket of goods in year t over the cost of the same market basket in year 0 (multiplied by 100).

Alternatively, one may use weights that reflect the importance of the product in the current year, a Paasche Index, i.e.

$$I_{Pt} = \Sigma_i(P_{it} \times Q_{it})/\Sigma_i(P_{i0} \times Q_{it}) \times 100. \tag{3.11}$$

This represents the comparison between the cost of purchasing a market basket of goods bought in year t with the cost of the same goods bought in year 0.

The consumer price index, CPI, is traditionally a base weighted index, using an occasional detailed survey of consumer expenditures as a basis for determining the weights. The deflator for GDP has until recently taken the form of a current weighted index. Is there a difference? Unfortunately, index number theory teaches us that the base weighted index is likely to overstate the rate of inflation. This results from the fact that consumer spending on particular products is likely to be negatively related to price. Consumers are likely to purchase fewer goods that have gone up in price. As a result, goods that have gone up in price are likely to be over-represented in a base weighted index (but under-represented in a current weighted index). As spending patterns change, this problem is likely to be more serious the further back in history is the base year. New procedures include averages of the two indexes and chaining of index numbers from one year to the next have been introduced to deal with this difficulty.

Whether price indexes measure price change with precision is important since, as we have noted, measures of inflation are frequently used to translate statistics of nominal changes in GDP into data on real changes in GDP. In that case, an underestimate of inflation of 2% might mean an overestimate of GDP growth of an equal amount. (It has been argued, for example, that the very high growth rates of Chinese GDP may reflect inadequate allowances for inflation. In place of 8% per year GDP growth, growth may only be 6%, still a large number.

There has also been much discussion of price measurement in the countries where the inflation rate in recent years has been comparatively low. The point is that, in the US, there may not be any inflation at all. The "new economy" involves such radical changes in communication and distribution services that there is often no consistent way to make price comparisons. The statistics handle changes in product quality, introduction of new products and changes in channels of distribution only very inadequately. The important point here is that if inflation is overstated, output and productivity growth have been understated, a big issue! The US economy may actually have been running with faster growth of GDP and productivity and with lower inflation than the official statistics suggest. The Federal Reserve took this possibility into account by delaying restrictive monetary policy in 1998–1999 even though the economy was growing more rapidly with lower unemployment than had earlier been anticipated. Eventually, the Fed did impose higher interest rates, after all, in order to slow the threat of overheating the economy.

The National Income Accounts

Government statisticians have linked the various aggregates into an accounting system. This system, which we discuss here, provides a logical framework. In many aspects, the National Income and Product Accounts are organized to reflect the theoretical structure that makes up the macroeconomy and to distinguish the activities of the principal participants — producers, households, etc. In contrast to business accounting, which is typically based directly on micro information, the national accounts are estimated from surveys and other approximate sources. The National Accounts framework helps to assure the consistency of the figures.

Table 3.2 outlines the main accounts and their interrelationships. (For purposes of clarification, we have simplified this material somewhat.) The national accounting system can be summarized in five interrelated accounts:

Account 1: National Income and Product Account — measuring total output and income of the economy.

Account 2: Personal Income and Outlay Account — measuring household income and its allocation.

Account 3: Government Receipts and Expenditures Account — measuring government income and spending.

Account 4: Foreign Transactions Account — seeing international transactions from a the Rest of the World perspective.

Account 5: Gross Saving and Investment Account — showing saving and investment.

(Be sure to link the verbal discussion as you go along below with the material in Table 3.2.)

Note that the total of both sides of each account must be equal. The right side, the Receipts side, must equal the left side, the Allocations side. Each item will appear on one side of one account and on the other side of another. To make that more clear, we have numbered each item, on the left for the account in which it first appears, and on the right for the counterpart entry in another account. For example "(1-1) Personal Consumption Expenditures (2-7)" means that the entry for Personal Consumption Expenditures appears as entry (1-1) on the receipts side of Account 1, National Income and Product Account, and as (2-7) on the allocations side of Account 2, the Personal Income and Outlay Account.

The principal Product and Income Account corresponds to our discussion of the alternative ways to compute GDP, above. It deals with the producers of the economy; how much they produce and how much income they generate. On the right-hand-side, typically called the Receipts side, we sum together total output from the perspective of sales of goods and services adjusted for inventory change. The component parts are: Consumption, Investment

Table 3.2   United States National Income amd Product Accounts.

Account 1   National Income and Product Account

Outlays	Receipts
(1-7) Compensation of Employees (2-1)	(1-1) Personal Consumption Expenditures (2-7)
	Durable goods
(1-8) Proprietors' Income (2-2)	Nondurable goods
	Services
(1-9) Rental Income of Persons (2-3)	
	(1-2) Gross Private Domestic Investment (5-5)
Corporate Profits	Nonresidential Structures
(1-10) Dividends (2-4)	Equipment and Software
(1-11) Undistributed Profits (5-2)	Residential Construction
(1-12) Corporate Profits Taxes (3-2)	Change in Inventories
(1-13) Net Interest (2-5)	
	Net Exports of Goods and Services
National Income	(1-3) Exports (4-4)
	(1-4) Less Imports (4-1)
(1-14) Indirect Business Taxes (3-3)	
	(1-5) Government Consumption (3-1)
(1-15) Consumption of Fixed Capital (5-3)	
	(1-6) Government Investment (3-2)
Gross National Product	
(1-16) Less Income Receipts from RoW (4-2)	
(1-17) Plus Income Payments to RoW (4-5)	
Gross Domestic Product	= **Gross Domestic Product**

Account 2   Personal Income and Outlay Account

Outlays	Receipts
(2-7) Personal Consumption Expenditures (1-1)	(2-1) Compensation of Employees (1-7)
(2-8) Personal Tax Payments (3-1)	(2-2) Proprietor's Income (1-8)
(2-9) Personal Saving (5-1)	(2-3) Rental Income of Persons (1-9)
	(2-4) Dividend Income (1-10)
	(2-5) Interest Income (1-13)
	(2-6) Government Transfers + Interest (3-6)
Personal Taxes, Outlays and Saving	= **Personal Income**

Table 3.2 (Continued)   United States National Income amd Product Accounts.

Account 3   Government Receipts and Expenditures Account

Outlays	Receipts
(3-4) Government Consumption (1-5)	(3-1) Personal Taxes (2-8)
(3-5) Government Investment (1-6)	(3-2) Corporate Profits Taxes (1-12)
(3-6) Government Transfers + Interest (2-6)	(3-3) Indirect Business Taxes (1-14)
(3-7) Surplus (+) or deficit (−) (5-4)	
Government Current Expenditures and Surplus =	**Government Current Receipts**

Account 4   Foreign Transactions Account

Outlays	Receipts
(4-4) Exports of Goods and Services (1-3)	(4-1) Imports of Goods and Services
(4-5) Income Receipts	(4-2) Income Payments (1-16)
	(4-3) Net Foreign Investment (5-7)
Receipts from Rest of World =	**Payments to Rest of World**

Account 5   Gross Saving and Investment Account

Outlays	Receipts
(5-5) Gross Private Domestic Investment (1-2)	(5-1) Personal Saving (2-9)
(5-6) Gross Government Investment (1-5)	(5-2) Undistributed Corporate Profits (1-11)
(5-7) Net Foreign Investment (4-3)	(5-3) Consumption of Fixed Capital (1-15)
	(5-4) Government Surplus or Deficit (3-7)
Gross Investments =	**Gross Saving**

Source: Survey of Current Business, December 1999 (with some simplifications).

(including inventory accumulation), Government Purchasing, and Exports minus Imports. Note that Government Consumption includes payments to government employees as well as purchases of goods and services. Also note that Exports and Imports consist not just of physical commodities. Increasingly, in the "new economy," they are made up of services such as consulting, financial services and patent licenses.

On the left of the account, the Allocations side, we show the flows of income generated. These consist of Compensation of Employees (wages and salaries), Proprietors' Income (earnings from self-employment and small firms), Rental Income, Corporate Profits and Net Interests, adding up to National Income. This represents a measure of income, national product measured at factor prices, whereas GDP is measured at market prices. To get to GDP, we must adjust for this difference. Three adjustments are needed: the first one is for Indirect Business Taxes. Indirect taxes, like sales and gasoline taxes, are passed on to consumers in the market price of the product. The second adjustment is to add back in the allowance for the Consumption of Fixed Capital (that has been taken out in the first place when National Income was computed). Gross National Product (GNP) is a gross measure — this means it does not allow for capital depreciation. National income, on the other hand, is net. It includes corporate profits after allowing for depreciation. Consequently to get to GNP we must add back in Capital Consumption Allowances, an estimate of the depreciation of capital stock. Finally, the third adjustment is needed to get from GNP to GDP, the concept that is now central to the US National Income and Product Accounts (NIPA). GDP represents GNP plus earnings on foreign assets in the US less US earnings abroad. (The latter are, of course, included in foreign countries' GDP.) The GNP concept represents income and product of the nation, a measure of our total income, including what we earn abroad less what foreigners earn on their assets held in the US. Domestic product (GDP) refers to production in the geographic boundaries of the US without regard to whether it belongs to citizens or foreigners. To get to GDP, we subtract Income Receipts from the Rest of the World and we add in Income Payments to the Rest of the World. The latter represent the foreign share in production activity that took place in the US. In the past, the US held substantial earning assets abroad, much more than foreigners held in the US. As a result, GNP exceeded GDP. But today, after the US has run current account deficits for many years, US earnings from foreign assets are about the same (a little less, actually) as foreign earnings in the US. It does not make much difference quantitatively whether we use GDP or GNP, so that we have turned to the internationally used GDP concept.

In this example, we assume that the statistics from the demand side and from the income side come out exactly the same, as they should. In practice, since national accountants draw on various sources of data, the total from the product side and the income side may not come out the same and a statistical discrepancy-adjustment item may be necessary. This adjustment is usually not large relative to other magnitudes in the accounts. Some countries show separate figures for GDP from the product side and another from the income side, but that is confusing.

Next, we turn to the account for households (Account 2). In contrast to producers, households receive income and use it to purchase consumer goods, pay taxes, and to save. On the receipts side, we sum together income receipts of consumers — Compensation of Employees, Interest, Proprietorship Income, Rental Income and Dividends. In addition, we add Transfer Payments. Transfer payments are made by government to the household sector for welfare and unemployment compensation — they are seen by consumers as income, but in contrast to wages, they are explicitly not payments for current productive effort. The total of household receipts adds up to Personal Income. On the left of the account, we allocate this total. There are Consumer Expenditures and Personal Taxes. The rest represents Personal Saving. (Note that there is no statistical discrepancy since saving is computed here as a residual. Computations based on original data sources for saving, from the Federal Reserve's Flow of Funds data, for example, may yield a different figure for saving.)

The Government Account aggregates all government agencies, federal as well as state and local. On the right, the Receipts side, we show all tax receipts. On the left, the Expenditure side, we show total government spending. When that spending is less than receipts, there will be a Surplus. That is treated here as a "non-spending" item like saving in the Household Account. Of course, if spending exceeds receipts, the deficit will show here as a negative figure. Government purchases of goods and services for consumption and investment also show up on the Receipts side of the National Income and Product Account. Transfer payments show up, as we have just noted, on the Receipts side of the Household Account. The government's aggregate Surplus or Deficit has its counterpart on the Receipts side of the Gross Saving and Investment Account.

Next, we turn to the Foreign Transactions Account which accounts for our relationships to other countries. The account is seen from the perspective of foreigners, so that an expenditure by the US, i.e. imports is shown as a positive receipt to the Foreign Transactions Account. On the receipts side, we have

Imports of Goods and Services, Income and Net Foreign Investment. The last term which accounts for the flow of foreign capital is somewhat of a misnomer since the reference is to financial asset flows rather than to real investment. Moreover, this figure is computed as a residual. If US exports exceed imports, from the foreign perspective there is an inflow of capital from the US, a positive net foreign investment. If, as is more typical in recent years, US imports exceed exports, there is a flow of foreign capital to the US that is treated as a negative entry for Net Foreign Investment on the Receipts side of the Foreign Transactions Account. On the allocations side, Net Foreign Investments is in the Gross Savings and Investments Account. Note that the difference between exports and imports in the Foreign Transactions Account shows up in the right-hand-side items of the Income and Product Account, exports with a positive sign and imports negative.

Next, we turn to the Gross Saving and Investment Account. The best way to see this is as a piggy bank into which savings flow and from which funds for investment purposes are channeled. On the Receipts side, this account shows, Personal Saving, Corporate Saving, Capital Consumption Allowances, and Government Surplus or Deficit. Note the corresponding items on the left-side of the Household, Government, and National Income and Product Accounts. In each case, the components of Gross Saving represent an allocation item in one of the other accounts. On the Allocations side, this account shows Private and Government Investment and Net Foreign Investment. As we note below, the account shows the fundamental equality between saving and investment.

The national accounts provide a quantitative picture of the economy's performance. Looking backward from an accounting perspective, the accounts are always in balance. Suppose at the beginning of a recession, a new survey signals that the figure for consumer purchasing should be revised downward, inventory change will need to be revised upward if output is to remain the unchanged. And, of course, consumption in the Personal Income Account must also be revised downward with a corresponding rise in saving, etc. Alternatively, if there also was a decline in output, there must be an appropriate revision on the income side as well, etc.

We consider the basic identities of the system below.

Some Important Identities

The national accounting system embodies some important conceptual identities. One of the critical issues is to place investment and savings into perspective. The national accounting framework is useful for this purpose. We have already noted that

$$GDP = C + I + G + X - M \qquad (3.12)$$

from the demand side.

An equivalent amount of GDP income is generated and allocated

$$GDP = C + T + S \qquad (3.13)$$

where C represents consumption, T represents taxes, and S is the residual not allocated to current consumption, i.e. saving. Consequently,

$$C + T + S = C + I + G + (X - M). \qquad (3.14)$$

Reshuffling the terms and canceling out the C's, we get

$$I = S + (T - G) + (M - X). \qquad (3.15)$$

This identity makes an important point. The level of investment (I) is determined by:

1. Saving (S) — here including corporate as well as personal saving — the first term on the right;
2. The government surplus (T − G), the second term; and
3. The net foreign capital inflow (M − X). Note that this corresponds to the current account deficit, the extent to which imports exceed exports.

The identity makes the point that investments requires saving. The more saving, the more the possibility for investing in new productive capital. And that represents a basic underpinning of economic growth.

This approach to investment applies to an economy that is operating at full employment, i.e. fully utilizing its resources. As we will see in our discussion of the business cycle in Chapter 7, in a recession, unused resources may be used to increase income and saving and that will permit more investment. But, so long as the economy's resources are in full use, more investment depends on more saving, either from domestic or foreign sources.

One of the striking contrasts between the developed economies and the countries of East Asia is with respect to saving and investment. The advanced countries have very low aggregate saving rates; private saving rates are low and governments often run deficits, i.e. they dissave. In contrast, extraordinarily high saving and investment rates have been one of the sources of rapid growth in East Asia.

Financial Statistics — Money

Financial flow statistics and interest rates represent an important aspect of the economy for most businesses, and particularly, for the financial sector. The meaning of these data has been changed in many regards with the changes that can be related to the "new economy." A very simple example during the 1980s was the spreading use of automated teller machines (ATM) and credit cards that greatly reduced the need to use currency. Some developing countries have been moving in one bound from the cash economy to the ATM and even computer or cell phone-based transactions. The development of e-business promises similar far-reaching changes.

As we will note further below, the relationship between money supply and economic activity was one of the tenets of Monetarism. The idea was that controlling money supply could be a way to control the entire economy. This meant that measures of money supply and of its relationship to GDP were very important for policy makers. If money grew too rapidly, we might run into inflation. If it grew too slowly, we could have recession. The difficulty is that there are several measures of money supply and that their relationship to GDP was not always stable. This is illustrated in Table 3.3, which shows data for four concepts of money supply (currency, M1, M2 and M3) and for nominal GDP. The annual growth rates of nominal GDP

Table 3.3   United States Financial Flows 1960–1999 (averages of daily figures, billions of dollars).

Year	M1	M2	M3	Currency	GDP $	M1	M2	M3	Currency
	Currency, Demand Deposits	M1 Plus Savings Deposits, and Small Time Deposits	M2 Plus Large Time Deposits		Percent Change Per Year				
1960	140.7	312.4	315.2	28.7	3.9	0.5	4.9	5.2	−0.3
1965	167.8	459.2	482.1	36.0	8.4	4.7	8.1	9.0	6.2
1970	214.4	626.5	677.1	48.6	5.5	5.1	6.6	9.9	6.3
1975	287.1	1016.6	1171.9	72.8	8.9	4.7	12.7	9.5	8.7
1980	408.1	1600.4	1996.3	115.3	8.9	6.9	8.5	10.3	10.0
1985	619.4	2497.4	3209.8	167.9	7.1	12.4	8.0	7.3	7.6
1990	824.6	3279.1	4155.6	247.0	5.7	4.0	3.8	1.6	11.0
1995	1126.9	3649.3	4618.6	372.3	4.9	−2.0	4.2	6.1	5.1
1996	1081.6	3824.2	4955.8	394.1	5.6	−4.0	4.8	7.3	5.9
1997	1075.2	4046.7	5403.4	424.5	6.2	−0.6	5.8	9.0	7.7
1998	1093.7	4401.4	5995.7	459.2	5.5	1.7	8.8	11.0	8.2
1999ᴾ	1125.4	4662.7	6484.9	516.9	5.6	2.9	5.9	8.2	12.6

Note: ᴾ is provisional.

and of the various money supply measures are also shown. The money supply concepts are:

Currency
M1: Currency and demand deposits.
M2: Currency, demand deposits, savings deposits, and small time deposits.
M3: Currency, demand deposits, savings deposits, and small and large time deposits.

All of these are monetary instruments, serving as a "means of exchange," and potentially, as a "store of value." In the US, currency is used only for smaller transactions. Most payments are made by credit card and/or settled by check against demand deposit balances. Today, the distinction between demand deposits and savings deposits has largely disappeared. We would expect, that M1 or M2, that are used for business transactions, would be closely related to the growth of nominal GDP. Table 3.3 shows that, from year to year, the percent changes in current GDP are not well matched by changes in the monetary aggregates; see for example, in 1990s, a period of sustained cyclical recovery. This is an important question since it undermnes the idea proposed by some "monetarists," that a smooth path of monetary growth would lead to a smooth path for GDP.

In the long run, there is clearly a relationship between growth of money supply and growth of GDP. There should be, since money serves to facilitate transactions in the economy and is one way in which people hold their assets. But, just because money supply has increased does not mean there will automatically be a corresponding increase in GDP. That said, it is important to note that massive expansion of money supply, by printing money to cover the government deficit, has been a source of runaway inflation in many countries. Hyperinflation is usually a monetary phenomenon.

Financial Statistics — Interest Rates and Stock Prices

The interest rate represents the cost of borrowing money or of holding assets in the form of money rather than in interest bearing assets. There are numerous interest rates dependent on the time horizon and risk involved.

Some of the most important are summarized in Table 3.4. US Treasury securities come in various maturities, ranging from three-month bills to 30-year T-bonds. Under normal circumstances, as we show below, the rates on long term bonds are higher than on short term paper since the market value of bonds is likely to vary prior to maturity. Corporate bonds are rated on the basis of risk. We show interest yields on the best Aaa and on lesser quality bonds, Baa. Commercial paper represents short term commercial borrowing against outstanding bills. The prime rate is the rate charged by banks to prime commercial borrowers. The discount rate is the rate charged by the Federal Reserve to lend reserves to member banks. It is one of the tools used by the

Table 3.4   United States Interest Rates and Bond Yields (percent per annum).

Year	US Treasury Securities				Corporate Bonds (Moody's)		Prime Rate	Discount Rate	Federal Funds
	Bills	Bonds			Aaa	Baa			
	3-month	3-year	10-year	30-year					
1960	2.92	3.98	4.12	—	4.41	5.19	4.82	3.53	3.22
1965	3.95	4.22	4.28	—	4.49	4.87	4.54	4.04	4.07
1970	6.45	7.29	7.35	—	8.04	9.11	7.91	5.95	7.18
1975	5.83	7.49	7.99	—	8.83	10.61	7.86	6.25	5.82
1980	11.50	11.55	11.46	11.27	11.94	13.67	15.27	11.77	13.36
1985	7.48	9.64	10.62	10.79	11.37	12.72	9.93	7.69	8.10
1990	7.51	8.26	8.55	8.61	9.32	10.36	10.01	6.98	8.10
1995	5.51	6.25	6.57	6.88	7.59	8.20	8.83	5.21	5.83
1996	5.02	5.99	6.44	6.71	7.37	8.05	8.27	5.02	5.30
1997	5.07	6.10	6.35	6.61	7.26	7.86	8.44	5.00	5.46
1998	4.81	5.14	5.26	5.58	6.53	7.22	8.35	4.92	5.35
1999	4.66	5.49	5.65	5.87	7.04	7.87	8.00	4.62	4.97
2000	5.85	6.22	6.03	5.94	7.62	8.36	9.23	5.73	6.24
2001 (September)	2.87	3.14	4.53	5.33	7.17	8.03	6.5–6.0	3.0–2.5	3.07

Source: US Joint Economic Committee, *Economic Indicators*, September 2001.

Fed to influence interest rates throughout the economy. Finally, the Federal funds rate is the shortest rate of all, the rate banks charge each other for overnight money needed to meet the central bank's reserve requirements.

One perspective on interest rates is the yield curve (Fig. 3.1). The interest yield of various assets is shown on the vertical axis. The maturity of these assets is shown on the horizontal axis. We would anticipate that long term instruments, like the 30-year Treasury bond would yield a higher return than short term instruments like three-month T-bills or the overnight Federal Funds rate. For this reason, the yield curve is normally upward sloped. There are times, however, when the curve is flat or inverted, as is shown on Fig. 3.1. Many analysts see an inverted or flat yield curve as a signal of tight money.

Stock prices are another important aspect of financial markets and have important implications for the rest of the economy. Figure 3.2 shows the recent movement of various stock price indexes. In the second half of the 1990s, US stock markets surged. This has been referred to as "bubble" economy. It not certain whether this stock market increase reflected a real change, what we have termed a "new economy." Certainly the sharpest swing was in technology stocks and in the NASDAQ index which contains newer high-tech companies. Federal Reserve Chairman, Alan Greenspan, long argued that the rise in stock values represents "irrational exuberance" that cannot be supported by anticipated future earnings. There are serious implications for the whole economy, not just for financial markets. In late 2000, the bubble burst. Financial institutions and banks could be in trouble and have been hesitant

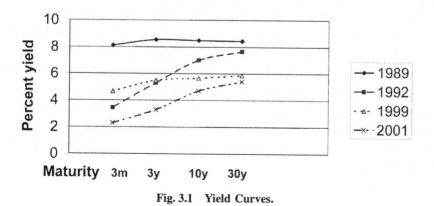

Fig. 3.1 Yield Curves.

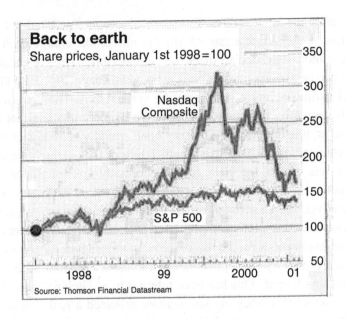

Fig. 3.2   Recent Stock Market Trends.

to make loans. Many stockholders, who by now make up almost half the US population, were hurt. They, in turn, seeing their wealth reduced, cut back on luxury spending on vacations, big houses and luxury cars. A sharp decline in the stock market could provoke a recession. Policy makers have been well aware of the problem, but they face a conundrum. Should they impose tight money and high interest rates at the potential cost of a stock market crash and a recession? Or should they loosen money and risk inflation? No wonder, the Fed hesitated, before it eased monetary policy in early 2001.

Stock markets are important and large in scale in developed country financial markets — the London Stock Exchange and other European exchanges are considering a giant merger. There are also active stock markets in many of the world's developing country capitals. In many cases, they serve as a base for speculation and are highly volatile. Let the buyer beware!

International Trade

International trade, the exchange rate and capital flows play an important role influencing economic performance. The phenomenal progress of East Asian countries is related to the rapid expansion of their exports and their increasing participation in world markets. However, turmoil in the world economy created by the East Asian crisis in 1997 was closely linked to international financial developments. As the global economy becomes ever more interrelated, as transportation and communication costs decline and capital flows proliferate, international payments stability has become the *sine qua non* of stable economic growth.

We will be considering the implications of internationalization in greater detail in Part IV of this book. They are central to maintaining economic growth and stability in the "new economy." At this point, we will consider only the basic statistics on trade as they relate to the national accounts. Data for US imports and exports are shown in Table 3.3; trade is shown in billions of current dollars. The flows of goods and services were quite well balanced until the 1980s, when the US turned into a deficit country, a recipient of large inflows of foreign capital (Net Foreign Investment). This is also shown on Fig. 3.3. As we will explain below, the inflow of capital into the US has helped

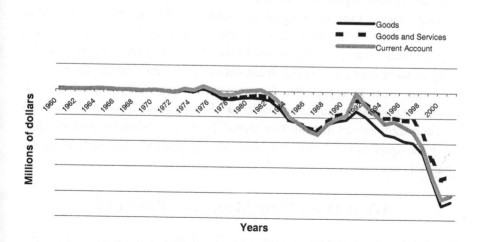

Fig. 3.3   US Balance of Payments (1960–2001).

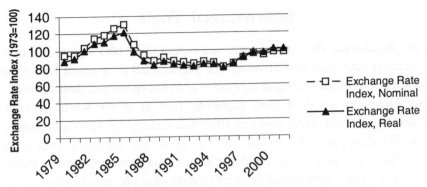

Fig. 3.4   **US Exchange Rate Index (Against Major Currencies).**

to supplement domestic shortages of saving. It is not damaging so long as US debts do not become excessively large and as long as foreigners retain confidence in the US economy.

The exchange rate of the US dollar has depreciated against foreign currencies since the early 1980s but it has shown substantial strength in the late 1990s (Fig. 3.4). This suggests that foreign investors still have substantial confidence in their holdings of US financial assets. There is not yet reason for serious concern about the US balance of payments.

Many developing economies operate much closer the limit, however. The exchange rate is a critical issue in determining trade competitiveness and in influencing the ability of debtors in these countries to pay their foreign currency obligations. The experience of the 1980s and 1990s suggests that for many of these countries, foreign trade deficits represent a substantial risk. On one hand, it can be argued that these countries need foreign capital inflows. Large flows of foreign capital are welcome. But, particularly, when these flows are short term money that must be repaid if foreign lenders become worried, there are significant risks of exchange rate depreciation, and often, domestic financial disarray.

What Does This Mean for Business?

In observing the economic environment, the challenge to business is to keep one's eyes on the broader picture, the macroeconomy, at the same time as

Table 3.5 Foreign Transactions in the National Income and Product Accounts (1960–1999) (billions of dollars).

Year	Receipts from Rest of the World				Payments to Rest of the World				
	Exports		Income Receipts	Total	Imports		Income Payments	Transfers	Net Foreign Investment
	Goods	Services			Goods	Services		Total	
1960	20.5	4.8	5.0	30.2	15.2	7.6	1.8	2.4	3.2
1965	27.8	7.6	8.1	43.5	22.2	9.3	2.7	3.0	6.2
1970	44.5	12.4	13.0	69.9	40.9	14.9	6.6	3.6	4.0
1975	109.6	26.7	28.2	164.4	99.0	23.7	14.9	5.4	21.4
1980	225.8	53.2	81.8	360.7	248.6	45.3	46.5	9.0	11.4
1985	222.2	80.8	113.1	416.1	343.3	73.9	87.8	22.1	-110.9
1990	398.5	158.6	188.3	745.5	508.0	120.6	159.3	26.8	-69.2
1995	583.8	234.7	232.3	1050.8	757.6	145.2	211.9	34.0	-98.0
1996	618.4	255.8	245.6	1119.7	808.3	154.8	227.5	39.8	-110.7
1997	689.0	279.0	282.6	1250.6	885.1	171.2	278.4	39.6	-123.7
1998	681.3	285.1	285.3	1251.6	930.4	185.5	295.2	42.0	-201.5
1999	697.5	298.8	—	—	1048.9	204.2	—	44.7	—

one keeps track of the detailed information reflecting the performance of the business and of the sector in which it operates. Clearly, trends in sales and costs will be the first information available to the business manager and these must be acted upon without delay. But broader information about what is happening to the industry or to the economy as a whole is often very important, particularly from a somewhat longer time perspective. There is no doubt, for example, that Thai managers who recognized the slowing of Thai exports in 1996 or who saw the buildup of vacant office space in the middle of a construction boom, were likely to make better strategic decisions than those who "kept their heads in the sand." On the other hand, for many managers it would have been difficult to predict the "meltdown" of the baht and of financial institutions in 1997, considering that this was not reflected in published statistics and considering that many private and public agents were still proclaiming the continued strength of the East Asian miracle. One can only draw the conclusions that economy entails substantial risks and that business managers must be well informed at all times.

Questions for Discussion

* What are the principal measures of an economy's macroeconomic performance?
* How are these measures linked together into a consistent accounting system?
* Discuss some of the problems of accurately measuring price change.
* Do the identities of the economy hold when the economy is operating below full employment? What are the implications of full employment or recession of the meaning of these identities?
* Is there a close relationship between money supply and the growth of GDP? What would you expect? Why?
* What are the principal relevant international statistics and how can they influence the domestic economy?
* Is the US running a surplus or deficit on its trade? What are its implications?

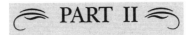

PART II

Growth and Development

This part is concerned with the theory of growth and development. We consider the basics of economic growth theory as it applies to industrial and to developing countries. The "new economy" has helped to redirect thinking about growth. We discuss the development experience, with special emphasis on East Asia. What special factors have allowed the East Asian countries to jump-start themselves into what has been termed the "East Asian Miracle?" Then, we study policy, specifically the relationship between policy and growth and development.

Chapter 4

Economic Growth and the "New Economy"

In this chapter, we lay out the theoretical background of the determinants of economic growth. We focus on the production function and its inputs, and on the concept of Total Factor Productivity (TFP) and growth accounting. We discuss the growth record of the United States and East Asia. We discuss the new theories that endogenize the growth process. Finally, we consider the implications of the "new economy" for thinking about economic growth.

Introduction

Economic growth and economic development are closely intertwined. But theoretical views on how growth and development take place have, until recently, gone down very different conceptual paths. Growth theorists have generally looked at the economy as an aggregate. They have asked how growth is determined and what long-run prospects for growth are likely to be. They have been concerned primarily with mature economies using a common technology, though their theories can be applied to a range of economies at different stages of development.

Development economics, on the other hand, is the study of economic change, from the primitive low income economy to the advanced high income economy. Development economists have focused on the duality of the less developed economy, on the sharp differences between its subsistence rural sector and its more advanced urban and manufacturing industries. Development economists have been concerned with the barriers to growth and the strategies that countries can use to overcome these constraints to achieve higher living standards.

In recent years, still another perspective has been that of the economic "transition" from the socialist command economy to the free market. This transition applies in some cases to fairly advanced industrial countries, like those of Eastern Europe, and in others, to low income developing economies like Vietnam or Cambodia.

The "new economy" has changed much thinking about the growth process. What were once seen as the "mature" economies, today, are at the threshold of a new era of technical change. What makes the new knowledge-based developments so different is that they break many of the constraints that have traditionally been associated with resource use. New discoveries may be costly to make and to bring to commercial application, but once made, their expanded use incurs very low marginal costs. Once an advanced computer program has been built, it can be applied widely at little cost. In many cases, there are enormous externalities, with widespread benefit beyond that captured by the developer. Moreover, innovations originating in one country can often be taken advantage of in other countries, poor as well as advanced. Satellite communications have opened worldwide television and the Internet to developing countries like India and China. The value of computer network applications like the Internet increases exponentially with the number of interacting subscribers. This means that there are enormous economies of scale. On the other hand, the new developments call for specialized human resources, like computer expertise, that are scarce except in the most advanced countries. How does the "new economy" alter our views of economic growth? How does it change the prospects for the mature countries and for the developing economies?

In this chapter, we will focus on economic growth. The next chapter will be concerned with the economic development experience.

Theory and Measurement of Growth

The production function serves as the basic framework of the theory of economic growth. The production function is simply a recipe for how inputs are combined into output. A nation's aggregate output depends on inputs of capital (K) and labor (L). How these inputs are combined depends on technology (A). We begin by assuming that technology remains unchanged. The production function can be shown graphically (Fig. 4.1). In the vertical direction we show labor productivity, output per unit of labor input (Y/L).

Y/L

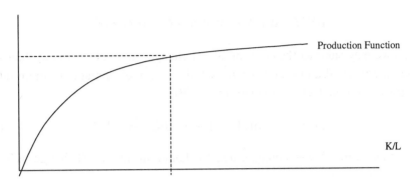

Fig. 4.1   The Production Function with Diminishing Returns.

In the horizontal direction, we measure capital intensity, capital per unit of capital input (K/L). Note that output, here shown as output per worker (Y/L), increases as more capital is used per worker (K/L), but the increases are not proportional to capital input. Diminishing returns are shown by the fact that the production function gradually flattens.

Algebraically, the typical production function written as

$$Y = A_t L^a K^{(1-a)} \tag{4.1}$$

is equivalent in logarithms to

$$LnY = LnA_t + a\,LnL + (1-a)LnK. \tag{4.2}$$

This simple form is known as the Cobb-Douglas function. The terms a and (1 – a) represent the elasticities of output with respect to inputs of labor and capital, respectively. Note that they add up to 1, so that as shown here, proportional increases in inputs translate into corresponding proportional increases in output. (In technical economics, this is called constant returns to scale.) We assume that technology can shift over time, the subscript t on A. In logarithms, the function is additive and we see clearly that the effect of technical change is simply additive to the effect of inputs of labor and capital — it is assumed that there are no interactions.

We may translate this function into percentage differences

$$dY/Y = dA/A + a \times dL/L + (1-a) \times dK/K \tag{4.3}$$

and we may subtract the contribution of changes in inputs from the changes in income to yield a measure for growth that is not attributable to more inputs, known as total factor productivity (TFP).

$$dY/Y - (a \times dL/L + (1-a) \times dK/K) = dA/A \tag{4.4}$$

%change in GDP − %change due to change in inputs = %change in TFP.

In equation (4.4), TFP, dA/A, is computed as a residual. It is sometimes referred to as the Solow residual or the "residual element in economic growth." This is an appropriate nomenclature since, as we see further below, it contains all the things that are not accounted for directly by the contribution of K and L.

The way in which economic progress involves increasing use of capital *and* shifts in technology is illustrated in Fig. 4.2. The curve marked "Traditional Technology" assumes that a country continues to use old-fashioned technology and simply increases capital inputs. Productivity increases as more capital per worker is used. But, because of diminishing returns, output does not rise proportionally with increasing use of capital. Indeed, after a certain point, additional inputs of capital yield little or no gains in productivity. This was the situation observed in heavy industry in the former Soviet Union and in some Chinese state-owned enterprises. Early in their development, the heavy industries in these countries showed substantial gains in output and productivity as huge new plants were constructed. By the 1970s, the payoff from these investments was beginning to diminish. The heavy industries became increasingly capital intensive, but they showed few gains in productivity because of failure to update technology.

The curve marked "Technological Frontier" shows the results of using advanced technology, like that available in the industrial countries. In this connection, the term "technology" must be interpreted broadly. It includes all sorts of considerations in addition to purely engineering/technical ones. It includes the organization of production, management, education of workers,

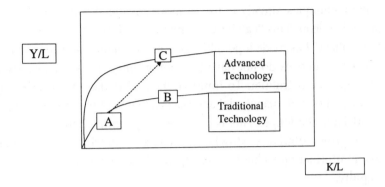

Fig. 4.2   Production Possibilities with Traditional and Advanced Technologies.

control of quality, product specifications, shifts from inefficient to efficient industries, etc. At the technological frontier, there are also limits to the profitable utilization of capital, but productivity is much higher all along the line than using traditional technology.

Beginning with point A, a country can make only limited progress by increasing capital intensity, for example to point B. It is necessary not only to use more capital, but also to improve technology, going from point A to point C. The shift from one curve to the other represents the improvement in productivity that is achieved through higher level technology, through shifting to more highly productive industries, and through economies of scale. Such changes are frequently related to investment, which is often a means to introduce new technology. For simplicity, the discussion of TFP assumes that the gains in TFP are independent of the use of capital. This is a way to disentangle the contribution to production of elements other than inputs, but it is not realistic. As we note in our discussion of endogenous growth below, in practice, it may not be possible realistically to account separately for gains in TFP since investment is often a means to introduce new technology and/or to utilize technically skilled labor. Moreover, new technology may itself be determined endogenously as a result of price and cost incentives.

The developing countries of East Asia began on the lower production curve but have had the opportunity to shift to a higher production curve. By borrowing techniques already in use in more advanced countries, they made a technological leap. This "catch up," sometimes referred to as "the advantage of backwardness" has made it possible for some of them to advance so rapidly. More mature countries do not have this opportunity. They are already close to the technological frontier. To improve their TFP, they must develop new technology and/or new managerial approaches that shift the "frontier" upward, a more difficult challenge. This is a reason why, until recently, productivity tended to grow relatively slowly in mature countries. Today, massive progress in information technology is apparently allowing them again to grow more rapidly.

Growth Accounting

How can we put some quantitative dimensions on such a computation? A very simple approach would be to estimate the values of (dA/A), (a), and (1 − a) by doing an empirical regression of changes in output (dY/Y) on changes in inputs of capital and labor (dK/K and dL/L). The value of (dA/A) would be the constant of the regression. The difficulty is that such a regression is not likely to have much precision since K and L are likely to move quite closely together over time. And the implied assumption that A moves smoothly over time may not be realistic. We need another way to get at the value of A and we need to be able to compute the values of A as they change, perhaps irregularly, over time.

Economic theory can come to the rescue. In purely competitive markets, wages will be equal to the marginal product of labor (MPL) since employers will hire workers up to the point where the wage equals MPL. The marginal product of capital will equal the return to capital. Assuming competitive markets and constant returns to scale, a and (1 − a) will equal respectively the share of labor and capital in total output.[1] Over time, the residual change in

---

[1] a is the elasticity of output with respect to labor, (dY/dL)/(Y/L). If the wage (w) equals the marginal productivity of labor (dY/dL), we can write: a = (dY/dL)/(Y/L) = (w × L)/Y where the term on the right is the labor share of GDP. A similar calculation can be made for the capital share. Assuming constant returns to scale, the terms (1 − a) and a add up to 1.

factor productivity, A, can be estimated as in equation (4.4). This approach has been the mainstay of TFP estimation and growth accounting for many years.

The factors contributing to the growth of output are shown quantitatively on Table 4.1 for the United States. Total growth in the US over a period of over 30 years is estimated at 2.9% per year of which 1.9 represents the effect of increases in inputs. The remaining 1% per year is TFP.

Whether TFP has made a substantial contribution to East Asian growth, or whether the rapid growth in the area is largely "input based," i.e. the result of very massive investment, has been the subject of vivid controversy. For the East Asian countries, the results vary and are very much in discussion. On Table 4.2, we show estimates based on the factor share calculation discussed above. Some of these calculations (Young 1995 and Kim and Lau 1994) imply that there has been little or no TFP in some Asian countries like Singapore, i.e. that rapid growth has simply been the result of massive factor inputs. However, these results seem counterintuitive. Even casual visits to East Asia over a period of years would suggest that rapid changes in the ways in which production is carried on, in products and in their distribution, have been going on. In contrast, other estimates which take a different approach attribute a substantial share of growth in East Asia to TFP, i.e. to technology or other

Table 4.1 Decomposition of Growth in the US 1960–1990 (% per year).

Total growth of GDP	2.9
Contribution of labor	1.5
Contribution of capital	0.4
Contribution of L and K	1.9
Total factor productivity (TFP)	1.0
Of which attributable to:	
Economies of scale	0.1
Shifts between sectors	0.4
Increased regulation	−0.2
Education/experience	0.2
Improvements in technology	0.5

Table 4.2   Total Factor Productivity in East Asia.

Country	Period	Growth of TFP (% p.a.)	Share of Total Growth (% when available)	Source
Indonesia	1960–94	0.8%	23.5%	Collins and Bosworth (1997)
	1970–90	−0.47%	−9.6%	Marti (1996)
Thailand	1960–94	1.8%	36%	Collins and Bosworth (1997)
	1970–90	1.65%	42.5%	Marti (1996)
Singapore	1966–90	0%	0%	Kim and Lau (1994)
	1960–94	1.5%	27.8%	Collins and Bosworth (1997)
South Korea	1966–90	−0.5%	−6%	Kim and Lau (1994)
	1966–90	1.7%	16.5%	Young (1995)
	1960–94	1.5%	26.3%	Collins and Bosworth (1997)
Taiwan	1966–90	0%	0%	Kim and Lau (1994)
	1966–90	2.6%	27.6%	Young (1995)
	1960–94	2.0%	34.5%	Collins and Bosworth (1997)
Hong Kong	1966–90	0%	0%	Kim and Lau (1994)
	1966–91	2.3%	31.5%	Young (1995)
Japan	1970–85	1.2%		Marti (1996)
	1970–90	0.9%	25.8%	Marti (1996)
Philippines	1960–94	−0.4%	−37.9%	Collins and Bosworth (1997)
Malaysia	1970–85	1%		Young (1994)
	1960–94	0.9%	23.7%	Collins and Bosworth (1997)
	1970–90	0.4%	12.9%	Marti (1996)

Source: Data drawn from Felipe J. (April 1999), "Total factor productivity growth in East Asia: a critical survey," *Journal of Development Studies* **35**(4), 1–41.

References:
Collins S. and Bosworth B. (1997), "Economic growth in East Asia: accumulation versus assimilation," *Brooking Papers in Economic Activity* **2**, 135–203.
Kim J. and Lau L. (1994), "The sources of economic growth of the East Asian newly industrialized economies," *Journal of Japanese and International Economics* **8**, 235–271.
Marti C. (1996), *Is there an East Asian Miracle?* Economic Research Working Paper, Union Bank of Switzerland.
Young A. (1994), "Accumulation, exports, and growth in the high performing Asian economies, a comment," *Carnegie-Rochester Conference Series on Public Policy* **40**, 237–250.
Young A. (August 1995), "The tyranny of numbers: confronting the statistical realities of the East Asian growth experience," *Quarterly Journal of Economics*, 651–680.

shifts in the production function. The explanation for the differences in results is not so much in the reality as in the computation. If one views technical change as an endogenous phenomenon, linked to capital accumulation, or if one argues that "knowledge capital" does not incur diminishing returns, the residual left to explain is very small. If on the other hand, one visualizes technological change as exogenous or separate, the residual turns out to be substantial. Some claims and computations notwithstanding, technological and structural change have played an important role in the rapidly developing countries of East Asia. Nevertheless, growth in East Asia does involve high rates of increase of inputs based on high savings rates. It is the combination of high inputs with technical change that accounts for the spectacular growth in the region.

Growth accountants have, also, tried to break down TFP into component parts. The forces that account for TFP growth are considerably broader than what we customarily think of as technology. All the factors other than the contribution of labor and capital at constant returns to scale show up in the residual. A breakdown is an instructive though inexact exercise. We show examples for the US but it would be difficult to quantify such a breakdown for the Asian countries. Important gains showing up in the "residual" reflect the shift of resources out of low to high productivity sectors. For many years, in the US this meant shifts out of agriculture into manufacturing. For a long time, these gains have been muted as shifts have been from manufacturing into the service sectors, some of which have low levels of productivity, but more recently shifts have been toward high productivity services like finance and technology. Some gains are attributable to the contribution of economies of scale, a reason for growing consolidation of e-businesses.

Strikingly, some contributions to the growth of productivity are negative. In the US, the productivity trend attributable to public sector regulation is thought to be negative. This is not, as some might imagine, just "the dead hand of government regulation." Much of it represents the cost of tighter environmental regulations. On one hand, there is a resource cost to pollution control; on the other, the gain in terms of a cleaner atmosphere is not measured in GDP!

As we have noted, some gains may be attributable to better quality labor inputs. Education and experience have not been measured in the labor inputs considered above. Instead labor input is, basically a count of manhours. In many countries, the labor force has become more educated. In recent years, it has also become more mature and experienced and this has increased its productivity. Finally, what is left may be called technology. To some extent, this represents technological improvement, in the traditional sense, i.e. better machinery and production processes. But to an important degree it may also represent improved management, attributable to the business schools rather than to engineering schools!

The "New Economy" and the New Growth Theory

From a theoretical point of view, the traditional TFP approach has serious shortcomings. TFP is exogenous. Over time, technical progress just proceeds on its merry way without a true economic explanation. The assumption of constant returns to scale, that is so convenient as a means of separating technological change from input-based growth, is unrealistic in many cases. Moreover, since capital runs into diminishing returns, it can be shown that, once the optimal capital stock has been built up relative to labor supply, additional savings and investments will not speed up growth. Once the system is in equilibrium, the rate of growth is independent of the savings/investment rate. GDP growth depends entirely on the rate of technical change (and population). The production function shifts upward in equilibrium as a result of technical change. But technical change is not explained in the model at all, leaving a system whose long-run equilibrium growth rate is determined by external forces. No wonder, economists were not satisfied with this approach. More complex theories are now providing a more sophisticated explanation.

The new approaches reflect what we see in the real world as the "new economy." The term "new economy" refers to rapid expansion of knowledge-based activities. We speak of information technology (IT), biotech, telecom, wireless, e-business, business to business (B2B) and business to consumer (B2C), etc. These cases have a number of common aspects; all of them represent contributions of new knowledge, the potentials of new science and technology. All of them are based on research or technical development. Generally, after the initial development has taken place, the new procedures can be extended widely at low marginal cost. An important aspect of knowledge is that there is benefit to society or to outsiders in addition to that obtained by the developers, i.e. there are externalities. Consequently, one may argue that knowledge represents a form of capital without diminishing returns. For the developer, there will undoubtedly be diminishing returns. But for the society, where there is room to extend use of the new ideas widely, the assumption of constant returns (no decline in marginal returns as use expands) may be appropriate for long periods of time. There may also be increasing returns to scale, many of them associated with the "network" aspects of the new technologies.

Modern growth theory has gone some steps further than the standard growth theory. Whereas in the discussion above, we see a production function shifting upward with changes in technology, the new growth theorists like to see only one production function which embodies all the forces contributing to the growth of output — hence the term endogenous growth theories. The idea is to explain endogenously as part of the economic system all the forces contributing to growth, leaving little or no "residual."

One way to accomplish that is to introduce human capital into the production function. We can write:

$$Y = A \times f(K_p, K_h, L) \tag{4.5}$$

where K_p and K_h stand for physical and human capital, respectively. There is no doubt about the importance of human capital reflecting levels of education and experience. Improved education and specific computer skills are particularly important in the "new economy." On the other hand, it is difficult to establish the appropriate coefficients measuring the contribution of human capital. There are, moreover, interactions between human capital and other aspects of the economy, like its capital stock and its communications and transportation infrastructure. A poor economy may not be able to use sophisticated technology and high level engineers.

A closely related approach introduces efficiency directly into the production function. For example, we may insert A directly into the function by seeing capital inputs as enhanced by the technological factor A. A similar approach can be taken with labor input by measuring it in terms of efficiency units or by introducing investments in human capital explicitly. This leads to a production function like

$$Y = f(K \times A, L \times E) \qquad (4.6)$$

where A represents the technology embodied in capital and E represents the impact of human capital or labor quality as improving the labor inputs. This approach potentially introduces technical progress directly into the production function. It avoids the problems of the Solow function (4.2) that the improvement of technology is left entirely outside the system, an unexplained external contributor to production. Ideally, only random variations are left unexplained. Technology takes the form of improvements in capital and labor efficiency and is counted as inputs.

Endogenous growth theories add some other important assumptions. For example, Romer (1986) argues that knowledge once developed can be applied widely at little or no cost. In terms of technical economics, knowledge capital is subject to constant returns. We can summarize this in a production function as follows:

$$Y = A(R) \times f(K, L, R) \qquad (4.7)$$

where R stands for the stock of knowledge. This would mean that output can increase proportionately with increases in knowledge capital, given other factors. How is this possible? Here, Romer makes an important distinction between private and public returns. As we have noted, from the perspective of the individual firm, accumulation of capital, knowledge as well as physical capital, always runs into diminishing returns. You cannot expect to increase output proportionately with inputs of more and more capital (but not more labor) *ad infinitum*. But one firm can develop new ideas and use them. Other firms can pick them up at no cost. This represents imitative technology, an externality that helps to increase productivity in the overall economy, by more than the gain made by the originating firm. Such knowledge externalities can be produced in a number of ways — as a result of research and development, "learning by doing" experience, even the knowledge of international trading partners. The important point is that, at the level of the national economy, there may be ample room to use new ideas with constant (or increasing) returns even though the individual firm that introduced the innovation may be running into diminishing returns.

The introduction of new technology may also change the economics of scale. In place of constant returns to scale, there may be times when there may be increasing returns to scale. Modern growth theory has integrated the theory of research and development, seeing inventive activity as purposeful, granting the inventor temporary monopoly advantage. Efforts to develop new products and production technologies may, themselves, depend on economic considerations like prices and costs.

Government plays a significant role in some of these approaches, providing support for education and research and development and setting up the legal and infrastructure framework in which growth can take place. By relating the equilibrium growth path directly to the rate of investment in physical or human capital, the new growth models have overcome the limitations of the standard approach growth model that in equilibrium growth is simply the growth of technology (and population).

Which of these views, the traditional approach with shifting production functions or the endogenous growth theories are most useful for studying economic progress empirically and for prescribing policy? Which ones are most relevant to explaining economic development?

There is no doubt about the sophistication of endogenous growth. Endogeneous growth theorists have pointed out that the growth process contains important interactions, the potential for interaction between new investment and the introduction of technical change, the role of education and knowledge, and the potential that new technology can be valuable more widely than to the original developer. But one may question the fundamental assumption of some of this work, that all countries are on the same production function. If knowledge were fully mobile and available to all, one could argue that everyone is on the same production function and has the same opportunity to use knowledge. But that is not the case. Production processes in poor countries are inefficient not because producers choose to make them so. They are inefficient because producers do not know how to produce more efficiently or because they lack the combination of skills or suppliers that allows the use of the most advanced production methods. The flip side of that view leads to an optimistic outcome. The transfer of knowledge, through education, learning by doing, foreign direct investment, production for export markets etc., pays tremendous dividends in improved productive ability. Much of the growth of the developing world can be called imitative technology, using methods that have been pioneered in more advanced countries. Some of these factors are measurable, others are not. The very fact that some countries are still "backward" in terms of technology, broadly defined, means that they have opportunities to modernize by using technology available from more advanced countries. In effect, in developing countries many gains are made by shifting from traditional production methods to more advanced techniques.

The process of economic development in East Asia, which we describe in greater detail below, illustrates how effective shifts from a primitive production function to one closer to the technological frontier can be. These shifts involve combinations of various factors like physical capital, human capital, as well as advanced technology and management. We will discuss the policies that have facilitated the development process.

Implications for Business

While growth theory operates on a highly aggregated level, it has serious implications for business. Our first concern is with the prospects for business in the advanced countries. As we turn to developing countries, we ask whether growth theory has any implications for the individual business enterprise.

For the advanced industrial countries, the "new economy" offer opportunities that traditional growth theorists had not foreseen. Instead of a plodding pace of technological change along a predetermined trend, the new views see potential for another industrial revolution, leading to more rapid economic progress. These developments are likely to change the structure of the economy toward increasingly sophisticated services. These call for a high level of technical training. The risk is a growing educational and income divide, between people who have the appropriate skills, who will do well indeed, and those who lack the requisite education and will fall behind. Business strategists must adapt their firms to this new environment, keeping their firms up to date and taking advantage of new opportunities.

From a broad forward-looking perspective, a less developed but growing economic setting offers opportunities that are not available in a mature society.

Most less developed countries are only just beginning to participate in the "new economy," though some like Taiwan and Singapore are basing their development strategy on new technology. There will be opportunities to introduce new products and services and to utilize advanced techniques that may already be "old hat" in more advanced regions. For many products, the barrier of geographic distance has been reduced or, in a few cases, eliminated. It is astonishing to hear that check processing, customer service, and computer programming are increasingly being outsourced to developing economies — airlines are doing data processing in Barbados! A country economy that is undergoing rapid technical change, where the production process is changing, will provide openings for new higher technology services and equipment. There will be linkages from one industry to another: needs for parts suppliers, for technical services, for finance, etc.

We should note here that the process is not simply from the macroeconomic environment to business. On the contrary, the very process of growth reflects the actions of thousands of businesses. Economists look at data that are aggregates of millions of micro actions, in this case the decisions of business managers to make investments, start new business endeavors, or expand toward marketing new products and services. The rapid growth of East Asia is built on the actions of enterprises, multinational as well as domestic, taking advantage of business opportunities created as countries move along the path to economic development. While economists are primarily concerned with aggregate economic performance, business executives must deal every day with detailed business decisions such as what to produce, where to produce, and how to produce. They must see not only the business environment but also the actions of competitors, the opportunities related to new technology, the possibilities in new markets, as well as meet many other complex challenges.

Questions for Discussion

* What explains economic growth? Is it different from economic development?
* Are growth prospects for advanced countries different from those of developing countries? Why?

* What exactly is a production function? How might one handle technological progress in a production function framework?
* What is total factor productivity? What might be its principal components?
* Discuss the interactions between inputs and technology that may govern the growth process.
* Does the "new economy" offer new and different prospects for growth? Explain.

Chapter 5

Economic Development:
The East Asian Experience

This chapter illustrates growth, economic development and crisis largely in terms of the East Asian experience. First, to explain the East Asian miracle, we put together the notions of growth theory and development theory. We do so by developing a product cycle theory that provides the basis for an economic development ladder. We consider the role of this process in the economic development of East Asia. Then we extend our view to the developed countries, evaluating the evidence for a "new economy." Finally, we consider the implications of the "new economy" for the developing countries. The role of government policy in the growth and development process is considered in the next chapter.

Approaches to Economic Development

Four decades ago, W.W. Rostow, 1961, proposed that economic development could be described as a sequence of stages.

The traditional society — Subsistence agriculture, largely rural, low incomes, high birth and death rates, and no significant increase in living standards.

The preconditions for takeoff — A surplus of product and labor force in agriculture, some savings, the beginnings of urban commercial banking development, and basic transport and communications infrastructure.

The takeoff — A period of rapid transformation, urbanization, beginning of labor-intensive manufacturing, a switch toward production of manufactures for export markets, need for infrastructure, high saving and investment, and rapidly rising living standards, particularly in urban areas.

The drive to maturity — A period of sustained rapid growth as industry develops and shifts from labor-intensive manufacturing toward more high-tech, capital-intensive methods, high levels of savings and investments, rising wage levels, appreciating currencies, and rapidly expanding GDP.

The age of high mass consumption — The period of maturity characterized by high living standards, increased service production and high-tech manufacturing but with relatively slower and relatively more modest improvements in productivity than in the previous periods.

According to Rostow, these stages would follow one another like the takeoff of an airplane seeking its normal flight altitude, an S-curve of development, starting slowly when the economy was ready, accelerating rapidly for a rapid growth spell, and then slowing again at maturity.

This happy analogy was derided by serious economists. The most serious charge against the Rostow approach was that it lacked substantive content. Rostow did not explain what forces made the development process take place? Why does one country "take off," while others languish in poverty? He did not suggest what policies assure continued progress toward maturity. The Rostow approach does not deal with the many cases where takeoff has not taken place. Some of the countries of Africa have lost their traditional society but have never "taken off." It does not deal with the many other failures or interruptions of development — wind shear or air pockets in terms of the Rostow analogy. Latin America, which showed so much promise in the 1960s, ran into serious problems of debt, inflation and recession in the 1980s. Modifying a favorite Brazilian saying at the time of the boom: "God is (not) a Brazilian!" after all.

Until 1997, the Rostow analogy fits East Asia astonishingly well. The four East Asian "tigers," the newly industrializing economies (NIEs), have come close to achieving industrial country status after less than three decades of rapid growth. They are fast becoming high mass consumption economies. And other East Asian countries — Malaysia and Thailand, among the more advanced, and Indonesia and Vietnam, further down the list — were at earlier stages of a similar path. The takeoff and drive to maturity was well under way until the financial crisis. The challenge is now to restore confidence and to return to a self-sustaining drive to maturity.

It is essential to explain why development takes place. Such an explanation would provide a basis for informed development strategy: better management of economic policy in poor countries aspiring to development, and more useful programs of overseas development assistance provided by advanced countries and by the international organizations.

It is also interesting to examine what progress in East Asia has meant for the more mature countries, now more focused on services than on manufacturing. How have trade patterns changed and what have been the implications for the structure of production in the mature economies? What are the implications of the "new economy" on the mature countries and on their relationship to East Asia?

Vicious and Virtuous Circles of Economic Development

Forty or fifty years ago, development economists still saw their field as the "dismal" science.[1] Prospects for development in the world's poor countries looked bleak, indeed. This pessimism about development had strong foundations since developing countries were seen to be facing almost insurmountable barriers, vicious circles that would prevent their escape from underdevelopment. For example:

1. The less developed countries were thought to be in a Malthusian trap. High birth rates seemed biologically inevitable. And resources were limited. As population tended to outrun a country's productive potential, living standards would remain close to subsistence.
2. The demand for the primary products, that represented the bulk of the Third World's exports, is inelastic with respect to price and income, so that the

---

[1]With reference to economics, Thomas Carlyle, 1872, wrote, "The Social Science — not a 'gay science' but a rueful [one], — which finds the secret of [t]his Universe in 'supply and demand' ... what we might call, by way of eminence, the dismal science."

long-run trend of earnings from growing commodity exports was likely to be unfavorable.

3. Modern industry is capital-intensive. But poor people do little saving. Consequently, in the developing world, savings were thought to be lacking for investment and capital accumulation.

4. Developing countries lack the technology and management skills required by advanced industry.

5. Local markets are too small to achieve the economies of scale and competition necessary to develop efficient industries.

Economists held out limited hope for raising incomes in the Third World. The developing countries would not be able to grow successfully except with outside help in the form of massive foreign aid from the industrial world or programs to support the prices of primary products exports.

But history has proved the pessimists wrong! The most dynamic part of the world consists of the countries of East and Southeast Asia. These countries, among the poorest in the 1950s and 1960s, have been on a "fast track" to development. Some, like Korea, have already graduated from "less developed" status and are joining the OECD, the "club" of the industrial countries.

What appeared to be vicious circles have, in many instances, turned out to be benign or even virtuous ones:

1. Population growth does not inevitably wipe out the potential gains of economic progress as Malthus predicted. On the contrary, declining birth rates have been a common feature in many of the rapidly growing East Asian countries. What was once considered largely the result of educational campaigns and other population control programs — legal restrictions on family size in China, for example — is more likely an economic phenomenon reflecting rising living standards and urbanization causing families to have fewer children. With economic progress, typically, a decline in birth rates follows by many years the drop in the death rate associated with improved living conditions. Initially, there is rapid population growth. But decline in the birth rate ultimately limits population growth. Population does not simply absorb the growth in output, though

urbanization may entail social and environmental costs that are not well measured in the GDP statistics.

2. The shortage of capital has not been binding in East Asia. One of the striking common factors among the high growth economies of East Asia is their high savings rate. This is not just a reflection of a common culture. Rapid growth promotes saving, as consumers are slow to adjust their spending patterns and as they seek to save for a high living standard in their retirement years. Growth promotes saving, and in turn, saving and investment promote growth. The capital investment required by the East Asian countries has been raised in large part from domestic sources. In addition, there has been plentiful foreign capital inflow attracted by high anticipated returns in the booming region.

3. The scale of production was quite limited at the beginning of the growth process. For that reason, some of the East Asian countries, Hong Kong and Singapore, for example, turned to export production to take advantage of world markets as a basis for high rates of production that would be efficient and competitive. Export markets continue to be one of the bases for East Asian growth, but increasingly there is a domestic market. Middle class people seek to buy cars, fashionable clothing, and electronic gadgets just like consumers in the mature countries. Moreover, the lowering of trade barriers worldwide, under the World Trade Organization (WTO), and in East Asia, as a result of the ASEAN Free Trade Area (AFTA), will also allow these countries to increase their scale of production.

While there are virtuous circles like those described here, there remain substantial barriers to development that are not easy to overcome. Some countries like Taiwan and Korea are much more advanced in their educational systems than are others like Thailand and Indonesia. Education, particularly of skilled workers, managers and engineers, is an enormously high priority. Building an educated labor force is not a problem that can be solved quickly; it may take 10 or 20 years or even more. Similar barriers exist with regard to infrastructure, where many countries lack sufficient transportation, communication and power. Fortunately, physical barriers like these can be fixed, though at considerable resource cost. Finally there are institutional and cultural barriers that make development difficult, such as the lack of an appropriate legal system, the need for a work ethic, etc. Social and cultural values are more difficult to change than physical barriers.

Perhaps, economic growth in East Asia should not come as a surprise after all. Most of today's high income industrial countries started out many years ago as poor countries engaged largely in subsistence agriculture. And they became mature high income countries! The astonishing aspect of East Asian development is that it has been so rapid. What took Western industrial countries one or two centuries is being repeated in East Asia in one or two generations! This is why the World Bank has termed it "The East Asian Miracle."

The Growth Process and the International Product Cycle

Until recently, East Asia represented a case study, perhaps a prototype, of rapid growth with relative price stability and balance of payments equilibrium. We see growth in East Asia as a regionally integrated process, a "development ladder." Progress in the more advanced countries of the region pulls along the more backward countries as their respective comparative advantage undergoes change. This represents an extension of the long-standing notion of the Vernon's "product cycle," 1966, to a new geographic setting. The beginning of sustained economic growth involves production and exports of primary products and labor-intensive manufacturing. As countries move up the development ladder, cost conditions for labor-intensive production become less favorable. The response by increasing the capital intensity of production leads to a switch to more sophisticated products while entrepreneurs shift simple labor-intensive activities to less advanced countries. The changing patterns of trade — agricultural products and labor-intensive manufactures from the less developed countries and high-tech products and services from more advanced countries — reflect the underlying changes in production economics.

The S-Curve of East Asian Development

A striking perspective on the growth process is provided by a cross-sectional view across the East Asian countries, focusing on the fact that, at one point in time, each of the countries in the region was at a substantially different stage of development (Fig. 5.1). In the vertical direction, the chart shows the level of per capita income in the mid-1990s, on a purchasing power basis.[2] The horizontal axis "years" requires some explanation. It measures the number of years since "rapid growth began." That is obviously an arbitrary choice. In the case of Korea, for example, we date the beginning of development from the ending of the Korean war, some 40 years. In the case of Thailand, the choice of 20 years is more arbitrary, from the time in the 1970s when the strategy of promoting exports and foreign direct investment was initiated.

The pattern observed is an S-curve. As noted above, this is a one-time cross-sectional view. But the countries appear to be following such a path in turn, although movement along the path is far from smooth. When we look at growth over time, there are ups and downs of the business cycle that must be smoothed out. The graph suggests a growth path beginning slowly, then rising rapidly, and finally slowing again as maturity is approached. Indonesia and the Philippines are still at an early stage in this process. Korea, Taiwan, Hong Kong and Singapore are in the full swing of growth, perhaps even a little beyond it. Thailand and Malaysia are only a little behind. Japan, which pioneered the pattern of export-led growth in the 1950s and 1960s, is now a mature country growing much more slowly.

We have noted Rostow's "takeoff" growth theory above. The pattern observed in Fig. 4.1 is similar. However, as we will see below, there is now a compelling logic behind it.

It is interesting to ask where China fits into this picture. It has been about 20 years since Chinese leaders opted to switch toward a "socialist market" economy. That makes the Chinese position on the horizontal axis quite firm. With regard to the vertical axis, per capita GDP, things are more complicated. On an exchange rate basis, China's per capita GDP was extremely low (less than US$500) in the mid-1950s. But the RMB yuan was extremely undervalued. On a PPP basis, Chinese per capita GDP was between US$1500 and US$2000. That puts China squarely on the S-curve!

---

[2]We use the mid-1990s because the 1997 East Asian crisis has thrown the pattern out of kilter temporarily.

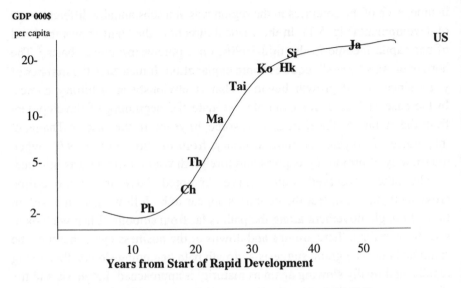

Fig. 5.1   The S-Curve of East Asian Growth: Mid-1990s.

Steps of Economic Development

As countries travel along the growth curve, they undergo fundamental structural transformation. One way to categorize these changes is by classifying the countries according to their comparative advantage as follows.

Development Level 1: Primary producers — Countries that produce and export mainly primary products. These are countries with large fractions of their populations engaged in agriculture, lumber and mineral industries. Land and labor are the abundant resources.

Development Level 2: Labor-intensive manufacturing — Countries that produce and export large quantities of labor-intensive manufactured products. The growth of export industries based on cheap abundant labor supplies and favorable exchange rates has been a central element of East

Asian development. The goods involved are typically light manufactures like textiles, footwear, apparel, household equipment and simple electronics. In some cases, this category includes processed foodstuffs, like frozen chickens and shrimp, linked to the agricultural sector. In these countries, comparative advantage lies in a large labor supply.

Development Level 3: High-tech manufacturing — As the labor supply is absorbed, wages rise and the comparative advantage of unskilled labor fades. Industries adapt by engaging in high-tech production. Initially, these efforts may involve components for products of more advanced countries, like disk drives. Eventually, the goods produced consist of more specialized equipment, like personal computers, chips and high-end electronics. As countries advance, they turn to making and exporting technically more sophisticated products, like machinery and equipment.

Finally, if we take a broader geographic perspective, we may visualize a still more advanced stage of economic development. (In East Asia, only very small countries like Singapore and Hong Kong can be visualized in this category.)

Development Level 4: The post-industrial service economy — This is the economy where comparative advantage is no longer in manufacturing but rather in services. These services tend to be in advanced, high productivity activities, like communication, finance, transportation and entertainment. They are the heart of the "new economy."

Is there still a more advanced level of development ahead? The concept of the "new economy" might suggest still a more advanced stage. One way of responding to this question is that the concept of the stage of development is not a rigid one. In Level 4, we visualize a high productivity service economy that can take many forms. It includes the technologically advanced services that make up the "new economy," the network connections, e-commerce, and the development of more sophisticated computer programs. An interesting issue, to be discussed in more detail below, is the extent to which the East Asian economies will be able to participate in these developments.

Of course, countries do not move abruptly from one development level to another. As the advantages of one type of activity fade, others are introduced gradually. At one time, a country is likely to have activities associated with various levels, but the proportions of these activities change as countries move from one development level to another. This "pattern of development" following Chenery and Syrquin, 1986, noted in Chapter 2 (Table 2.3) illustrates the shares of agriculture, industry, and the other sectors over the development process. Agriculture, representing the bulk of primary products output, except for petroleum and mining, declines as countries advance. Industry, in this case, labor-intensive mass production, increases with economic development, and finally begins to decline as countries approach maturity. A breakdown between labor-intensive and high-tech industries would show that the share of labor-intensive industry rises rapidly reaching a peak in the middle income developing countries. High-tech industry becomes increasingly important as countries advance. Industries like machinery and electronics are at a maximum, of course in Japan, and they are rising rapidly in Singapore, Taiwan and Korea.

Capital and technological knowledge are necessary for industrialization to occur as we have shown in Chapter 4. At first, the needs are fairly modest. Level 1 products are basic commodities which call for little capital or skill. Since the production process in Level 2 is based on cheap labor, only simple machinery may be required although the product must be of suitable design and sufficient quality to sell in the world market. Inputs of design consulting and management assistance from the foreign purchaser or from a multinational firm may make the difference between producing competitively or not. As the sophistication of products increases, needs for imported capital equipment and technical help increase. More advanced products like computer chips are often built in turnkey plants entirely constructed by foreign contractors. Indonesian footwear manufacturers often use Korean-made equipment and Korean management. The sophistication of local engineers and managers has improved greatly in recent years, but countries like Malaysia, Thailand and Indonesia still lag behind in this respect as compared to their more advanced neighbors like Singapore, Taiwan and Korea.

In Fig. 5.2, we have classified the East Asian countries according to their level of development at various times during the post-World War II period.

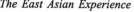

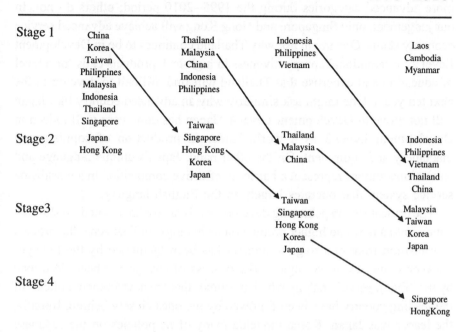

Fig. 5.2   The Stages of the Product Cycle Process.

In the first 15 years (1950–65) only Japan and Hong Kong appear in Development Level 2. Other countries in the region were still largely primary product producers. During the next 30 years (1965–95) many of the East Asian countries shift into Development Level 2, becoming manufacturers of labor-intensive mass production products, in large part exported to the industrial world. Japan, Taiwan, Singapore, Hong Kong and Korea moved into Development Level 3. Only Indonesia, a heavily populated country and a big oil producer, and the Philippines, with a decidedly spotty development record, remained primarily in Development Level 1.

At the turn of the century, all of the East Asian countries have focused their development planning on moving ahead on this scale, some seeking to advance to Development Level 3 and others, like Singapore and Hong Kong, setting targets on Development Level 4 as the financial, trading and communications centers for the region. Some of the countries move into more advanced categories during the 1995–2010 period; others do not. In our judgement, only Singapore and Hong Kong will achieve advanced service economy status. One might ask why Thailand continues to be in Development Level 2? International competitiveness in high-tech products calls for a level of education and expertise that Thailand will find difficult to develop in the next ten years. One might ask similarly why an advanced country like Japan will not move to Development Level 4? Japan has done very well indeed in Development Level 3 as a world leader in production of sophisticated machinery and equipment. On the other hand, Japan's unique language and cultural institutions represent a barrier to effective competition in a worldwide service system that operates largely in the English language.

The critical step in achieving development is, as we have noted, to shift the nation onto a new and higher production technology. In East Asia, the process of transition from one stage to another has been facilitated by the linkages between countries in the region. The process of change has been described by the "flying geese" analogy which presumes that the development policies of the leading country have been followed by the ones closely behind. Initially, the leader was Japan. Korea modeled many of its policies on the Japanese precedent and, to a lesser extent, so did Taiwan. In recent years, the linkages between countries have become more tangible links between business operations rather than just policy. Businesses operating in more advanced, and often more costly, countries are moving production operations, sometimes entire sectors, that lack comparative advantage to countries at a lower position on the development ladder where the economics are more suitable. With rising labor costs, Hong Kong has shifted much of its labor-intensive production to Guangdong province, and Taiwan has started extensive production operations in Fujian province. Singapore has developed electronic manufacturing in neighboring Malaysia and Indonesia, and even, Korea is shifting operations to China. Japan, long a laggard in supplying its domestic needs from abroad, has begun to outsource production of components and some assembly operations to other East Asian countries reserving for its domestic industry only high-value and high-tech operations. This relationship between the countries that are higher on the development ladder with countries still on a lower rung can be likened to a relay race where the production operations being shifted from one country to another represent the baton. Such a process has mutual benefit for the country outsourcing uneconomic industries and for the recipient. For the latter, it offers not only capital but also more advanced technology, and importantly, modern management.

We are describing an ongoing process rather than some isolated events. Indeed as the Level 2 countries are benefiting from the industries being shifted from their Level 3 neighbors, they are in turn shifting industries to Level 1 countries in the region. The process is well illustrated by the experience of the manufacturers of athletic footwear. (Case Study 5.1). It reflects the close geographic and cultural relations between many of the countries in the region. We anticipate that the process will continue and that it will ultimately link the entire region into a closely intertwined economic area.

Rapid growth in East Asia was abruptly interrupted in 1997–8 but appears to be back on track today. The crisis has been attributed to a combination of causes: business cycle factors, balance of payments disequilibrium and exchange rate contagion, bank failures and policy mismanagement.

We can relate the sudden change in economic conditions of some East Asian countries to the development ladder discussed above. A proximate cause of the crisis was the slowdown of exports that affected several of the East Asian countries in 1996 and 1997. Most observers attributed this slowdown to poor economic conditions in the export markets of Japan and Europe, and to difficulties in the semiconductor and small computer industries. On further consideration, it appears that an important factor for some countries, like Thailand, Indonesia, Malaysia and South Korea was a loss of competitiveness. As their economies boomed and costs rose, these countries were no longer able to compete successfully, particularly with respect to their largest supply competitor, China. There is much ad hoc evidence of manufacturers in Thailand and Indonesia who found that they could no longer sell their products at prevailing costs and exchange rates. This is a natural occurrence in the development ladder process. Either exchange rates must adjust downward, as they eventually did, or industrial sectors must proceed to a more advanced stage of development. That is not always a painless process. It is now apparent that Thailand and Indonesia did not yet have sufficient high-tech engineers and managers and lacked the infrastructure necessary for more advanced production processes. These represent difficult challenges. Hopefully, as financial market confidence is restored, these countries will take the steps necessary to make their continued participation in the East Asian development ladder possible.

Implications for the Mature Economies

Does the East Asian development ladder have implications for the mature economies? Indeed, did East Asian development come at the cost of jobs and/or welfare in the industrial world?

The massive changes in production structure and trade observed in East Asia could not have been made without corresponding changes in trade of the industrial world. Trade flows have increased vastly from the principal East Asian countries to the US, Europe, and Japan and back. The patterns observed are consistent with the growth of East Asia as a supplier of consumer products to the US, Europe, and a little later, to Japan. At first, these were primary products and simple manufactures, but over time the East Asian countries have increasingly turned to more advanced goods. During the same period, East Asia has been an important importer from the more advanced countries, drawing on them for capital goods and high productivity services.

Implications of the "New Economy"

The "new economy" is the most advanced stage of development, as we have noted. It represents a special kind of "service economy," making use of advanced information technology (IT), science and finance. The focus of this economy is not so much on manufacturing as on computer programming and communication, e-commerce, and creation of networks and linkages that replace old forms of personal service and communication. The introduction of electronic networks to handle many of the tasks of business represents a sort of industrial revolution that is giving mature countries like the US prospects of further rapid growth.

Reich in *The Work of Nations*, 1992, has called the people working in this type of economy "symbolic analysts" to contrast them with ordinary service workers and production workers. The "new economy" calls for a trained and experienced labor force different from that employed in manufacturing. On one hand, this will mean that the mature economies that have the required education and research and development institutions will have special advantages in this field. A few of the developing countries, like Taiwan, Singapore, Israel, etc., may also quickly become part of the "new economy." On the other hand, the "new economy" may represent serious challenges to some of the East Asian countries, and to developing countries elsewhere. This is because the "new economy" calls for "new" skills and networked development that are still absent or scarce in many parts of the world. Some "nodes" of technology have formed in Asia, but they represent the exception so far. It may take many years and much effort before the educational and cultural structures that lie behind the "new economy" will be dispersed widely even in the rapidly growing countries of East Asia.

Conclusions about the Growth Process

East Asian economic growth has been the envy of the rest of the world. Growth has been astonishingly rapid. The East Asian countries appeared to have unlocked the secret to rapid development. Perhaps, words like *miracle* are too strong, but certainly East Asia has been part of a development process with significant momentum. One important word in this discussion is *process*. It is no accident that all the countries of the region were moving along together. Nor is it simply a matter of *leadership* by some countries, though the leading positions, first of Japan and then of Korea, Singapore, Hong Kong and Taiwan cannot be disputed. The critical issue here is *linkages*. These tie the less advanced countries to the more advanced countries in numerous ways. The transfer of "sunset industries" from the advanced to the less advanced countries represents only one dimension. The search by advanced countries for outlets for their capital and for markets for their high technology products is another. These linkages are very broad for they involve transfers of knowledge and technology, on one hand, and opening of consumer markets on the other.

While there clearly will be interruptions in the growth process, as the one in 1997, what is being created in East Asia is a remarkably integrated modern economic system. If we look far enough ahead, this regional economy may ultimately be comparable in size and income to the European Union (EU) and the North American Free Trade Area (NAFTA), indeed, if we include China, one that might be very much larger than both combined.

From the Perspective of Business

The development ladder has important implications for business. Decisions of where and how to produce are greatly influenced by changing economic settings as countries advance in the development process. On one hand, as we describe in the Nidas case study (Case Study 5.1), lower costs and, consequently, competitiveness cause firms to seek advantageous production sites. This is clearly not just a matter of low wage rates or undervalued exchange rates. The level of technology and skill in many low wage countries simply is not sufficient to produce the consistent high quality demanded by modern consumers. Transportation systems may not be up to the task of getting the product to market quickly and in good condition.[3] The legal system may not be sufficiently developed to protect the interests of foreign investors.

The domestic market in the developing economy is another important consideration. As per capita income rose in the East Asian countries, a significant middle class of consumers has developed. They purchase many of the same products — automobiles, appliances, electronic equipment and clothing — that these countries have been exporting to the US and Western Europe. Since many of these countries are relatively small, these markets are not yet big enough to sustain competitive mass production industries. But very large countries, like China and India, offer growing potential, and the ASEAN Free Trade Area (AFTA) will also offer a large market place for modern products.

---

[3]An interesting example is the strong competitive advantage of Mexico in the US as a result of the fact that trucks carry goods into the US market much more expeditiously than shipping from other sources like Southeast Asia.

The pattern of development we have described in East Asia offers business opportunities for managers within the area and from the outside. Within the development ladder region, managers must be fast on their feet to recognize when comparative advantage is shifting, when competitiveness in one country declines and when it is time to shift production into another location. The Nidas case about production of athletic shoes illustrates how companies can exploit changing cost conditions to minimize their production costs.

Foreign direct investment from outside the region has made a substantial contribution, particularly in the 1990s. This has been much more than simply a contribution of capital. Multinational enterprises have come with advanced technology. Setting up operations, often with domestic partners, they have introduced systems of technology and management that have greatly benefited the host countries. In turn, they have developed reliable low cost sources for the products they sell throughout their worldwide markets.

This means that there are business opportunities as the East Asia develops. Globally-minded businesses would do well to keep their eyes open to these possibilities.

Questions for Discussion

* Is modern development experience best described as one that represents a "vicious" or a "virtuous" circle? Discuss.
* The "development ladder" involves important linkages between countries. Explain.
* How does comparative advantage in various sectors change as countries mature?
* What constraints may hinder some countries from participating fully in the development ladder?
* Will Africa join the development ladder?
* What are the implications of the "new economy" for East Asian development?

Case Study 5.1
Nidas Shoe Company:
Sourcing Production in Asia

The Nidas Shoe Company began as a producer of athletic shoes in the northwest of the US in the mid-1950s. By 1970s, all production had gone offshore to Asian countries that were at various stages of economic development. Today, Nidas is one of the largest producers of athletic shoes worldwide. Most of these shoes are tailored to specific athletic activities and have leather uppers, rubber soles and a number of patented features. Nidas shoes retail for as much as US$125 a pair although their production cost is only a small fraction of their retail price. The technology used by the athletic footwear industry is now far more complex and sophisticated than it was in the 1950s, but much of the assembly work still relies on relatively simple hand labor. High quality athletic shoes require precision metal molds made by high-tech computer-controlled milling machines.

Nidas goes offshore

Manufacturing costs of the original operations in the US were not sufficiently remunerative. Labor costs were too high and US factories did not keep up with the latest technological developments in the footwear industry. By the early 1970s, Nidas had turned to Asian manufacturers in Korea and Taiwan to make their product. As production moved to Asia, Nidas found it was possible to improve labor productivity by using semi-automatic machinery but fully automatic shoe production was not economic. Parts of the production process continued to be labor-intensive. All the shoe producers in Asia paid about the same for raw materials. Some of the raw materials like PVC and rubber could be sourced locally while other materials, like leather, were imported from Australia and other countries.

Nidas did not then and does not now own or operate footwear manufacturing facilities anywhere in the world. It operated through licensing agreements with local independent manufacturers, some owned by Taiwanese interests and managed by Koreans. Nidas provided the suppliers with purchased raw materials, models and the associated product specifications. Contracts were made with the suppliers who were expected to deliver specified quantities of shoes of a desired quality on a planned schedule. Nidas helped producers by maintaining support staff at the production sites to assist the plants in producing the product to specifications. The number of factories producing for Nidas varied from time to time, expanding and contracting with changes in sales requirements and producers' performance with respect to quality, delivery and cost.

The 1980s

In the late 1980s, production conditions in East Asia were changing and additional changes were anticipated. By then, Korea was the principal production center with about 50% of Nidas's total output. The remaining output was equally divided between Taiwan and Thailand. Production had been initiated in China and Indonesia.

Korea's footwear manufacturing industry was mature. The labor force was experienced. Capital and labor-saving technology had helped to improve labor productivity, though further investments yielded only marginal additional gains. On the other hand, wage rates were relatively high, some US$600 to US$700 per month, and organized labor applied continuous pressure for further substantial annual increases.

The situation in Taiwan was roughly comparable. There, too, additions of new capital and labor-saving technology tended to offset the relatively high labor cost. Despite the political antagonism between the governments of Taiwan and China, many businesspeople in Taiwan had family and business links to China. As China opened up to new investment, Taiwanese manufacturers became the conduit for technology transfer in the athletic footwear industry.

The Early 1990s

As production moved out of Taiwan and Korea seeking lower labor costs, Thailand, China and Indonesia became competitors, particularly at the lower end of the footwear market. All three were relatively low wage countries. The average monthly wage was less than US$90 in Thailand, although higher than the US$30 to US$50 per month found in China and Indonesia.

Thailand

From a country perspective, Thailand had advantages in terms of economic and political stability. On the managerial level, however, Thai factory owners failed to develop their middle management. Highly trained managers were expensive and most manufacturers, with some striking exceptions, failed to hire the quality of management required. Although workers were productive, they lacked the leadership and training needed to meet Nidas' quantity and quality standards consistently. Instead of taking advantage of technological advances, Thai managers tried to reach their goals by using cheap poorly trained labor. This lack of vision resulted in frequent manufacturing problems and prevented the production of high quality and high level technical products. The range of products that could be produced in Thailand remained limited to less sophisticated lower quality goods.

China

China presented different problems from other countries in the region. Factories were largely state-owned and had obsolescent machinery and inexpert management. In the 1980s, the few private operations there came mainly from Taiwan. While still in their infancy, they were already demonstrating improvements over state-owned companies.

Indonesia

Indonesia had an advantage over Thailand and China in operations. Ethnic Chinese Indonesian businesspeople collaborated with Korean footwear manufacturers to bring their technology and management systems into local factories. Until 1998, the Suharto government created a stable and predictable business environment.

The mid-1990s

By the mid-1990s, consumers were demanding a high-tech product but at a lower price, making it even more important for Nidas to produce shoes at as low a cost as possible. As a consequence, the sourcing of production changed. One-third of the product was manufactured in China and another third in Indonesia. Korea, Taiwan and Thailand each accounted for some 10% of the market. Vietnam was beginning to produce, albeit with a great deal of difficulty. Government corruption, poor infrastructure and poorly trained workers made Vietnam a difficult place in which to do business regardless of the low wage structure. Moreover, since Vietnam lacked a commercial agreement with the US, shoes produced there were subject to a 35% tariff in the US and were, consequently, shipped mostly to other markets.

Labor costs were the principal reason Nidas looked for low wage countries in which to manufacture. Wages in Korea, for example, had risen to US $1000 per month, a level that could not be offset by improved production equipment. By the late 1990s, Korean companies only manufactured high-end footwear.

The situation in Taiwan was similar. Taiwanese firms were setting up satellite operations in China. Korean investors and experts directed activity toward Indonesia. Production in Thailand had lost comparative advantage as wages rose. Though, at US$160 per month, workers were still much cheaper than Korean or Taiwanese, their wages were higher than in the competing countries. The depreciation of the baht exchange rate beginning in 1997 temporarily improved Thailand's competitive position, but the failure of Thai producers to upgrade their production process continued as a barrier to expanded production in that country.

China and Indonesia became the principal producers. By this time, the majority of Chinese factories were privately owned. There was a massive transfer of technology from Korea and Taiwan, helping Chinese producers to upgrade the quality of their product and their productivity. Because wages rose rapidly in South China's Guangdong province, where many of the firms were located, some producers considered relocation further inland. The potential of an immense 1.3 billion people, Chinese domestic market was a further attraction although production remained primarily export-oriented.

Indonesia, like China, benefited from substantial technical transfer, but local ethnic Chinese partners suffered huge financial setbacks when the reins of government changed hands from President Suharto to Habibie and then to Wahid and Megawati. In the short run at least, an uneasy political situation coupled with a cutback on the number of Korean and Taiwanese managers in local factories, made Indonesian competitiveness more problematic.

Vietnam, a socialist economy in transition to the market system had not improved as a place to conduct business operations. Red tape, vast quantities of paperwork, and an inadequate legal system caused extensive delays and problems. Nevertheless, the best firms from Korea and Taiwan began to install modern factories with the newest equipment. Workers were highly motivated but received wages that amounted to only US$50 per month at the prevailing exchange rate. These low wage rates were, nevertheless, approximately twice the prevailing wage in other industries. By the end of the 1990s, Nidas supplier factories in Vietnam employed 45,000 workers and shipped more than 10% of Nidas shoe output.

Social Issues

Critics of Nidas and other athletic footwear companies charged that Nidas deliberately sought investment in countries that were "havens of repression." Although they stopped short of accusing Nidas of leaving South Korea and Taiwan for operations in more politically repressive countries, they noted that while Nidas did not overtly support repression, it certainly profited from it. In recent years, Nidas came under attack from opponents of child labor. They charged that children worked in factories rather than going to school. In addition, children were neglected when their mothers worked overtime and were physically harmed when their mothers were exposed to noxious fumes while pregnant.

Nidas asserted it did not knowingly employ children and was careful about the environment. A minimum employment age of 16 was established. Harmful solvents and glues were gradually replaced by somewhat less effective but much less harmful water-based products. Large fans were installed for ventilation. But it proved impossible to eliminate all risks to employee health.

The company maintained that in the low income countries of Asia, people begin to work at an early age and for low wages. Even if the nature of the job is potentially hazardous to health, it was better than being jobless. Nidas further asserted it did not have full control of the plants as they were operated by supplier companies.

Nidas also struggled with how to respond to charges by American labor unions that by putting low wage Asians to work, Americans were losing jobs and incomes. The question whether to protect jobs at home while still making a profit abroad remained unsettled.

It was not clear how Nidas could meet the challenges of political activists nor how effective the activists would be in boycotting or otherwise hindering Nidas's athletic shoe business.

The Future

With rising labor costs worldwide, efforts to improve production efficiency will be necessary everywhere. Production costs in Korea and Taiwan will continue to rise. Thailand will need to improve production and managerial efficiency and quality to retain its place. With technological and management knowhow from Korea and Taiwan, production can be expected to increase further in China, Indonesia, and after signing a commercial agreement, in Vietnam. A critical consideration will be whether these countries will be able to support the high level of technology necessary to produce the top-of-the-range footwear that, until now, is still being produced in Korea. Further ahead is the potential development of still other supply sources in low wage countries like Cambodia, Laos, Myanmar, or Bangladesh. Such production would depend on the comparative advantage of these countries and on the availability of foreign capital and production technology.

Questions for Discussion

* What are the principal ways in which this case supports the notion of the economic development ladder? In what respect does it violate

this theme? What countries are the source of capital, technology and management?

* What is likely to be the next (or ultimate) location of the industry? Will the geographic product cycle process, illustrated here, extend to countries outside East and Southeast Asia?
* Can a country like Thailand maintain its role as an athletic shoe producer in the face of rising wages and competition from low wage, favorable exchange rate countries like China? Explain.
* What would be Nidas's optimal organization of production in respect to product quality and specification, cost, security of supply, etc.?
* Can Nidas make good use of the Internet to optimize the integration of parts supply, production, inventories and deliveries?
* How can Nidas deal with the challenges posed by political activists?

Chapter 6

Growth and Development Policy

This chapter is concerned with policies for growth and development. An important issue is whether these policies should be different in a "new economy" than they have been in the past. We outline the policy approaches to growth. We consider the dispute between economists who argue that government has played an important role in fostering growth and development and those who believe primarily in market mechanisms. We consider the role of other participants in the development process, the function of financial markets, domestic enterprise and foreign investors.

Introduction

Most countries see the encouragement of growth and development as one of the central responsibilities of the public sector. The balance between countries that use the government to plan and direct the development process and those that rely primarily on unguided private sector initiatives has changed. Thirty years ago, the world's economies could be divided into three broad groups:

1. The Western industrial countries operated as market economies. This is not to say that they were entirely unfettered free competitive markets. Indicative planning, state-owned businesses, regulatory interventions, and trade and financial market restrictions applied to some degree in almost all of them. But, arguably, economic decisions were largely made by businesses seeking profit.
2. The socialist block, including China, which was run as a bureaucratic, planned, command economy. Again there was substantial variance, particularly with respect to agriculture and small business, but in most of the socialist countries a central plan guided production and allocation by publicly-owned and directed businesses.

3. The Third World, the poor countries that operated in a kind of "third way" between capitalism and socialism. In these countries, development was frequently sought by government-led industrialization. While state enterprises played an important role, particularly in basic industries, much business transpired in private firms subjected to a vast amount of public control.

This division all but disappeared in the 1990s. All over the world, the pendulum has swung toward the market economy. The industrial countries have deregulated and privatized many previously public enterprises. (Privatization is discussed in Case 6.1.) The socialist block, now called the "transition economies," is well on the way toward a market economy, though one may still dispute in many cases how private, free and competitive the market in many of these countries really is. The developing countries have staked their progress largely on the growth of private export-oriented firms. They have also sharply reduced regulations, and privatized state-owned enterprises, though many of them still protect their domestic industries.

The world economy has been globalized, creating new trade links among many countries, particularly between the developing and developed worlds. Trade has been the mainstay of the East Asian development experience. Trade goes in both directions, raw materials and simple manufactures from East to West, and capital goods, financial flows, sophisticated services from West to East. The growth of trade has been much more rapid than the growth of GDP as costs of transportation and trade barriers have been reduced. Economic historians remind us how much the reduction of shipping delays and costs — fast ships, container vessels, air freight — has facilitated international trade.

Substantial progress to reduce trade barriers has been a basis for a vast expansion of international trade in the post-World War II period. The framework of the General Agreement on Tariffs and Trade (GATT), now the World Trade Organization (WTO), attracted many countries seeking liberalization of international trade. Unhindered markets do not yet apply in international trade the way they do within nations or trading areas like the European Union (EU) or the North American Free Trade Area (NAFTA). Further steps for liberalizing world trade are well underway. In the past few years, there has been progress in establishing the WTO, tariff reductions under the aegis of the Asean Free Trade Area (AFTA) and in discussions of wiping out trade barriers across the Pacific, the Asia Pacific Economic Cooperation (APEC) forum.

At the same time, there has been an enormous internationalization of financial flows. There is much agreement about the benefits of foreign direct investment and most, but not all, countries have sought to attract it. Multinational companies make long term investments, often bringing in domestic partners. They accompany their capital with new technology and high production and management standards. Fears that foreign firms will dominate domestic industries have caused many countries to impose limits on the foreign investor — some sectors like telecommunications and banking have been sharply restricted — but these limits have been fading rapidly in recent years.

With respect to other financial flows, such as bank lending or debt, recent experiences have been less favorable. There is a consensus, for example, that foreign capital inflows fueled the financial booms of most East Asian countries in the first half of the 1990s. Some observers have argued that when financial markets plunged, foreign capital, which was mostly short term, withdrew which contributed to, or even caused the financial crisis.

More recently still, the integration of the world market involves linkages of information and knowledge through the Internet. We are only at the threshold of this development. But already, e-business relationships are opening markets to East Asian business; software and data entry are being developed in Asia and transmitted instantaneously to users in Europe, Japan and the United States. The potentials for further increasing the linkages between developed and developing countries are immense, but then so are the barriers.

The Role of Government

Few politicians and even fewer economists would advocate a turn back toward planned, regulated, or protectionist economies. But there is still much difference of opinion about the role government has played in the past in the successfully developing economies and the role that government should play in the future. In this regard, economists can be divided into two camps:

1. The free marketers, who argue that most progress has come from allowing competitive markets free rein. This position is that the less government intervention the better. It is important to "get prices right" to allow them to be determined by market forces. Then competitive business will do almost all that is necessary to advance growth and development. According to the free marketers, the role of government is very limited, to maintaining a legal system, to protecting property rights, to asssuring competition, and to dealing with broad social needs like education and prevention of pollution.
2. The development managers, sometimes called revisionists, who see an important role for government to plan and initiate development and growth. (This tradition goes back to Alexander Hamilton's "Report on Manufactures" in 1791.) Post-War Japanese development shaped by the guiding hand of the Ministry of International Trade and Industry (MITI) is often seen as the most successful example of government-led development. Similar strategies, first building strategic heavy industries and protecting the domestic market but promoting exports have been used with considerable success in most of East Asia. The "development managers" would argue that such policies, with more or less specific industrial targeting, are a necessary ingredient to achieve rapid economic growth.

What is today's consensus among the experts on this issue? Robert Wade, perhaps the foremost authority on this issue, has argued that such development management policies are helpful so long as they work closely with private enterprise and are consistent with the market. In Wade's opinion, the "developmental state" involves strategic interventions by government. The success of development in Taiwan and South Korea, he would say, in large part reflects the fact that government officials aimed for objectives that were in accord with eventual market outcomes and operated cooperatively with private enterprise. In its *East Asian Miracle* study [World Bank (1993)], the World Bank reached somewhat similar conclusions, albeit somewhat reluctantly. The World Bank study suggests that there is little assurance that policies that worked in some settings will work in others. Much depends on the quality and sophistication of government officials and on their relationship with business. Directives that seem to have worked at early stages of development when critical linkage industries were not available may not work so well as countries achieve higher levels of development. Sophisticated technology industries cannot be guided and developed as easily as the basic industries that served at earlier stages of development. We are inclined to agree with that view. We have yet to see whether the measures that helped set Korea and Taiwan on their course to modernization, to build steel, auto and consumer electronics industries will serve as well to back up the knowledge-intensive industries of the "new economy."

The precise meaning of the term "market economy"[1] has not been clearly defined. But there appears to be broad consensus that it means individual enterprise decision-making guided by the profit objective in the light of market-determined prices. As we have noted, it contrasts sharply with the centralized decision-making of the planned economy. There is much less consensus however on the role governments should take in a market economy. Indeed, there have been striking differences in the role of government between the industrial countries and the less developed countries.

The contrast between the role of government in the industrial world and in the developing countries is summarized in Table 6.1. In the vertical direction, we list various possible functions of government, from the most general down to the most specific. We indicate whether government performs these functions in the mature (DCs) and the developing economies in general (LDCs), and in East Asia in particular (EA).

Growth and Development Policies

The very different challenges faced by policy in the mature economies and in the developing countries account, at least in part, for the differing scope for government intervention in the two types of economies. There is need to promote growth in both. In the advanced countries, the challenge is to move the technological frontier outward. In the developing countries, the challenge is to accumulate more capital and to adapt technology to methods already being used in more advanced countries.

---

[1]Curiously, the Chinese speak of a "socialist market economy." That sounds like an oxymoron.

Table 6.1   The Role of Government in Industrial and Developing Countries.

	DCs	LDCs	EA
Macroeconomic Policies for Growth	F↑	I	I
Macroeconomic Policies for Stabilization	I	F	F
Balance of Payments and Exchange Rate Policy	F	I↑	I↑
Protectionism	O↓	F↓	F↓
Export Promotion	O	F	I
Attraction of Foreign Investment	N	F	I
Exchange Rate Intervention	O	F	F↓
Income Distribution Equity	F	N	O
Environmental Protection	I	O↑	O↑
Infrastructure	F↓	I	I
Science and Education	I↓	F↑	O↑
Intervention in Business	O	F	F
Planning of Industrial Structure	O	F	F↓
State Enterprises	O↓	F↓	F↓

Code: I = very important; F = frequent; O = occasional; N = not a policy target;
↑ = increasing in importance; and ↓ = decreasing in importance.

Two important points must be made:

1. This is not just a matter of technology in the narrow definition of the word. We do not mean simply technical progress but more broadly also progress in management, communication, transportation, marketing, distribution, etc. We do not mean only how products are produced but also what products are produced. As economic progress is made, on one hand, resources are used with greater efficiency, using more advanced methods, and on the other, more valuable, more advanced products are produced.

2. Policies depend greatly on the degree of advancement already attained. In developing countries, provisions for basic infrastructure, education and social services dominate. In the advanced economies, where much of this basic fundament is already being provided, emphasis is likely to be on advanced education, scientific research and sophisticated communications infrastructure — the information superhighway, for example.

Here we consider policies in more detail.

Macroeconomic policies

Macroeconomic stability is a *sine qua non* of sustained economic growth. Until 1997, most of the East Asian countries had maintained a remarkable record of stability on the macro level. While there were certainly periods of slowdown and even recession, by and large, demand was well maintained. Most of the East Asian countries kept good control of their money supply and avoided the inflationary excesses that occurred in Latin America. Most were able to stabilize their exchange rates so as to reduce uncertainties and risks for import and export business. How important such stability is for sustained growth was demonstrated by its failure in the 1997 crisis in East Asia.

Even those policies that are primarily intended to achieve short run stabilization objectives, are likely to have impacts on a country's long run growth path. A simple example is monetary policy tightening, like the restructuring programs suggested by the International Monetary Fund (IMF) to deal with the East Asian crisis. Such policy moves will raise interest rates. In turn that will reduce investment, potentially slowing the path of economic growth. Some economists have opposed recent IMF proposals on the grounds that they impose hardships and impede long term growth. On the other hand, as we will see in our discussion of the "open economy," such policies may help to restore confidence and attract foreign capital.

The details of macroeconomic policy, fiscal policy, monetary policy and exchange rate policy will be discussed in greater detail in later parts of this volume.

Trade and exchange rate policy

Appropriate trade and exchange rate policies are an essential ingredient of a rapid economic development strategy, as we will outline in more detail below. The switch from protection of domestic producers to a more open trade policy favoring exports was basic in encouraging the development of industries that are capable of competing in world markets. These industries can take advantage of low-cost labor and other domestic resources to produce competitive products. They must produce products that meet world market specifications in terms of design and quality. The importance of an appropriate exchange rate is often underestimated. Politicians are frequently proud when their country has a strong and stable currency. There is, consequently, the temptation to maintain the exchange rate fixed regardless of what happens to a country's competitive position. But from the perspective of competition, it is usually better for the exchange rate to be undervalued. Systematic undervaluation of the exchange rate has helped to make products of the East Asian countries competitive in the markets of the developed world. Exchange rate policy also has important implications from the perspective of avoiding financial crises like the one that occurred in East Asia in 1997.

Education policy

A well-trained labor force is an essential of modern production. This means not only skilled workers for assembly operations but also engineers, managers and entrepreneurs to build modern companies. The developed countries have achieved a high level of education even though it is not yet always suited to produce the skills required by the "new economy." In the developing world, education is much more problematic. In a few countries, like Singapore, Taiwan and Korea, education has been given a high priority and an educated workforce has been created. Other countries have lagged behind, despite substantial efforts. This means, for example, that when the economy is booming in Thailand, there is inevitably a shortage of skilled workers even though the population is abundant and many people are out of work. Many economies of East Asia must greatly improve their educational systems and expand them if they are to participate actively in the "new economy."

Social policy

Most of the developed countries have extensive social policies, a social safety net that protects their workers when they are laid off or in other difficulties. This includes unemployment compensation, retirement plans, aid to dependent children, retraining and other educational programs, etc. The cost of social benefits has become so large that they have impeded economic growth and employment in Western Europe. On the other hand, in the developing countries, workers have very little social protection. If business slumps, workers must work in the informal sector, on the streets, or return to their villages. This made the 1997 crisis very hard, particularly for people who had only recently joined the middle class.

Industrial policy

As we have noted, one of the basic debates on development policy has been whether government policies favoring specific industries help to advance the growth process. Other economists place faith in non-intervention. It can be argued that many countries that did not engage in systematic market intervention, like Hong Kong and Thailand, are also success stories. Most development economists, however, support the notion that government incentives should stimulate investment and growth in general without introducing systematic biases Thailand's Board of Investment (BoI) tax incentives, or favorable exchange rates and credit terms to export industries tend to meet such criteria.

Industrial policy is much more controversial. It involves government intervention to build specific industries or firms. It often ends up building projects that do not turn out to be commercially viable. The World Bank's East Asian Miracle study (World Bank, *The East Asian Miracle: Economic Growth and Public Policy*, Oxford, 1993) lent some support to the notion that in some cases, industry-specific promotional policies have been useful, but reached the conclusion that for most countries such policies would not be useful in the future.

In practice, there have been great differences in how countries have dealt with this issue. In addition to macro policies, should a country have more focused growth policies selecting the industries or sectors that merit special encouragement and phasing out the ones that have adverse prospects?

In the US, the idea of an industrial policy flared briefly and then fizzled quickly in the late 1970s. Most economists argued that government officials are not well equipped to make choices of industries and technologies. Such decisions are better made in the private sector where the gain or loss of private capital is at stake. At best, it was argued that the government might implement general, non-selective policies, like reducing interest rates, providing support for basic research, and expanding technical education, policies that would not require specific industry choices. The Reagan administration handled the matter more forcefully: "The best industrial policy is no industrial policy!" Yet, many observers credit the Defense Department's support for programs of scientific research for many of the basic inventions that lie behind the "new economy." In other developed countries, too, the swing toward more conservative free market approaches and privatization has reduced the role of public support for specific industries. Even *national champions* like the airlines and phone companies have been privatized and sector-specific intervention is less likely to be growth-oriented than to be simply a response to political pressures.

The Japanese have long maintained that industrial policies of its MITI helped the rapid recovery and growth of the Japanese economy in the 1960s, when MITI supported the development of industries like steel and autos thought to be basic building blocks of an advanced economy. MITI still supports selected industrial research and development programs in high technology fields. In Europe, too, particularly in France, there have long been policies to support the "industries of the future," but the results have been quite mixed. The French *plan calcul*, to build a computer industry failed; on the other hand, the Airbus, a pan European project, is a thriving but costly enterprise.

In the developing world, public support for specific industries and state-owned firms has been quite widespread until recently. In Malaysia, the Proton was built as a national car, and in Indonesia, Korea and even Taiwan, public support for specific industries and even specific firms has been widespread. But, in recent years, privatization has become fashionable in the developing countries. In many cases, the justification for selling off ownership shares to private investors, often from abroad, has been a financial one. This represents a way for developing countries to bring in foreign capital and to balance the budget. Fortunately, private foreign participation in formerly state-owned businesses frequently brings in important measures of competitive dynamism and modern technology (Case 6.1).

Case 6.1
Privatization: A Survey

The beginnings of privatization in the 1970s had a strong theoretical and ideological content. In the late 1960s, economists were turning away from planning and public sector governance toward free market economics. This was the background of the return to a conservative majority in Britain under Margaret Thatcher and of the Reagan presidency in the US. In the United Kingdom, there was the privatization of coal mines, electric, gas and water utilities, transportation, etc. The US began with the deregulation of the airlines, and more recently, the public utilities. Among the developing countries, Chile was clearly the leader, again motivated by philosophical and economic theory considerations. Beginning in 1974, the state-owned enterprises created by the Allende government were unraveled and in the 1980s, privatization was extended through incentives to stock ownership, so-called popular capitalism, to social institutions, like public pensions, where private plans had not been tried before. Other countries in Latin America and East Asia followed, particularly allowing private foreign participation in airlines and communications. Privatization of steel, petrochemicals, and petroleum and petrochemicals and mining has been more difficult.

In the developing world in the 1980s and 1990s, privatization had more prosaic and immediate underpinnings. State-owned enterprises had turned out to be large, inefficient operations, frequently guided by political considerations, and most important, imposing heavy burdens on the state budget. Compared to privately-owned enterprises, these firms were remarkably rigid and costly. It was time to take these firms in hand and call for changes in management and control as well as in ownership.

In the US, the organizational changes toward private sector control represented deregulation rather than privatization, since most enterprises were privately owned but subject to public regulation, by the CAB, the FCC, and the state public utility commissions. Deregulation began in 1978 with airlines, and was extended to other forms of transportation such as trucking and railroads and is now being applied to public utilities. The breakup of the

ATT telephone monopoly was also part of this process. These changes have opened markets to competition and have made them much more dynamic. In Europe, corresponding moves are being made in the telecom field and in transportation, with the UK serving as the leader.

Many developing countries have also recognized the dynamic forces implicit in private enterprise and have shifted many national companies to private ownership, often with foreign participation. Early steps in that direction was the sale to private interests of national chemical plants in Taiwan, and many other countries are now going in the same direction. In India, this move is termed *disinvestment* and *parallelization*.

Technological change has also been an important influence promoting deregulation and privatization. National and/or regulated companies have often found it difficult to keep up with the latest technology. As technological change has occurred, they have been forced to compete, sometimes in markets where there had been no competition earlier. The case of the phone companies challenged by microwave (the origin of Sprint in the US) and satellite transmission is an example. The entry of private enterprises into cellular phone service and the opening of public phone systems to private competition are a result. The introduction of the combined cycle gas turbine for power production, equipment that can operate at much smaller scale than traditional power plants, promises to have similar impacts in electricity generation.

Public sector financial needs became a dominant consideration after the debt crisis in the 1980s in Latin America and budgetary difficulties in the mid-1990s in East Asia. It was not only a matter of stopping state-owned enterprise deficits, but increasingly, became a question of raising capital funds outside the government's budget constraint. Partial privatization, in the form of sales of minority equity, like in Thai International Airways, appeared attractive because international interest rates were often well below domestic ones. In this case, capital market considerations were dominant and it is not clear how much, if any, change occurred in management or organizational objectives. As a result of foreign exchange crises, as in Brazil in 1998, in many cases, privatization became a question of raising foreign exchange as well as covering the domestic budget deficit, as in Brazil in 1998. These transactions involve sales to foreign interests. This is like selling a country's "crown jewels," though it may also be justified as a way to realize implicit value that cannot be realized on domestic capital markets. Often, these transactions also bring the benefit of advanced management, modern technology, and efficient scale available to the foreign purchaser so that they may be consistent with today's underlying political-economic philosophy regardless of their immediate financial or foreign exchange motivation.

Revenues from privatization in the developing world, particularly in Latin America, have been increasing sharply in the mid-1990s, representing a total of US$82 billion of which US$35 billion is foreign exchange during the 1990–96 period (World Bank statistics).

Finally, in recent years the limits of privatization have been stretched. Activities that have been considered public sector concerns are being privatized. Chile pioneered the private investment of social security funds, a move that has been taken or is actively being considered elsewhere, including the US. While there have long been private schools, along with public school systems, the move now is toward profit-making schools, often in competition with public ones. The thought is not simply that private schools may be better, but that they will impose welcome competitive pressures on the public school system. Private, profit-making entrepreneurship is also being extended to other public sector activities, even to running prisons. Since there are often national interest imperatives for public sector activities — control of the curriculum or fair administration of justice, for example — it is not clear whether, in the end, the advantages of private business will be sufficient to offset the other implications of privatization in these cases.

Development policies

Over the past three decades, many dimensions of development strategy have undergone substantial change, even reversal:

1. From social and development planning to free markets;
2. From state-owned industries to private and joint venture enterprises; and
3. From import substitution to export promotion.

The initial post-World War II model for the developing economy was one based on traditional ideas of underdevelopment. A poor country, exploited by the former colonial industrial powers, needed to focus its energies. Using its limited resources optimally required an organized planned effort, led by government officials. Lack of private capital implied that large-scale basic enterprises would be supported by public funds. Building local industries called for tariff and quota protection. Only in a protected market would they reach a level of scale and experience that would allow them to operate efficiently.

It would be too strong a statement to say that these efforts were not successful, for many countries built infrastructure and achieved a modicum of industrialization with such a government-led protected industry approach to development. The deficiencies of this approach became apparent as the level of development rose. Government planning lacked rationality and flexibility, aiming at targets that were often more symbolic than economic and unable to modify these aims once they were established. Public enterprises were notably inefficient, employing too many workers and lacking entrepreneurship. Protected industries operated at too low a scale, lacked incentives to reduce costs, and often failed to modernize and maintain the quality of their products. Some classic cases were:

1. The Mexican petroleum industry, Pemex, with staff numbering many times that of an equivalent private enterprise;
2. The Latin American or Indian automobile industries that continued to produce the same product designs many years after they had been phased out elsewhere; or
3. Economic policies in Argentina until the end of the 1980s.

The changes began in East Asia, with Japan followed by Hong Kong, Korea, Taiwan and Singapore. These countries began policies of export promotion to meet their needs for foreign exchange. It became apparent quickly that competition in world markets served multiple purposes:

1. It required industries to be competitive, not simply in terms of manufacturing costs but also in terms of product design and quality;
2. It attracted foreign capital and frequently foreign design and technology; and
3. It brought the desired hard currency earnings.

It has been difficult to phase out protectionist import substitution policies entirely. Indeed, for political reasons, most countries, mature and developing alike, still maintain certain measures of protection. Export promotion has become the mechanism of choice for advancing economic development. In the 1980s, the East Asian countries were fortunate because they had important advantages for the production of manufactures at a time when the more mature countries, like the US and Western Europe, were willing to accept an increasing import flow of such goods. It is not clear to what extent these imports were stimulated by the increasing ability of the East Asian countries to produce them, and to what extent they were expanded by the explicit efforts of importers in the advanced countries. At one time in the late 1970s, mass merchandisers in the US explicitly planned on increasing the import share of their sales. Their managers helped to organize foreign production to their product specifications, including fashionable designs and high quality. Multinational corporations from the US, Europe and Japan played an important role in this process, but it appears that indigenous companies, sometimes imitating the actions of their international competitors also were important. In recent years, local companies from Korea, Taiwan and Thailand have developed export production in neighboring countries, particularly in China.

Growth and Development Policies for the "New Economy"

The "new economy" offers new potentials and new challenges. How should policy makers respond to promote economic development?

It is essential for policy to take into account the characteristics of the "new" industries and the setting in which they are to be fostered. A critical distinction is between "new" and "old" traditional industries. The new information technology (IT) field includes hardware (chips, cellular phones, routers and optical cables) as well as software (operating systems, application programs, internet controls, e-business software, etc.). All call for higher, more specialized, and newer technology than traditional "old industries."

The computer has its roots in the research activities of large companies like IBM, Fujitsu and Xerox, and the Internet can be traced to research funded by the US Department of Defense. But recent applications like the PC and the "new economy" originated in a series of new enterprises, many of them beginning at a very small scale. Steve Jobs started Apple Computer in a garage and Bill Gates is said to have begun Microsoft in his bedroom. Many of the IT companies are now very large — like Intel, SAP and some others have near monopoly power. But the advanced frontiers of the IT industry and other advanced industries like biotechnology are still characterized by many new small companies with an entrepreneurial spirit. Most of them are located in a few regional centers where interaction with other inventors and users is facilitated, e.g. Silicon Valley, Austin and Boston in the US. A few such network centers have developed in other countries, for example, PC-related hardware in East Asia, cellular in Finland and programming in Israel. Some of the most promising developments have come from new firms. These enterprises have heavy needs for capital that comes from venture capital funds, offerings of new stock, or acquisition by larger firms.

The development of an IT industry, thus, calls for special attributes: the availability of other related IT firms with which to interact, a technically trained labor force, and plentiful venture capital. A few developing countries like Taiwan and Singapore have been able to participate in aspects of the new economy, mostly as producers of the requisite high-tech hardware. A few others, even surprisingly in India, Bangalore, have been able to leapfrog into the world of software. But most of the developing countries including some of the most successful in East Asia so far have found it difficult to bring together the special attributes required. Industrial policy to foster new technology applications is even more challenging than using industrial policy to promote traditional industry. The Japanese found that building IT firms is quite different from creating steel or automobile industries. As a result, in place of selecting specific development plans, MITI has supported a variety of different research and development initiatives hoping that among them one or another will succeed. These efforts have had only limited success. Yet, some countries like Singapore and Taiwan have made substantial progress in this direction. These are small countries already endowed with high incomes. Singapore, in particular has put enormous resources into developing higher education. Taiwan has fostered a series of high-tech research parks and has encouraged the return of its "sons and daughters" who have been successful abroad. The hope that local and foreign entrepreneurs would work together to build new advanced industrial companies has been realized in Taiwan, but it has been more difficult to achieve these objectives in other countries. Malaysia, which has benefited from Singaporean entrepreneurship in its Penang growth pole, is using public money to build an electronic network to its new capital. Whether that will help to promote "new" industry remains to be seen.

To summarize, the essentials for the "new" industries appear to lie more in the availability and interaction of highly trained entrepreneurs and the availability of capital than in government expenditures. Appropriate infra-structure must be available, often in scientific and industrial parks. Beyond that, a challenge to the public sector is to develop a suitably educated labor force. This may involve basic education, particularly in regions where even elementary education remains deficient. Importantly, it also involves advanced education, oriented toward science, technology and management. Financial institutions that provide venture capital need also to be developed, though the actual investment in new venture is best left to the private sector.

Implications for Business

What does the growth and development policy environment mean for business? Policy measures frequently provide opportunities that business managers can exploit. Policy measures also, frequently, set up barriers that must be overcome.

Investment promotion has been central to development policy in many developing countries. Such incentives may involve tax preferences, subsidies, support for R&D, infrastructure development, etc. In some cases, the benefits are general without sectoral preference, but in many countries they are directed at particular industries that appear to planners to be central to the economy's growth. Unfortunately, some of these preferences may be available only to domestic entrepreneurs. Some countries sharply limit the role of foreign business particularly in sectors like banking, communications and the professions. Others limit foreign shareholding, making it necessary to bring in local partners. As the financial crisis in East Asia unfolded, opportunities for foreign business to take over ailing local firms, even banks, have multiplied.

The problems faced by foreign investors have often been legal and cultural. Only a few developing countries maintain the high legal standards available in the US, Western Europe, or Japan. That means that formal contracts may not be enforceable, that intellectual property is not adequately protected, that there is often no formal system for bankruptcy. In some countries, widespread bribery and corruption pose another difficulty. Cultural norms in the developing world also differ greatly from those in the advanced countries. Policies to bring legal and cultural institutions in the developing countries closer to Western standards are being enacted widely.

Questions for Discussion

* Contrast the role of government in developed and in developing economies.
* What are the arguments *for* and *against* industrial policy?
* Is privatization always a useful way to advance the economy?
* Contrast the merits of the import substitution and export promotion approaches to economic development.
* Can developing countries participate in the "new economy." Do they have any advantages? Do they face any barriers?

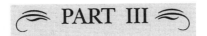

PART III

Stabilizing the Economy: Domestic Perspectives

In Part III, we are concerned with the domestic aspects of economic stabilization in a closed economy. From a pedagogical perspective, it is useful to deal first with a closed economy and then, in Part IV, to extend the model to include international interactions. Much of the material covered in Part III is relevant to large economies like the United States or the European Union, particularly at times when economic activity is not dominated by international forces. In Chapter 7, we introduce a simple aggregate demand model of the economy. We consider the forces that determine demand by consumers, investors and government. Chapter 8 is concerned with the operation of the monetary sector, money supply and interest rates are discussed. Together, the real and the monetary parts of the economy determine aggregate demand. In Chapter 9, we consider the supply side and the interaction of demand and supply. Then, we integrate these forces in a more complex and realistic model. How are the aggregate demand and supply side elements affected by the "new economy"? Fiscal and monetary aggregate demand policies are discussed in Chapter 10. The increasingly important international considerations and policy in an open economy are the focus of Part IV.

Chapter 7

The Aggregate Demand Model

The aggregate demand and supply curves are a simple, largely self-explanatory approach to consider the factors that determine the economy's production and price performance over the business cycle. We begin this chapter by considering the nature of the business cycle. Is it affected by the advent of a "new economy"? In this chapter, we focus on the determinants of aggregate demand. Can we build a simple aggregate model of the economy? What are the forces that influence the purchasing of consumers, investors and government?

Business Fluctuations and the "New Economy"

The ups and downs of the business cycle — booms and recessions — are a traditional concern of economists and politicians in developed countries. But developing countries must also be concerned with economic stabilization. Indeed, historical experience suggests that stabilization of demand, prices and the balance of payments is essential in these countries to maintain investor confidence and continued growth.

To begin, we ask: is there a business cycle? In developed countries like the United States, there are ups and downs in economic activity, but if we look for regular cyclical patterns, we will not find them. The cycles may average three to four years in length, with the downswing somewhat shorter than the upswing, but they vary greatly in duration and amplitude. The upswing in the US during the 1990s lasted almost ten years. It was interrupted by a slowdown in the growth rate engineered by the Federal Reserve, only about one year long in 1994–5, and that was followed by a growth spurt in 1997–2000. The long expansion of the 1990s and its acceleration in the most recent years, reflects widespread technological innovations — hardware, software and electronic networks. Here, we see clearly the influence of what has been termed the "new economy."

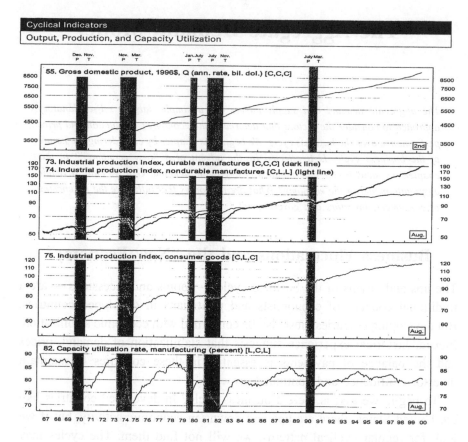

Fig. 7.1   The Business Cycle and Manufacturing Capacity Utilization.

Some optimists have gone so far as to say "The business cycle is dead!" They argue that the new technology will wipe out business fluctuations. That is unlikely, though the cycle may be delayed at a time of burgeoning investment. It may be attenuated in an increasingly service-dominated economy. The Fed believes that the US is in a "New Era" of faster productivity growth, but it fears that low unemployment and high capacity utilization will rekindle inflationary pressures. In mid-2000, an increase in interest rates and a decline in stocks caused many observers to bet on slowing of the economy's rapid expansion, and possibly, on a recession (Fig. 7.1).

Until recently, the cycle was less apparent in the rapidly growing countries of East Asia. The slowdowns did not show up as definite downturns of economic activity, only as a slowing of the rate of growth, say from the trend of 7 to 8%, as in Thailand, to growth of 3 or 4% during the down phase. But in 1997–8, the cycle came back with a vengeance.

There has been much discussion about the sources of business fluctuations. In some cases, the origin is clear, for example, with regard to the recessions of 1974–5 and 1981–2 which were linked to the Middle Eastern oil price increases. Other recessions reflect policy, for example, monetary tightening by the Federal Reserve in an effort to contain inflationary pressures in 1990–1.

Business cycles may also have their origin in the natural dynamics of the economy. The business cycle is not so much a regularly spaced rhythm, as a tendency for booms to create an environment of inflation and excess capacity that leads to a downturn. Finally, *real business cycle theory* argues that business fluctuations are caused by shocks on the supply side of the economy. In this connection, we can see the "new economy" as a source of exogenous productivity gains. As new technologies are introduced, there is impetus both on the demand and on the supply sides. The economic boom in the late 1990s can be seen as a real business cycle phenomenon.

Cyclical swings have widespread consequences. The period of expansion produces increases in employment and wages, high levels of investment and growing profits. Politicians as well as consumers welcome the boom. As the expansion continues, it runs into capacity constraints. Labor markets tighten and wage pressures mount. Order books build up and backlogs begin to increase. Prices of basic materials rise. With increasing pressures between demand and available production capacity, inflation begins to accelerate. Interest rates rise. The balance of payments deteriorates, as imports rise and exports tend to lag. The monetary authorities, usually a central bank like the US Federal Reserve, begin to tighten credit. Rising inflation and higher interest rates begin to cut into investment demand and consumption, causing involuntary inventory accumulation and presaging a downturn. Excessive inventories cause cutbacks in production and employment and declines in productivity, characteristic of the start of the recession period. Layoffs translate into rising unemployment. Capacity utilization declines and new office buildings, only now being completed, remain empty. While demand pressures ease, there is little, if any, decline in prices, since wages and prices tend to be sticky.

As the recession proceeds, the overhang of excess inventories is gradually worked down, underutilized office and factory space is absorbed. The Central Bank eases monetary policy. Eventually, when interest rates have fallen and business people become aware of renewed demand, new orders increase, production schedules are expanded, and workers are re-hired. Finally, the recovery has begun.

Government policy seeks to stabilize the cycle. But often, the best governments can do is to moderate the cycle and sometimes the very policy that monetary and fiscal authorities impose in order to tame the expansion and inflation leads to the downturn. A so-called "stop-go" cycle is frequently the result.

A Simple Demand Side Model

Turning now to the underlying theory: if output and employment are not always at the full employment, full capacity level, we must first try to explain what determines the level of output. What are the forces that determine how much the economy will produce?

What is the most simple aggregate demand model that we can think of? A diagram like Fig. 7.2 shows the relationship between the various components of aggregate demand and aggregate production. It works on the assumption that the nation's production is driven by aggregate demand. The horizontal arrow pointing toward aggregate demand (AD) sums together the major demand forces in the economy: Consumption (C), Investment (I) and Government Spending (G). (Note that for simplicity, we have left out exports and imports here.) One might suppose that forecasting only involves summing the estimated values of the various demands to obtain AD. Then the level of production activity and income (Y) will adjust to meet market needs. If production exceeds demand, inventories would pile up and firms would

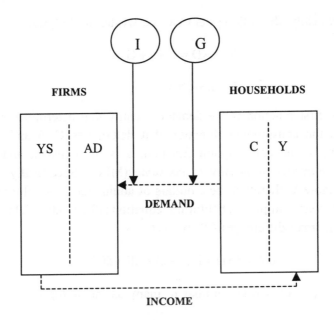

Fig. 7.2 A Simple Demand Model (Demand Determines Output, Output Determines Income, and Income Determines Demand).

soon reduce their production schedules. If aggregate demand, AD exceeds output, Y, inventories will be drawn down, and businesses would increase production generating additional employment and income. Here's the rub. Additional income would flow to consumers who would in turn increase the consumption spending. There is *feedback* from Y to consumption, shown in the diagram by the dashed line (Fig. 7.2).

For forecasting, we assume the investment and government spending are determined outside our little system by business sentiment and by government budgets, respectively. Effectively, we make an informed guess to predict these values. Using econometricians' terminology, these variables are exogenous. It is not possible, however, to make a similar guess about Y without simultaneously saying something about C, since C depends closely on Y. Both variables are simultaneously determined.

Algebraically, the little system can be written as follows:

$$Y = AD = C + I + G \qquad (7.1)$$

$$C = a + c \times Y \qquad (7.2)$$

where the first function is the demand identity that determines Y and the second is the consumption function that determines C. a and c are the parameters of the consumption function, a is the constant and c is the so-called *marginal propensity to consume* (MPC). Specifically for every dollar of more Y, there will be c dollars of additional C. A solution for this system is very simple, substituting equations (7.2) into (7.1), AD and computing small differences (d), we get

$$dY = dAD = 1/(1-c) \times (dI + dG). \qquad (7.3)$$

The term $1/(1-c)$ will be familiar to many as the *multiplier*.

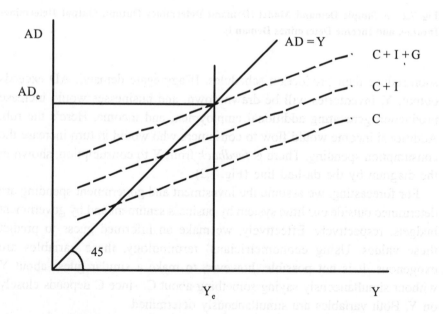

Fig. 7.3   Consumption, Investment and Government Spending Determine Aggregate Demand.

Another way to evaluate the model is to display it graphically as in Fig. 7.3. This diagram, sometimes facetiously referred to as the Keynesian cross, measures output (Y) on the horizontal direction and aggregate demand AD on the vertical. Equilibrium in the economy, the situation where aggregate demand is just sufficient to absorb what the economy is producing, i.e. Y = AD, is shown on this graph by the 45° line. Only points on this line represent equilibrium. To the right of the 45° line, output exceeds demand, inventories will accumulate, and businesses will revise their production plans downward. The left, demand exceeds output, and businesses will have incentive to increase production activity.

Next we introduce consumption into the chart. The line marked C represents consumption, drawn here with an upward slope because consumption depends largely on income. The intersection of the line with the vertical axis at Y = 0, is the "a" term of our equation above, representing autonomous consumption. The slope of the line, dC/dY, corresponds to the parameter "c" in equation (7.2). Keynes called this parameter, the *marginal propensity to consume*. In addition to consumer demand, we must include investment and government purchases (omitting exports and imports at this point). Since I and G are exogenous here, i.e. not related to income, we can simply draw them as at a constant level above C. So that the diagram shows a line for C + I + G. Where that line intersects the 45° line corresponds to the equilibrium level of Y, (Y_e), i.e. where production just corresponds to demand.

Now suppose the government proposes to increase spending from G_0 to G_1. Output will rise in response, by more than the increase in G, since higher aggregate demand will cause higher Y, and that in turn will produce higher C, etc. The new equilibrium will be where the new aggregate demand equals current production.

There is nothing in this graph to mark full employment or potential GDP. Presumably, the Y that corresponds to full employment must be somewhere to the right of Y_e, because only if there is sufficient spare capacity can real output expand to accommodate increased demand.

Case 7.1
An Application of the Simple Aggregate Demand Model

Returning now to our simple model, I asked a graduate student to turn this theoretical model into an *econometric model* and to test its performance. Building an econometric model involves, in this case, simply estimating realistic values for the parameters "a" and "c" of the consumption function. Using data for consumption and income from the US National Income and Product Accounts for the period 1961 to 1973, my student ran a statistical regression between the corresponding quarterly values of consumption and income. He obtained the following result:

$$C = -518 + 0.75 \times Y. \tag{7.4}$$

The consumption function thus had a constant of −518 (at $Y = 0$), and an MPC of 0.75; out of every additional dollar of Y, consumers would spend 75 cents. Then, substituting equation (7.4) for equation (7.2) and using the actual data available each year for the I and G variables, my student computed estimated values for Y, Y_{est}. He compared these estimated values out of the model solutions with the known values for each year's Y. Figure 7.4 shows his estimates of Y (Y_{est}) as compared to the actual values of Y.

At this point, he came back to me more than a little discouraged. "The model does not work! It's way off after 1973, just when we most need it." Note that this calculation was made just before the 1974 oil shock sent prices skyrocketing. Up to 1973, the values of Y_{est} corresponded very well, indeed, to the path taken by Y. My student's disappointment was that the model veered far from the actual Y at that point and continued to do so for several more years. Why? The explanation is simple. The model we have postulated here is an overly simple representation of the world. It includes only a primitive demand side picture of the economy. It deals only with real (price-adjusted) values. It contains no supply constraint, no monetary mechanism, no international trade. Its failure to operate effectively after 1973 is the result of the inflationary oil shock that occurred at that time and

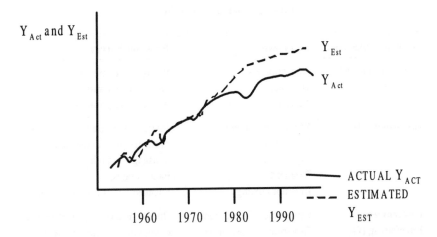

Fig. 7.4   Actual Y$_{act}$ and Model Estimated Y$_{est}$ Diverge with the Oil Shock in the Mid-1970s.

that introduced elements that our little model did not take into account. Such a simple system is helpful as a teaching device but not as a basis for forecasting or policy making. Ultimately this model picks up only the demand side. That's OK at a time when the economy is operating below capacity *and* if prices are relatively sticky. But to make the model really useful, we must consider the supply side as well.

Elaborating the Demand Side Model

What makes up the economy's aggregate demand? Purchasers of the economy's product include millions of individual consumers, business investors, government organizations, and purchasers from abroad (exports); and there are millions of different products. Economists deal with broad aggregates. In contrast, business managers, of course are concerned with detailed product-specific demand data.

Table 7.1   Demand Side Forces.

Demand Category	Sub-classes	Relevant Forces
Consumption (C)	Non-durables Durables Services	Personal income, prices, credit, interest rates, life- time consumption needs
Investment (I)	Private investments Structures Equipment Residential Inventory change	Interest rates, credit availability, needs for production capacity, mortgage and other interest rates, business needs for inventories
Government Purchasing (G)	Government investments Government consumption	Budget, needs for infrastructure, employment of government (including military)
Imports (M) Exports (E)		Exchange rate, income, relative prices at home and abroad

The model described above shows only the simplest aspects of the demand approach. At this point, we provide a somewhat more elaborate picture of the demand side forces of the economy. A summary of the demand side (Table 7.1) provides a quick perspective.

Consumption (C)

We begin with consumption. First we will consider simplified theory of consumption and then we will add some real-life complications. Consumer spending is for:

1. Durable goods like cars and appliances,
2. Non-durables like food and clothing, and
3. Services.

Each of these categories has very different characteristics over the business cycle, something that practicing business people are well aware of.

The underlying hypothesis is that consumption is largely determined by consumer income. At the micro level, there are millions of consumers, each receiving an income, and making decisions on whether to spend that income — consumption — or alternatively, to save it. The aggregate consumption function is an aggregation of millions of spending decisions. At best it is only an approximation.

In our simple model, we treated consumption as an endogenous variable. That is because in the model, consumption is determined by income. In the real world, consumer spending is closely linked to income as is apparent from Fig. 7.5. Panel A shows the movement of aggregate real income (GDP) in the US and aggregate consumption over time. Panel B shows the same information in an x–y diagram, consumption in the vertical direction and income in the horizontal. The best fit regression line shows the relationship. (This is the estimate my student used in our discussion of the minimodel above.) Note that this is a pretty good fit, but it is not perfect, particularly if we look at it in detail. Consumption does not always move synchronously with income. Note, the points below or above the regression line. Consumers do not react immediately to changes in income. They wait to see if the change in income is temporary or if it is likely to persist, to be part of what Milton Friedman termed *permanent income*. Only after consumers see that the increase in income is permanent, do they adjust consumption fully to an increase in income.

The theory of consumption is the counterpart to the theory of saving, since income less consumption equals saving. A theory of consumption

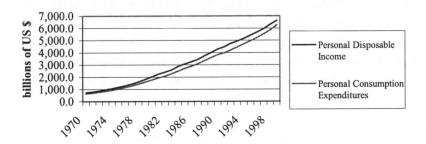

Fig. 7.5 Panel A: Personal Income and Consumption.

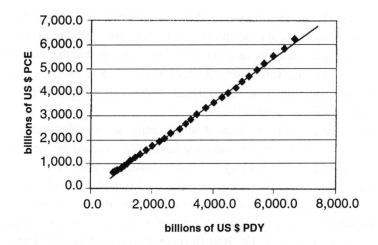

Fig. 7.5   Panel B Personal Consumption Expenditures in Relation to Personal Disposable Income.

will embody a theory of saving, and *vice versa*. It is obvious, of course, why consumers consume (spend). It is not so clear why they save (not spend).

The most fundamental approach to saving and consumption is Modigliani's *life cycle* hypothesis. The intuition here is that in an effort to maximize their well-being, consumers spread their income over their entire lifetime. When they are at their peak earning power, they save in order to meet their consumption needs later when they are retired.[1] This pattern is illustrated in Fig. 7.6. In Panel A, we assume that income is steady at W over the working life period and zero during retirement. The area of saving (a) must equal the area of dissaving (b) if the consumer is to have sufficient income to cover his/her needs during retirement. We assume, probably unrealistically, that consumers have no desire to leave anything to their children, what

---

[1]More typically, the retired worker will have social security and retirement benefits after the working phase of life is over. These represent part of the stream of income generated from savings made during the period of working life.

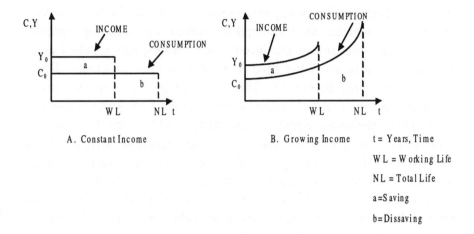

A. Constant Income

B. Growing Income

t = Years, Time
WL = Working Life
NL = Total Life
a = Saving
b = Dissaving

Fig. 7.6   The Life Cycle Hypothesis (with Constant Income and Growing Income).

economists have termed the bequest motive. The implications of this approach are:

1. That there is justification for consumers to set aside some of their income as savings for retirement.
2. That on average, consumers will try to save as much during their lifetime as they expect to require to maintain their lifestyle during the retirement years.
3. That a temporary increase in income will affect current consumption only little since consumer spending and saving is related to lifetime income rather than to current income.

The life cycle hypothesis has interesting implications. In the mature economies, the pattern of income is flat (or nearly so). Consumers will spend a share of their income that corresponds to the proportion of their lifetime spent working.[2] On the other hand, when income is increasing and

---

[2]I.e., $w \times wl = c \times nl$ where w is the wage rate and wl is working life, c is consumption and nl is total life. Note that this means the $c/y = wl/nl$.

living standards are increasing very rapidly, as they are in the East Asian developing economies, the consumption standard desired during retirement is very high compared to the income and consumption standard at the beginning. The result is the need to have high rates of saving. This is illustrated in Panel B, Fig. 7.6. This argument goes a long way toward explaining the high rate of saving observed in the East Asian countries.

Another interesting aspect of consumption and saving behavior is a problem of reconciling individual behavior and aggregate behavior. At the individual level, the theory posed above may well fit behavior — though admittedly lots of counter arguments and lots of counter evidence can be presented. The problem is that at the aggregate level of consumption and savings function, we are talking about the behavior of many individuals, some at every stage of the life cycle, some working, some retired. The aggregate saving ratio will depend not only on the need to support consumption during retirement, but also on the proportion of working people and the proportion of retired people. In a stable situation where the age distribution of the population is not changing, and income is not rising, the savings of working people will approximately offset consumption of the retired. While some individuals are saving, others are dissaving and the aggregate saving ratio will be zero. In a population that is aging, savings will be high in order to meet future needs, and the saving rate will drop as the population becomes progressively older. This means that saving depends also on the so-called dependency ratios of young people to working people and retired people to working people. Empirical work tends to substantiate these ideas. The age distribution and the need to save towards old age have been very important in explaining the high saving rate in Japan. As the population ages, a serious problem in Japan, there is reason to think that the Japanese saving rate will decline.

In the real world, numerous factors other than income also have important influence on consumer spending and must be taken into account. Some of these may determine long-run saving behavior — how much on average people in a society consume and save. Others contributed to the ups and downs of consumption spending over the business cycle. Theory and empirical observation suggest that the following are among the many influences that affect consumer spending:

1. Consumer assets and debt obligations;
2. Interest rates and the availability of credit;
3. Expectations about income and inflation;
4. Income distribution, high income people may save more than poor people; and
5. Cultural factors, publicity and advertising.

Case 7.2 provides a good illustration of how some of these factors interact.

Case 7.2
Recent Experience about the Uncertainties of Consumer Spending

The 2000–1 experience in the US provides some interesting illustrations about the difficulty of predicting consumer expenditure. In early 2001, expectations about consumer spending were quite pessimistic. The stock market bubble had burst and many consumers had seen their wealth drop drastically during the previous year. In the boom, consumers had piled up large quantities of debt. Finally, many high-tech firms were threatening layoffs. Unemployment was beginning to rise, albeit from a very low level, and the job situation was becoming more difficult. Electricity and natural gas prices were rising rapidly, leading to some fear of inflation.

The 2000 presidential campaign was also perceived as a source of difficulty. In order to sell their tax cut plan, the Republicans suggested that the economy was going into a recession. Fearing a self-fulfilling prophecy, the Democrats responded vigorously, arguing that all was well, that the ten-year boom was still on. It is doubtful, however, that political pronouncements about the economy had a great deal of influence on economic behavior.

Consumer sentiment dropped drastically in early 2001. But in the first half of 2001, consumer spending was surprisingly well maintained. There was fear, however, that if production and employment were to decline further, the second half of the year would see a more serious adjustment.

The September 11 terrorist attacks on the World Trade Center in New York had a major negative impact on consumer spending, but there is evidence that spending was already dropping sharply even before the attacks.

Various influences affect consumption spending in developing countries as well as in advanced countries. The duality of the developing economies means that much of the consumption of manufactured durables will depend on urban income where living standards are above subsistence and where people can buy goods and services in addition to the basics. As incomes rise, an increasing fraction of spending in developing economies goes for discretionary products like better quality clothing, household appliances and, particularly, motorcycles and cars. Well-to-do urban people also account for the most saving. Rural consumers spend most of their income on food, much of it produced on their own farm plots and do not have much left over for luxury goods or for saving. The unequal income distribution is an important consideration influencing consumption and saving in developing economies.

The discussion suggests that in the real world predicting consumption is not quite as simple as our consumption function based only on current income would suggest.

Investment (I)

Investment is one of the volatile demand factors that drive the business cycle. We have treated investment — purchases of new equipment, structures and inventories — as an exogenous variable in our simple discussion above, but we must try to make it endogenous. Our approach will be to discuss investment first in simple theoretical terms and then to add a degree of realism.

The investment decision — PDV and IRR

A number of factors enter into making the decision to make an investment. Suppose, for example, that we want to establish a McDonald's franchise.

Once the site is available, it will be necessary to make investments in a structure, the building and in equipment, the "Golden Arches," the deep fryer, the tables and chairs, etc. How can we put a quantitative dimension on the expenses and on the returns, and how do we make the decision that the investment is justifiable? Our friendly banker will ask us to submit a business plan which will include a simple calculation of present discounted value (PDV) or of the internal rate of return (IRR) of our projected investment. The parent McDonald's company may help in doing the figuring. The calculations are as follows:

$$PDV = -C_0 + GP_1/(1+r) + GP_2/(1+r)^2$$
$$+ GP_3/(1+r)^3 + \cdots + GP_n/(1+r)^n \qquad (7.5)$$

where C_0 is the cost to be incurred in year 0, and $GP_{1,...,n}$ is the annual gross profit to be earned each year from year 1 to years n. Future earnings must be discounted to bring them to present value,[3] i.e accomplished by dividing them by the $(1+r)$ term, where r is the rate of interest, one year out and again each year as we go into the future, so that two years out we must divide by $(1+r)^2$, at three years by $(1+r)^3$, etc.

The criterion on whether to do the investment here is whether PDV is positive or negative, assuming that r is the appropriate cost of capital, i.e.:

If PDV > 0   Invest
If PDV < 0   Don't Invest.

A more convenient way to get to the same point is to compute the internal rate of return. We use the same equation as (7.5) above, only this time we set PDV equal to zero and we solve for r, the IRR:

$$0 = PDV = -C_0 + GP_1/(1+r) + GP_2/(1+r)^2$$
$$+ GP_3/(1+r)^3 + \cdots + GP_n/(1+r)^n . \qquad (7.6)$$

---

[3]A dollar available in some future year is not the same as a dollar available today. Of course, we could borrow that dollar today for repayment later, but then we would have to pay interest on the loan. Consequently, future income must be discounted to establish its present value.

The IRR is the rate of interest (r) that would reduce PDV to zero. In this case, the investment criterion relates the IRR to the cost of capital (CC), the rate of interest at which the funds for the investment will be available, i.e.

If IRR > CC   Invest
If IRR < CC   Don't invest.

The basic theory of investment assumes that investments will be made so long as the return on the project exceeds the cost of capital. In Fig. 7.7, we show an approach to the investment decision. On the horizontal axis, we show various investment projects available, ranked according to their rate of return. The first project might be a high-tech factory with a high internal rate of return prospect of 20%; the second might be electrical generating machinery which yields 12%; the third might be a parking structure with an internal rate of return of 7%; and so on. We have approximated the different rate of return possibilities with a straight line. Now the decision of how much investment to make depends on the cost of capital, that is the rate of interest that must be paid to obtain capital. Many corporations call this the hurdle rate. In Fig. 7.7, the hurdle rate has been drawn in at 10%.

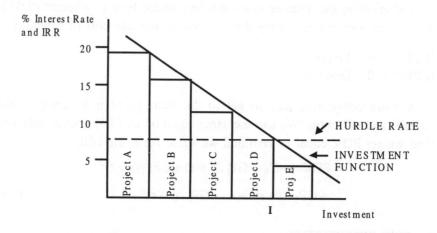

Fig. 7.7 Investment and the Interest Rate. Investment Opportunities and the Interest Rate Determine Investment (I).

The high-tech factory and the electrical generating machinery can be justified, but not the parking structure.

As we have shown above, investment depends on the cost of capital, which is of course in large part, the rate of interest.[4] This establishes a link between the market for goods and services and the financial market. We will be considering interest rates and the financial sector in more detail below.

The accelerator

The acceleration principle offers another perspective on investment and its relationship to output. The basic idea is that investment goes to build the economy's plant capacity. Suppose that production potential depends simply on the available plant capacity, a production function as follows:

$$Y = 1/a \times K \tag{7.7}$$

where K stands for capital stock. We can turn this around to say that required capital

$$K = a \times Y. \tag{7.8}$$

Now, recognizing that investment represents the change in capital stock and substituting

$$I = K - K_{-1} = a \times Y - K_{-1}. \tag{7.9}$$

Note that this equation describes a process of adjusting from the existing capital stock of the previous period (K_{-1}) to the desired capital stock of the present period $(a \times Y)$. When this adjustment occurs within the current period

---

[4]The tax treatment of interest and dividend payments and the way in which capital can be depreciated for tax computation purposes also affect the cost of capital. On some occasions, investment may be constrained by availability of investment capital. At times of financial crisis, funds for investment may not be available no matter how high the interest rate the borrower might be willing to pay.

of analysis, for example, the current year, we can substitute the $(a \times Y_{-1})$ term from equation (7.8) for K_{-1}.

$$I = a \times (Y - Y_{-1}). \tag{7.10}$$

The relationship between investment and the *change* in output (Y) is known as the *accelerator*. Note that the relationship is with the change of output, not its level. Such a relationship can be shown to account for business cycle fluctuations. Investment demand turns down when growth in general business activity slows. The simple accelerator can be modified into the flexible accelerator by recognizing that the adjustment of capital from its existing level to the desired level is not always accomplished immediately.

Returning now to our discussion of the comparison between the marginal product of capital and the cost of capital, considered above.

Assume a production function

$$Y = a_0 \times K^{a_1} \times L^{(1-a_1)}. \tag{7.11}$$

In terms of small changes, we can compute as

$$dY / Y = a_1 \times dK / K, \quad \text{and} \tag{7.12}$$

$$dY / dK = a_1 \times Y / K. \tag{7.13}$$

The criterion determining investment will be whether the marginal product of capital (dY/dK) exceeds or is equal to the cost of capital (r). The can be seen as

$$a_1 \times Y / K = r \tag{7.14}$$

where r is the cost of capital, broadly speaking the rate of interest. Using the information in equation (7.5) and rearranging, we may then write

$$I = (a_1 \times Y / r) - K_{-1}. \tag{7.15}$$

To summarize, investment depends directly on output, inversely on the interest rate and on the capital stock already in existence. These relationships are critical factors in accounting for the fluctuations of the business cycle. But the realities of individual investment decisions are likely to be a good deal more complex that we have shown here.

Investment decisions may be greatly affected by the investor's optimism or pessimism. Keynes called this psychological factor, *animal spirits*. (How such factors can affect the investment calculation is considered in Case 7.3.) No wonder then that investment may be volatile, high when expectations are high and interest rates are low, low or non-existent when the economic outlook is cloudy, when there is overcapacity, and when high interest rates make capital costly. A simple way to contrast the investment demand situation at the peak of the business cycle and at the trough to in the shape and position of the investment function as shown in Fig. 7.8. The graph shows investment, in the horizontal direction, and the cost of capital % in the vertical direction. In a recession, the investment function is steep and to the left. There are few investment opportunities. The investments that are made will be essential ones, like replacing a ruptured boiler, and will be carried out regardless of the cost of capital. That is why the investment function is steep. The boom investment curve is to the right and quite flat. There are lots of investment opportunities. Investment is held in check largely by the cost of capital. Obviously on investments whose IRR exceeds the cost of capital % will be carried out. But if the rate of interest is reduced, there are

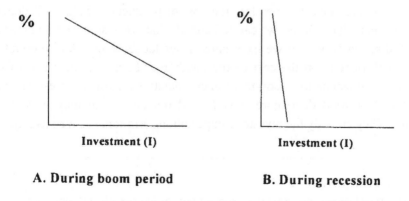

A. During boom period   B. During recession

Figure 7.8   The Investment Relationship During Boom and Bust

lots of opportunities out there to exploit. That is why the investment curve with respect to "%" is flat.

Financial market conditions, usually represented by the interest rate, influence some kinds of investments, like residential construction, more than others. As we will see Chapter 8, monetary policy may seek to raise interest rates to hold back investment when demand is excessive and reduce them during recessions to stimulate investment demand. Construction spending is usually the component of investment that is most affected.

Case 7.3
Optimism and Pessimism and the Investment Calculation

The investment calculation procedure considered above appears neatly mechanical. Indeed, spreadsheet programs enable us to compute IRR very easily on the basis of assumed values for the cost C_0 and for the gross profit (GP) trends into the distant future. But beware! All the numbers are likely to be subject to a wide band of error and to be greatly influenced by your current mood.

Even the costs incurred in the current year, C_0, are not known with precision — cost overruns are not unusual. The gross profits earned in future years, GP, are equal to sales less the cost of production. Sales will depend on how many hamburgers we can sell and at what price, an uncertain prospect depending on how well we have chosen our location, etc. And production costs will depend on the cost of the hamburger buns and meat and of the labor, etc. It stands to reason that the computations involved in establishing IRR look a good deal more reliable and objective than they may be in reality. They embody the investor's expectations, irrational as well as rational.

In developing economies, monetary considerations also influence investment. In these countries, bank loans play a much larger role in financing business investment than they do in mature economies where there are highly developed equity markets and venture capital firms. In developing countries, the availability of funds, or lack thereof, may be more important than the interest rate. Interest rates may be high, but for a variety of reasons, banks may not have credit available or may be unwilling to take on risky investments. For this reason much of the financing of investments in developing countries is through informal private lending, often from family sources.

In some of the rapidly growing countries of East Asia, there are sometimes opportunities for high return investments. The difficulty is, first, that risks are sometimes very high. These may simply be the risks of producing in an environment that lacks skilled workers, good transportation or communication, or adequate power supplies. It may also involve political risk, for example the risk of being expropriated without legal protection. Secondly, interest rates in developing countries tend to be very high. Neither of these issues seem to have dissuaded business from making investments in East Asia. Quite the contrary; until 1997, economic expansion in some East Asian countries was energized by booms in office building, hotel and housing construction.

Government purchasing (G)

Government purchasing of goods and services includes both public expenditures for current consumption — education, police, medical and military services, for example — and investment in roads, bridges, port facilities, etc. These represent direct demands by the public sector for goods and services being produced currently. In addition, the government also affects demand indirectly, in a positive direction through transfer payments which enter personal income and affect consumption, and in a negative direction, through the imposition of taxes.

Congress votes on the expenditure budget and on tax rates. The Office of Management and Budget (OMB) and the Congressional Budget Office keep careful tabs on various dimensions of government spending and receipts. It is convenient in simple forecasting exercises to assume that the government budget is exogenous, determined largely by political decisions. But, in fact, government spending and tax receipts are very sensitive to economic conditions. When GDP declines, public spending for welfare and unemployment compensation automatically increases as the eligible population for these payments grows. In the boom phase of the cycle, tax collections rise as corporate profit taxes and personal income taxes reflect the growth of these income flows. This means that a complex model would show government receipts and spending as endogenous in the economic system, though discretionary action to change spending or to alter tax rates must also be taken into account.

Case 7.4
Is the Government Budget Endogenous?

The US budget surplus in the late 1990s is an example of the endogenous nature of the government budget. It reflected high rates of income and corporate profits that brought in large amounts of tax revenues, though efforts to limit the growth of public spending may also have helped. While there was extensive discussion of how to "spend" the surplus, it would quickly disappear if the economy went into a recession.

The structural adjustment program proposed by IMF to Thailand in 1997 is an example for developing countries. It contained provisions for large cuts in spending and an increase in the value added tax from 7 to 10%. These policy changes would have caused a substantial cutback in demand and economic activity in Thailand, part of the structural re-adjustment being sought by the IMF and Thai authorities. But these actions would not have assured that the budget would be balanced since the resulting decline in income would also have reduced tax collections. In fact, such a cut would have had serious costs in terms of reduced social services and employment, directly and indirectly. Instead, the IMF subsequently permitted Thailand to cut taxes and to engage in stimulative spending.

Imports and exports (M and X)

Imports may also be considered as endogenous parts of the system. Imports are closely tied to economic activity of the economy, since imports represent parts and raw materials for production as well as imported consumer and capital goods. An aggregative approach might simply relate imports to general business activity (GDP), but more detailed treatment relating consumer imports to personal income, imports of materials and parts to production activity, and imports of machinery and equipment to investment in new plants might be appropriate. As we note further below, imports are also sensitive to prices of goods in the domestic market, prices of competitive goods available abroad, and of course, the rate of exchange. Import restrictions and tariffs may also affect the quantity imports.

Exports represent a demand originating abroad for our economy's product. Consequently, exports depend on economic conditions in foreign markets. Looking at one economy in isolation, we generally treat exports as exogenous. In fact, however, the level of activity in all countries is interrelated since output abroad depends on our imports, which in turn influence our exports (foreign imports). Domestic costs and the exchange rate will have an important effect since they determine the competitiveness of exports as compared to the price of goods produced domestically in those markets as well as the prices of competing suppliers.

Imports and exports will be discussed in greater detail when we consider the international aspects of the economy in Chapter 11.

Aggregate Demand and the "New Economy"

Some business forecasters have argued that we are in a "new" economy whose cyclical characteristics are very different from the "old." But, the fundamentals of aggregate demand theory remain the same regardless of whether we are speaking about the "old" or the "new" economy.

There is no avoiding the fact that the advent of information technology greatly increased demand and stimulated economic activity during the decade 1990s. High-tech equipment and software rather than "old" economy hardware accounted for much of the increase in investment spending that occurred in the US in this period. We had not anticipated how cyclically sensitive these expenditures were likely to be. As a consequence, the sudden slowdown in 2001 came as a surprise. Fortunately, other components of demand are not as volatile. Moreover, the pace of technical progress has become so rapid, that many new possibilities for investment were developing even as the economy entered a recession phase of the cycle.

Implications for Business

Forecasts of aggregate demand are an important ingredient in business planning. Even though, most often the concern will be with the demand for particular goods and services rather than with aggregate demand, the market for many goods follows the ups and downs of the cycle. Some goods are necessities and are purchased regardless of the general economic situation whereas others are luxuries, sensitive to general business conditions. Auto purchases, for example, mirror the business cycle closely. Evaluation of aggregate demand conditions and their translation to demand for particular goods and services is an important challenge for business economists.

Questions for Discussion

* Aggregate economic demand can be described as a *feedback system*. Explain.
* What are the principal considerations that influence consumer demand? Do they differ between different types of consumer products?
* In what way(s) are expenditures on investment characteristically different from consumption spending?
* Should we think of the government budget as exogenous or endogenous?

Chapter 8

The Monetary
Sector and Aggregate Demand

In this chapter, we consider how the demand and supply of money interact to determine the interest rate. We relate the financial sector and the real part of the economy and consider the aggregate demand curve.

As we have already noted, financial considerations have substantial impact on the real demands for the economy's product. We cannot provide an estimate of demand without at the same time saying something about conditions in financial markets. Specifically, it is necessary to integrate the financial markets into our description of the economy. That is the purpose of the following section.

A Demand and Supply for Money Perspective

The simplest way to look at interest rate determination is to view it in terms of demand for money and supply of money. By money, we do not mean just currency. Most liquid balances are held, not in currency but in bank deposits. As we noted in Chapter 3, there are various definitions of money, for example M1 which includes currency and demand deposits, M2 which adds certain types of savings deposits, etc. Here, we will be primarily concerned with demand deposits.

Demand for Money

Why would individuals hold liquid balances that pay no interest, money, when they could be earning a return by holding savings bonds, corporate bonds or equities or by lending out their money? This requires some

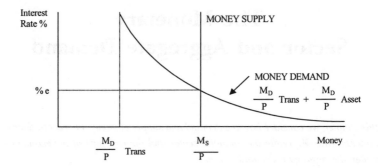

Fig. 8.1   Supply and Demand for Money Determines the Interest Rate.

explanation. Economists classify the motives for holding money balances into two categories:

1. Transaction motives, and
2. Asset motives.

Since we are concerned with purchasing power held rather than simply with nominal dollar balances, we will be dealing with real money balances here (M/P) where we divide by the price level (P) to allow for the fact that money is usually measured in nominal terms while related variables like GDP (Y) are typically treated in real terms. The two demands for money are shown in Fig. 8.1. The first part of the chart, to the left of the vertical up and down line represents transactions demand, and the part to the right between the up and down line and the sloping line represents asset demand. At any time, transactions demand depends on the volume of transactions while asset demand depends on the interest rate.

Transactions demand for money

Transaction motives for holding real money balances involve the common sense notion that you hold money in order to make expenditures. Of course, you need not hold a liquid balance, preferring to keep your assets in interest earning securities, but then you would have to run to the bank to get the funds every time you wanted to buy something. In the ordinary course of business, liquid balances being kept for transaction purposes are likely to be related to the amount of spending we plan to do or the amount of income we receive, i.e.

$$M_{D\,Trans}/P = k \times Y \tag{8.1}$$

where the term on the left represents demand for real transactions balances and Y represents real GDP. The parameter k is simply the amount of liquid transaction balances people keep per unit of GDP.

It is frequently argued that k is likely to be fairly stable in the short run since it depends on institutional arrangements, for example, whether people are paid on a monthly or weekly basis (Case 8.1). In the long run, however, k may shift as the introduction of ATMs or debit cards reduces the need to hold liquid balances. E-banking and other transactions over the Internet will also affect the need for transactions money. As we will see in Chapter 10, the stability of k is an important consideration in determining whether monetarism is an effective policy approach.

Case 8.1
Liquid Balances and Income

Suppose that you earn $5000 per month and that you spend approximately the same amount. Every month your employer deposits $5000 into your account. You spend this amount gradually to exhaust your balance at the end of the month when your employer deposits another $5000. The average balance over the month would be $2500. Now suppose you get a raise to $6000 and adjust your spending accordingly. Then the beginning balance would be $6000, the ending balance would be zero, and the average balance would be $3000. In this example, there is a clear link between the amount of income and the transactions balance. Suppose now that there is an institutional change. Your employer decides to pay, four times a month. In that case, the payment would be $1500 per pay period. If you exhaust the balance each pay period as before, the average balance would be $750. Obviously, the average balance depends on the typical arrangement with regard to making payments and spending. These arrangements are fairly stable from one year to the next. But there are potentials for change, for example as a result of credit cards and ATMs.

Asset demand for money

Why would people want to hold liquid balance as assets? There is clearly a cost involved since these assets could have been put into a form that brings a return. The simplest explanation is the so-called precautionary motive. The idea is that liquid balance are held in case an unanticipated need for liquidity arises. A homey example is as follows: every day I cross a busy street on my way to the swimming pool. I am afraid that one day I will be run over by a car. I make sure always to have $10 in my wallet so that I can pay the taxi driver to take me to the hospital. In the business world, there are many potential needs for liquidity. How much of the company's assets an asset manager might want to keep in liquid funds will depend on the interest rate, the higher the interest rate, the less the liquid balance, i.e.

$$M_{D\,Asset}/P = h \times r \qquad (8.2)$$

where the term on the left represents the liquid balance being held for asset purposes and r represents the interest rate. The parameter h is negative since a high interest rate will discourage holding cash balances, while people may well be willing to hold cash balances when interest rates are very low.

Another way to look at the question of holding liquid balances for asset purposes is called the *speculative motive*. The idea is that asset holders seek to maximize their total return, interest plus the change in the value of the asset they hold. If asset values are variable, indeed are related to what happens to interest rates, then it may pay to hold liquid assets rather than bonds. The process is described in Case 8.2. Financial people will be well aware of the phenomenon of switching assets into short maturities at times when interest rates are expected to rise. This is precisely because the prices of short maturity securities are less sensitive to interest rate increases than bonds. If you are sure that interest rates will rise, and the market value of your assets will fall, then hold liquid assets, i.e. money. This means that liquid asset holding will depend on expectations about interest rates. If interest rates are high, above their normal anticipated level, demand for liquid balance will be small. It is better to put assets into securities which may rise with a decline in interest rates. If interest rates are very low, and presumably can only rise, it is better to hold liquid asset to avoid losing capital value on other asset holdings. This suggests a negative relationship between demand for money and the interest rate. Moreover, it suggests that when interest rates are very low — the interest rate cannot fall below zero — asset holders will seek to hold as much of their assets in money as possible. This is an important point to which we will return.

Case 8.2
Asset Values and Interest Rates

A long term government bond selling for $10,000 represents a promise to pay annual interest of $600 for 30 years. The principal is repayable only after 30 years, but the bond is negotiable, so that it may be sold on the market for whatever it will bring in the meantime. When the prevailing interest rate is 6%, the bond will sell for its face value of $10,000 or at 100 in market parlance. The market price equals the annual interest payment divided by the prevailing rate of interest, or, in this example, 600/0.06 = $10,000.

At $10,000, the bond's yield will just equal the market rate of interest assumed here to be 6%. Suppose, now, that prevailing interest rates rise to 8%. The market value of the bond will fall, i.e. 600/0.08 = $7500. At that price, it will yield a return equal to prevailing rate of interest. Similarly, if interest rates fall, to 4% for example, the value of the bond will rise, 600/0.04 = $15,000. This means that if interest rates are so low that they are likely to rise, bond holders risk a capital loss and would do better to hold their assets in liquid form. On the other hand, if interest rates are very high and are expected to decline, the bond holder gets the reward of a high rate of return and the expectation of a capital gain, so that it pays to hold bonds rather than money.

Demand and Supply of Money

The total demand for money consists of the demand for transactions purposes plus demand for asset purposes, the former depending on income and the latter on the rate of interest, i.e.

$$M_D / P = M_{D\,Trans} / P + M_{D\,Asset} / P \tag{8.3}$$

$$M_D / P = k \times y + h \times 1 \tag{8.4}$$

The supply of money is determined by central bank authorities. Our discussion of monetary policy, Chapter 10, will consider how the central bank controls the money supply. We will also point out that with government borrowing, the government budget deficit will tend to expand the money supply. A surplus on the international current account also has the potential for increasing money supply. But for the moment let us take money supply, M_s/P, as exogenously determined.

The Interest Rate

The interest rate is determined by the intersection of the money demand and supply curves as in Fig. 8.1 above. In the vertical direction, this graph shows the interest rate. The appropriate interest rate here is a short-term rate like the federal funds rate. On the horizontal direction, we measure the demand for and supply of money. The demand consists of two components, the part that is related to transactions (Y), the transactions demand which is shown by the area to the left of the vertical dotted line, and the part that represents asset demand for money, shown as between the dotted vertical line and the sloping demand schedule. The point is that only asset demand for money is sensitive to the rate of interest. Money demand equals money supply, i.e. $M_D/P = M_S/P$ when the interest rate is at r_e.[1] The equilibrium interest rate is where the total supply of money is being held. If the interest rate were lower than equilibrium, some people seeking to hold liquid funds would be unable to get them and would bid up the interest rate. If the interest rate were above equilibrium, excess funds would be available and the interest rate would fall. Note also that if the central bank decided to increase the money supply, interest rates would fall. Except that as interest rates begin to approach their lower boundary, increases in the money supply would simply be absorbed as holdings of liquid assets since the demand for money at that point is highly responsive to the interest rate, i.e. the demand for money curve is almost flat. This has been called the *liquidity trap*, since further expansions of money availability will simply be absorbed by money holders without further reductions in the interest rate.

We have assumed so far that the price level, P, remains fixed. Suppose now that P changes, without there being a corresponding change in nominal M_S. In other words, if the central bank does not pump more money into the system as P increases, we would see a decline in real money supply. The money supply curve $(M/P)_s$ in Fig. 8.1 moves to the left and interest rates rise. Following through on the consequences, higher interest rates cause lower investment, and lower demand in turn causes lower Y. Such a phenomenon would not happen if the central bank adjusted money supply to allow for the higher price level, but if money supply is held in check, higher prices mean a higher interest rate and lower aggregate demand. We will revisit this concept in the next section.

We will discuss how monetary policy is managed and how it impacts on the economy in Chapter 10.

---

[1]Gertrude Stein, the writer and art collector, had a nice way to describe equilibrium in the money market. She said that the peculiar thing about money is that it always had to be in somebody's pocket. If it wasn't in my pocket then it had to be in yours. The point is that if the equilibrium interest rate, all the available money is willingly in somebody's pocket.

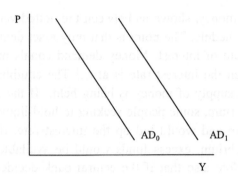

Fig. 8.2   The Aggregate Demand Curve Shifts with Changes in I or G.

The Aggregate Demand Curve

The concept of the aggregate demand curve summarizes the information about demand we have discussed above. The aggregate demand curve places the demand information into a new context. The aggregate demand curve in Fig. 8.2 is downward sloping to the right, as a demand curve should be, i.e. the lower prices, the greater the aggregate demand. Why is this? As we note above, a higher level of prices, given a fixed nominal money supply, will produce higher interest rates and these in turn will reduce investment demand. We note that a change in the level of prices, all else given, will not cause a shift of the AD curve, only a movement along it.

If there is an increase in exogenous demand, an increase in government purchasing or in exports, for example, the demand curve will shift to the right, from curve AD_0 to AD_1. In particular, we note that the AD curve will respond to government expenditure and monetary policy, a topic to be discussed further in Chapter 11 below.

Implications for Business

Financial market conditions are important for most business firms (Case 8.3). The availability and cost of credit are important ingredients in business planning and investment decisions. Business managers are concerned about more than the overall level of interest rates. They are concerned about the terms at which funds can be raised for various purposes, for short-term purposes like financing accounts receivable or inventories as well as for long term financing long term investments. They are also concerned with the availability of funds since at times and to some firms, credit may not be available no matter what the interest rate the borrower is prepared to pay.

Firms in the financial sector, like banks, insurance companies, and investment firms are highly specialized and may be more involved in purely financial matters than in the evolution of the real parts of the economy. In practice, the real aspects of the economy and the financial aspects are closely intertwined and must be considered jointly.

Case 8.3
Financial Information for the Beer Business

Many years ago, as a young inexperienced economist, I was asked to advise a large company on the economic outlook. Beer was the firm's primary product. Thinking that beer was a consumer product the demand for which would be closely linked to consumer income and expectations, I spent much of my time discussing the outlook for consumption. My audience was not very interested. Using surveys and data on promotional activity, they had a pretty good handle on the demand for their product. What they wanted to know was what was going on in financial markets. What would be the short-term interest rate and the yield curve? This information would help them set a company-wide hurdle rate and to make their investment plans.

Questions for Discussion

* What do economists mean by "money"?
* What are the factors that influence demand for money?

* When is demand for money sensitive to the interest rate? When it is low, or when it is high? Why?
* How does the supply of money influence interest rates?
* What is the nature of the aggregate demand curve? What will cause it to move?

Chapter 9

The Supply Side and the Aggregate Supply and Demand Model

In this chapter, we consider the supply side and the interaction between aggregate supply and demand. What is the economy's supply potential? What is the relation between output and prices? Then we combine aggregate supply and demand to determine output and price. We consider the adjustment of the economy to demand pressures, the concept of the Phillips curve. Finally, we ask about the implications of the "new economy" for the constraints on supply. Does the "new economy" reduce the pressure of demand on the economy's supply potential? Does the "new economy" reduce or eliminate the risk of inflation?

Introduction

In the previous chapter, we considered the aggregate demand curve. Here, we turn to aggregate supply. What determines how much product businesses will put on the market? How sensitive is the supply to price? What are the limits to an economy's output at any point in time? The "new economy" is the cause of substantial new debates on these topics.

Productive Capacity and Potential GDP

The limit of an economy's productive capacity is potential GDP. This represents the level of production at which an economy fully utilizes its available resources. In terms of the production function, potential GDP (Y_{pot}) is:

$$Y_{pot} = a_0 \times K^{a-1} \times L_{full}^{(1-a)}. \qquad (9.1)$$

This represents the output the economy can produce at full employment. Note that we assume full employment of labor (L_{full}) but not of capital. In the mature countries, capital is not usually a general constraint though it may be a problem in particular industries, for example, the recent electric power or gasoline refining shortages in the United States. Statistics on employment and unemployment are regularly available, and are typically our basis for evaluating business conditions.

If we estimate how many additional workers are available, beyond a minimum frictional unemployment, we can use the production function (9.1) to compute potential GDP. This approach uses what is known as Okun's law. Empirical calculations show that 1% of additional GDP can be produced for every 0.3 to 0.5% of unemployed labor force available above the frictional minimum. Recent experience suggests, however, that in the "new economy," we do not know very much about the flexibility of output with respect to available workers, or even how many additional workers may "come out of the woodwork" when job opportunities improve. The economy's potential output is sometimes quite uncertain.

Developing economies also frequently encounter bottlenecks, even though there may still be unemployment or spare production capacity. Their infrastructure is underdeveloped so that harbors or land transport may be inadequate for shipping the country's full capacity production. There may also not be enough trained engineers or managers. Production capacity of basic materials, like cement, may be insufficient so that, during the boom, raw material supply shortages may cause inflationary pressures.

Data on inflation often serve as an indication that a country is approaching the limits of its producing capacity. When the level of unemployment is high or when there is ample spare capacity, prices tend to be stable. As the economy comes closer to full employment, wage rates tend to rise as employers bid against each other to hire additional workers. At the same time, as output increases relative to potential GDP, costs of production rise as less efficient facilities must be used or as bottlenecks are encountered in the market for some material inputs.

As we note further below, the "new economy" has altered some of the underlying relationships. New information technology and new services make the concept of capacity much less clear than it was when physical commodities from agriculture and manufacturing dominated production. As a result, in recent years the US has been able to achieve much lower levels of unemployment without inflation that had earlier been thought possible.

The Aggregate Supply Schedule

Potential output represents a limit to the economy's production. What happens when the economy is operating at potential output and below potential is described by the economy's supply schedule.

At the micro level, a supply schedule relates output to price, a positively sloped curve since, within limits of capacity, higher prices will allow firms to offer more product on the market. At the macro level, we are dealing with the aggregate output of the economy rather than with individual products. In effect, the aggregate supply curve tells us the response of output to price for the entire economy (Fig. 9.1).

When the economy is operating below its full capacity, businesses can increase output in response to an increase in demand with little price increase. The supply curve is likely to be flat or almost flat over a substantial range. If demand declines, over the short and medium term, often a period of several years, firms will cut production to keep prices from going down too

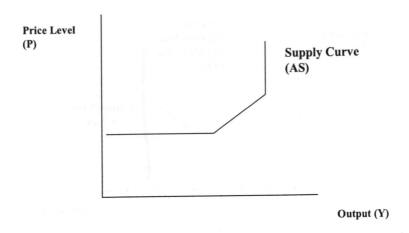

Fig. 9.1   Short and Medium Term Aggregate Supply.

much. After all, they want to cover the costs. Price cuts would sharply reduce profitability. Workers, moreover, do not willingly accept wage reductions. As we will see below, the issue of whether wages and prices are flexible in the long run, making the supply schedule steep rather than flat, is central to much of the discussion of modern macroeconomics.

As the economy approaches its full output potential, capacity constraints begin to bite, costs begin to rise, for example, as firms have to use overtime or bid higher wages for additional workers. The supply curve begins to turn upward. Often, if there are bottlenecks, firms may put their customers on "allocations." That means that they will only ship them a part of their orders. Of course, purchasers will respond by ordering more than they need and by building up inventories, if possible, increasing upward price pressures still further!

Once the economy reaches a level of GDP that approximates full capacity or full employment, physical output cannot be increased at all; the supply curve becomes vertical. In Fig. 9.1, we view the supply curve as having three segments: a flat area when there is lots of spare capacity, an upward sloping segment when we are getting closer to full capacity utilization, and a vertical region when full capacity output has been attained. In Fig. 9.2, we also show the full capacity constraint. If we take a very long run perspective, when

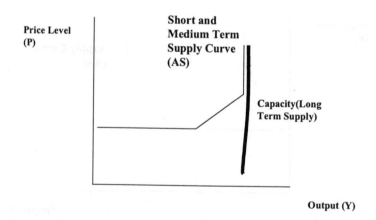

Fig. 9.2   Short and Medium Term Aggregate Supply and Capacity (Long Term Supply).

prices and wages adjust downward when there is excess capacity. As we explain below, we may think of this line as an aggregate supply curve in the long run.

Case 9.1
Defining Capacity in the United States

The recent situation in the US provides a good illustration of the difficulty of defining capacity. By traditional standards — an unemployment rate of 4% and a utilization rate near 87 — the economy came close to full capacity in 1999–2000. But the Federal Reserve faces a quandary because it could not be sure where full capacity was.

Conceivably output could increase further, perhaps even without creating inflationary pressures. Rapid technological change had contributed to extraordinary gains in productivity. But it was also possible that productivity was rising rapidly as firms responded to shortages of labor. If staff to handle paperwork was not available, employers would have strong incentives to automate, particularly as new web-based information technology made such automation easier. In that case, the capacity constraint is lifted by shifting to methods of handling transactions that require less labor. The "new economy" offers many such opportunities.

Below, we will consider first the relation between the *level* of prices and economic activity, the aggregate demand and supply curves. Then we will look at adjustment of prices, the *rate* of inflation.

Outline of the Aggregate Demand and Supply Model

A simple way to look at the economic situation in the short run is through the mechanism of aggregate demand and supply. Figure 9.3 shows the price

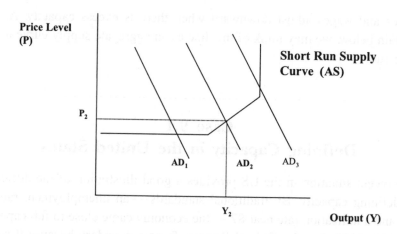

Fig. 9.3   Aggregate Supply and Demand: Determination of Output and Price Level.

level (P) on the vertical axis and real output (Y) on the horizontal axis. The downward sloping line (AD) represents aggregate demand for goods and services at various levels of price. The supply curve (AS) is upward-sloped. Output will be higher at higher prices. Equilibrium, where the curves intersect, determines the level of output (Y) and prices (P).

What is the role of demand and supply in determining the economy's level of economic activity? Suppose we shift the demand curve to the right from AD_1 to AD_2. Such an increase in demand could occur if the public sector increases spending or cuts taxes. It could also occur if monetary authorities cut interest rates and business managers increase investment spending. It could also happen if export markets expand. The expansion of demand, will call for an increase in production. Such an expansion can occur with little or no increase in prices, so long as there is ample spare capacity. In Fig. 9.3, this occurs from AD_1 to AD_2, resulting in an increase in output without much price change. A further increase in demand to AD_3, will encounter capacity constraints resulting in little increase in output but in substantial price increase. A still further increase in demand, would produce no more output, just inflation as the supply curve has become vertical indicating that supply constraints are preventing further output expansion.

(This point corresponds to the point when actual GDP encounters the potential GDP so that no further increase in output is possible.)

Analogous results can be observed if demand falls, for example in a recession. If demand shifts to the left, inventories may pile up, causing firms to cut back production. While some temporary price cutting may occur, most industries are "quantity adjusters." That is, rather than continuing to produce at lower prices, they will cut back output and lay off workers. Similarly rather than accept lower wages in order to find work, workers may remain unemployed, often supported by unemployment compensation, allowing wages to remain at prevailing levels. The result is a story of sticky prices and wages and underemployment of the capital stock and of the labor force in a recession. This represents a disequilibrium because resources are underutilized and more output could be produced. How long it will take before the economy readjusts, prices fall, and the economy returns to full employment is a matter of considerable debate, one that we discuss in the next section.

The Keynesian versus the Classical Approach

Theoretical economists have been widely split in recent years between those supporting a Keynesian view and those supporting a classical view. How is the difference between these two approaches relevant here?

The ideas of John Maynard Keynes (1883–1948) lie behind the economics of the post-war period and motivate many economists, particularly in business and government, to this day. Keynesian economics began with a concern with depression, unemployment and underutilization of production facilities. When there is excess capacity, output is largely determined by the market demand, as it was in our mini model discussed earlier. According to Keynesian economists, if demand is sufficient to absorb the current level of production, the economy will be in equilibrium, even if it is operating below capacity. There may be gradual tendencies to adjust through changes in wages or prices, but wages and prices tend to be sticky in a downward direction allowing extended periods of unemployment.

In the post-World War II decades, when inflation became a dominant concern, Keynesian analysis was extended to deal with situations when demand exceeds the economy's supply potential when demand pressures exceed capacity, causing inflation. Keynesian economists are primarily concerned with business cycle stabilization. Their tools are the instruments of fiscal and monetary policy. Importantly, Keynesian thinking suggests that government spending and tax policies, as well as monetary policies, can influence economic activity and employment. On this basis, Keynesian economists tend to be activists, proposing the use of the government budget and/or monetary policies to maintain the economy as close as possible to a full employment path. In our framework (Fig. 9.1), the horizontal segment of the supply schedule reflects a frankly Keynesian perspective.

Classical economists take a different view. Going back to the work of Alfred Marshall (1842–1924), they view the economy as tending to be at full employment. Recessions or inflationary pressures are seen as temporary, usually dealt with naturally by market forces. If there is unemployment, it is a temporary phenomenon until demand and supply are back in equilibrium at a new, presumably lower, level of wages. Since recessions are seen as temporary maladjustment until markets are back in balance, classical economists see little or no role for public stabilization policy. Expenditure policy and monetary stimulus should have little if any effect on output; mostly they just tend to raise prices. In our framework (Fig. 9.1), the vertical segment of the supply schedule can be seen as classical. A purely classical approach would view the supply schedule as being almost vertical throughout like the "Capacity" line in Fig. 9.2, an economy operating at full employment where changes in demand translate into changes in price. Another way to say this is to argue that prices are flexible. If demand changes, up or down, prices will adjust so that the economy remains near full employment. Long run equilibrium price determination is shown in Fig. 9.4. While at lower prices the economy is back at full capacity, the long run can be very long indeed.

In the 1970s, when economists like Milton Friedman and Edmund Phelps began to explore the theoretical microeconomic underpinnings of Keynesian theory, they discovered many problems. Making the assumptions of consumer

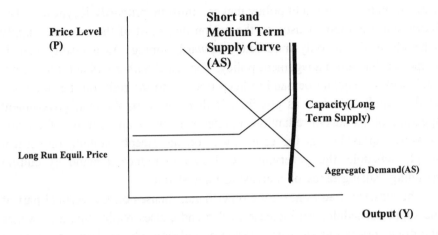

Fig. 9.4 Short and Medium Term Aggregate Supply and Capacity (Long Term Supply).

maximization and smoothly operating markets typical of microeconomics led to the classical result — the economy would tend toward a natural unemployment rate through adjustment of prices and wages. Recessions were seen as temporary aberrations. Policy recommendations based on this line of thought were largely non-interventionist — the best policy is the least policy — arguing that market forces would take care of the problem so long as macro policy was kept on a steady course. The more recent idea that consumers have *rational expectations*, i.e. that they take likely future developments into account, further suggested that macro policy interventions might be fruitless. Only unanticipated policy changes would have an effect.

Many, but not all, younger economists have turned toward such a neoclassical approach. Others still stick to what Paul Samuelson called the *neoclassical synthesis* that sees the Keynesian view as appropriate for short term macro, dealing with the problems of the business cycle, and uses more classical ideas to deal with questions of resource allocation and growth, primarily over the long run.

Our discussion looks at both the classical and Keynesian approaches. But, in our view, there is not enough time over the business cycle for full price adjustments to occur. Forecasting and policy management, like the view of many government policy makers, must be primarily Keynesian. The Keynesian tradition focuses on the notion that most of the time the supply schedule is flat or only moderately upward sloping. As a result, there is scope for demand management policy. The fiscal authorities and the central bank seek to regulate demand to keep it as far to the right on the flat range of the supply schedule as possible. If demand is insufficient, government spending or tax cuts or reductions in interest rates are appropriate. If demand pressure builds so that the economy is on the steeply sloping or vertical supply schedule, the government will seek to reduce demand by cutting spending, raising taxes or increasing interest rates.

The classical tradition, on the other hand, focuses on the vertical part of the supply schedule. An increase in demand causes readjustment in wages and prices not in output, since market equilibrium always implies the same full employment output. Demand changes affect prices but not output. When classical economists are challenged to explain unemployment, they respond that unemployment is temporary and will go away when market equilibrium is achieved. Here lies room for a compromise between the two warring factions of economists. We may well argue that market disequilibrium can persist in the short or medium run, say, over the business cycle. This may call for demand management policy response. On the other hand, a classical view may be appropriate in the long run, particularly if we are concerned with growth.

The Phillips Curve

The relationship between the unemployment rate and the rate of inflation, known as the Phillips curve, is an interesting example of the fragility of economic laws. The idea of the Phillips curve is that wages and prices will tend to rise as aggregate demand pushes economic activity toward its potential, measured by the unemployment rate. This corresponds to the ideas behind our discussion of the determination of prices by the AS and AD curves, except that here we are dealing with the rate of inflation, i.e. *change* in prices rather than the *level* of prices. A. W. Phillips drew a graph that showed in the vertical direction the rate of wage increase and in the horizontal

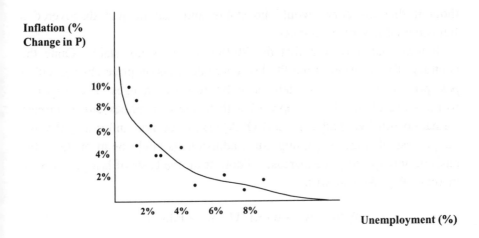

Fig. 9.5   The Phillips Curve.

direction the rate of unemployment (Fig. 9.5). The points representing the aggregate data for each year on price change and unemployment approximated a curved line, tending toward vertical close to the origin, when unemployment was low, and tending toward the horizontal as the unemployment rate increased. This made much sense since it was thought that inflationary wage pressures would depend on the tightness of labor markets. Note that this is a dynamic concept, the adjustment toward equilibrium. It relates the *rate of change* of wages to the unemployment rate.

Such a line can be summarized as follows:

$$\text{Wdot} = w_0 + w_1 \times 1/U \tag{9.2}$$

where Wdot represents the percentage rate of change of wages and U represents the unemployment rate, simply the percent of the workers in labor force who are not working (and looking for employment).[1] Phillips

---

[1]The unemployment rate is in the form 1/U in order to give the relationship a nonlinear form. When U is very small, the term 1/U is very large, indicating that a small additional reduction in U would have very large impact on wage increases.

thought that his curve would be stable and that he had discovered a fundamental law of economics.

It turns out, however, that the Phillips curve is not stable. Quite the contrary. The position of the Phillips curve depends on price change, either past price changes or expectations of future price changes. The wages of workers are often adjusted upward with increase in prices either through formal-cost-of-living adjustment (COLA) clauses or more informally through the process of wage bargaining. Such adjustments might be in made on the basis of anticipated price increases, $Pdot_e$ or on the basis of last year's price increase P_{-1}. We can write:

$$Wdot = w_0 + w_1 \times 1/U + w_2 \times Pdot_e. \qquad (9.3)$$

The means that wage increases will not only depend on the unemployment rate but also on expected (or past) price increases. This is not surprising since the decision to work must be made on the basis of real wages; if prices rise, workers will anticipate an offsetting increase in wages to maintain their real purchasing power.[2] The position of the Phillips curve depends on what is happening to prices as in Fig. 9.6.

This story can be elaborated by introducing a mechanism to explain prices. The idea here is that *of cost markup*. Producers set the price of their products as a markup on production costs. This means the prices are determined by labor cost per unit of output, and by cost of imported materials, as follows:

$$Pdot = p_0 + p_1 \times ULCdot + p_2 \times P_m dot \qquad (9.4)$$

where Pdot represents the percentage change in prices. ULCdot represents the percentage change in unit labor costs and $P_m dot$ represents the percent change in the prices of imported materials. ULC calls for explanation. It accounts for what is happening to labor costs per unit of output:

---

[2]Though often the escalation factor, w_2 will have a value less than one. That means that workers will absorb part of past price increase.

$$ULC = (W \times L)/Y. \tag{9.5}$$

The expression in brackets represents total labor cost — wages times employment. Divided by Y, this is labor cost per unit of output (ULC). The expression can also be seen in a different way,

$$ULC = W/(Y/L) \tag{9.6}$$

where the expression in brackets represents labor productivity. In terms of small changes, we can then say

$$ULCdot = Wdot - (Y/L)dot. \tag{9.7}$$

Wage increases tend to increase costs and prices. But increases in productivity tend to reduce costs and prices. An increase in wages translates into higher costs and then presumably into higher prices, only if it is not offset by a gain in productivity. Wage increases that do not exceed gains in productivity are not inflationary!

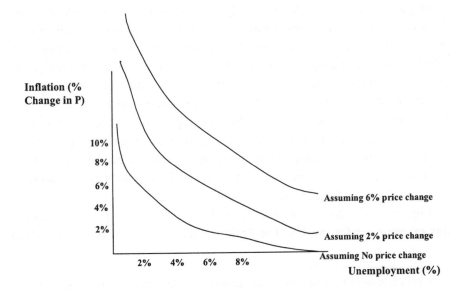

Fig. 9.6 The Phillips Curve with Different Inflationary Expectations.

Combining equations (9.3), (9.4) and (9.5), we have a system to explain prices. Wages explain prices and in turn prices explain wages. An exogenous increase in prices, perhaps as a result of rising costs of imported petroleum, Pm, causes production costs to rise. The resulting increase in price is passed to the wage equation, raising the Phillips curve and causing wage increase, which in turn is passed back to the price equation and causes further price increase. This was how the US economy was affected by the oil price shocks in the 1970s.

A similar story can be told about periods of inflationary boom. Low unemployment rates cause high rates of wage increase. The increase in wages causes increases in consumer prices. Workers in turn ask for still higher wage increases to offset their lost purchasing power. This process is described as a price-wage spiral.

In the framework of the Phillips curve, this means that the Phillips curve shifts with increases in prices as illustrated in Fig. 9.6. Phelps has argued that these upward shifts will mean that if workers are rational, their wage demands will always build in an allowance for anticipated price increases. The higher expectations about prices, the higher the pressure for higher wages, and in turn, the higher the need to adjust for anticipated price increase. As a result an unemployment rate less than the unemployment rate where pressure on wages is zero, or at least where wage increases are not fully offset by productivity gains, will result in infinite inflation. Obviously, this can only happen if the system is fully flexible and if monetary policy accommodates the price increases. If money supply were held fixed, then the rise in wages would soon cease because higher interest rates would drag down investment and reduce GDP and raise unemployment. Phelps calls the unemployment rate where there is no inflationary pressure, the *natural unemployment* rate.[3] Sometimes we also speak of the "Non-accelerating Inflation Rate of Unemployment" (NAIRU).

Figure 9.7 illustrates the process of shifting Phillips curves. The data in this example are for the US. The Phillips curve seemed to fit pretty well in

---

[3]It is an indication of the power of words that this term, the natural enemployment rate, has been adopted widely even though there is nothing natural about it.

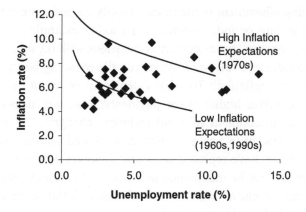

Fig. 9.7   Relationship Between Inflation and Unemployment.

the 1960s. It was shifted by the oil shock in the 1970s, causing recessions, and has gradually moved back down as price pressures have abated. We will consider the appropriate policy mix to maintain stable or minimal inflation in the next chapter.

Inflation and the "New Economy"

If the discussion above seems artificial, the reader should be reminded that inflation has been a real problem in many of the world's economies. In the industrial world, inflation rates have been held in check to 2 to 3% annually, except when there were periods of commodity market shocks as in the 1970s or times when pressure of demand has been unusually high. In the developing countries, too, there has been significant decline in inflation rates in the last decade as these countries have kept better control of their fiscal budgets and their money supply.

But history also shows periods of *hyper inflation* with serious conse-quences to economic management and assets. As we have noted, these periods of rapid inflation are largely monetary phenomena, resulting from huge increases in money supply. *Inertial inflation* in Brazil, where automatic adjustment of wages and bank balances to past price increases with accommodating adjustment in the money supply caused rapid inflation to be maintained for long periods of time, was another example.

The "new economy" poses numerous questions with regard to inflationary pressures. How close to full employment can the economy be pushed without causing excessive inflation? To what extent can we count on increases in productivity to offset higher wage payments? Can we measure inflation properly in an environment of rapid technical change? Are pressures for higher wages different in a world where high-skilled service workers, most of them non-union, have replaced unionized laborers on the assembly line? Can monetary control be maintained in a world of e-money and e-banking? To what extent do cheap imports keep domestic inflation in check in an increasingly global world economy?

There is no doubt that an advanced high-tech economy with all the informational links that the "new economy" can provide is different from the traditional old economy. To some extent, this applies to inflation as well as to other aspects of the economy. It is possible to get along with lower inventories and to recognize changes in economic conditions more rapidly. Wage determination in the "new economy," where many workers are in high-tech service and programming occupations, is quite different than union wage negotiations in "old" manufacturing industries. The meaning of money supply may be different in an e-banking world. Some economists have been arguing that inflationary pressures are reduced because we are in a "new economy." But it is not clear whether the "new economy" is more or less susceptible to inflation than the old.

Implications for Business

Inflation is a mixed blessing for business. On one hand, a period of strong demand may be beneficial. Rising prices are not all bad if you hold inventories whose value is appreciating or if you are heavily in debt and can pay back your debts in depreciated currency. On the other hand, inflation adds another degree of difficulty to rational business planning. Rising costs may reduce a firm's competitiveness especially in foreign markets. In an inflationary period, it may be difficult or expensive to raise capital. Long term contracts may require frequent adjustment to allow for changes in prices.

Most business are not too concerned if inflation is kept at a moderate predictable pace, say 2 or 3% per year. A very high rate of inflation, however, can get in the way of rational business decision-making, leading people to seek inflationary gains rather than profits from constructive investment. On the other extreme, declining prices and deflation may also be difficult for businesses, as recent experience in Japan appears to show.

Business people are more interested in the prices of particular commodities, their material inputs and capital goods, and in the wage rates of their employees, than in general price indexes. But, particular prices and wages tend to move with the price level in general. That makes inflation and its measurement a matter of broad business concern.

Questions for Discussion

* Depending on the underlying assumptions, the aggregate supply curve may be flat or upward sloped. Explain.
* Contrast the Keynesian and the classical approaches.
* The Phillips curve is not likely to be a stable relationship. Why? What lies behind the shifts in the Phillips curve?
* Increases in wages that are no bigger than increases in productivity will not be a source of inflationary pressure. Explain.

Chapter 10
Domestic Policy Considerations

In this chapter, we deal with domestic macroeconomic policy. While the "new economy" represents a revolution in the business world, the mechanisms of macroeconomic policy are not greatly changed. But the uncertainty about when and how policy should be applied is considerably greater. We introduce the concepts of stabilization and the nature of fiscal and monetary policies. We consider how these policies apply in the industrial world and how they can be implemented in developing countries. Finally, we discuss the impact of the "new economy" on policy making.

Introduction to Domestic Stabilization Policy

Government officials responsible for macroeconomic policy must take into account the various objectives we have discussed in greater detail above. Stabilization over the business cycle calls for a concern about all of the objectives simultaneously though priorities will differ depending on the economy's current situation. In Europe, primary emphasis must be on bringing down high unemployment that has plagued some of these economies for a generation. Japan has been suffering from repeated dips of recession, a "triple dip recession" since the early 1990s and needs demand stimulus. The United States, on the other hand, sees itself as a winner, a country that, during the 1990s, has been able to slay both the dragons of unemployment and inflation. Some have attributed this to the "new economy." However, it is too early to tell whether today's optimism in the US is as badly off the mark as the deep pessimism that pervaded US thinking only ten years ago. Even large productivity gains associated with the IT revolution may not be sufficient to offset recessionary tendencies.

The exchange rate and the foreign balance are also important considerations, sometimes central factors, influencing monetary and fiscal policies. In the interest of simplicity, we will focus on domestic policy in this Chapter. We introduce the complexities of foreign payments in Chapters 11 to 13.

Most economists will agree that countries that maintain a stable economy show better long run performance than those whose economies are unstable or that follow a stop-go pattern of policy intervention. Only with stability can there be an assurance of continued high employment, growth and low inflation.

In developing economies, questions of growth and social justice sometimes seem to overshadow short run stabilization objectives. Experience has shown that conservative fiscal and monetary policies may be even more important in the developing world than in the industrial countries. The developing country has much less leeway: many of its people are already living on the brink of poverty; it is dependent on the outside world whose investors seek a stable environment; and it lacks foreign exchange reserves. Even a perception of economic (or political) instability, not to speak of real swings in output or prices, may produce a financial crisis that could have adverse impact on the path of economic development at home. To give an example, East Asia's tradition of strong central banks working closely with the ministries of finance to assure economic stability paid off handsomely for many years. The 1997 crisis reflects, in part, failure by the central banks in East Asia to maintain stability.

The principal aim of domestic stabilization is to achieve as high a level of output and employment that is compatible with price stability. As we have noted in the previous chapter, it is not easy to define the maximum level of non-inflationary output numerically. Though we know that there is a tradeoff between achieving the real output objective versus achieving the price stability objective, reasonable people may differ on the precise definition of the target. Some will seek "zero inflation," tolerating a low of output and employment, while others will aim for higher output and more jobs, even if this creates moderate inflation. Few, however, will seek to expand output when the supply curve slopes steeply upward, risking massive inflation.

The traditional way to visualize the tools of stabilization policy is to see them in terms of the institutions to whom they are assigned:

1. Fiscal policy to the Treasury or Ministry of Finance, the agency concerned with government spending and with raising revenue.
2. Monetary policy to the central bank — the Federal Reserve in the US, the Bank of Thailand in Thailand, Bank Negara in Malaysia, etc.

Fiscal Policy Tools

The government budget is a detailed expenditure and tax plan to determine priorities for particular programs as well as to control spending, revenues and the surplus or deficit in the aggregate. We are concerned here not with the details of the budget but with the implications of aggregate expenditure and revenues on the level of economic activity. The composition of revenues and expenditures also may have macroeconomic effects as will be considered further below.

Government expenditures consist of three components:

1. Government consumption — purchases of goods and services for current use (G_C).
2. Government investment — purchases of goods and services embodied into capital projects (G_I).
3. Transfer payments — welfare, unemployment compensation, etc. (TR).

All affect aggregate demand, government consumption and government investment, directly as final demand, and transfers through their impact on personal income and, thus, on consumption.

Revenues, obtained from a variety of taxes (T) affect aggregate demand largely indirectly through their effect first on personal income and profits and, then on consumption and investment, respectively. Taxes may, of course, also affect the macroeconomy in other ways through their impact on incentives to work, save and invest.

The budget surplus/deficit, (S/D), is defined as the difference between tax receipts and expenditures:

$$S/D = T - G_c - G_i - TR. \qquad (10.1)$$

When expenditures exceed revenues, the deficit represents dissaving by the public sector. When revenues exceed expenditures, the surplus represents public sector saving. In broad terms, a deficit represents stimulative fiscal policy in that, on balance, government spending injects more demand into the economy than is taken out through taxes. A surplus, in turn, represents restrictive policy. Note also that a deficit is financed by increasing public debt, in effect by borrowing from the central bank which then issues money. Sometimes this is referred to colloquially, as "printing money," though the creation of bank credit may not involve actual printing of bills. Here, we have an important link between budgetary policy and monetary policy.

What then is appropriate budget policy? Should public officials aim for a balanced budget at all times, or may they live for extended periods with a surplus or a deficit. One proposal has been to balance the budget over the business cycle, running a surplus during the boom, when restrictive policy is appropriate, and a deficit during the recession when the economy needs fiscal stimulus. The idea is that the surplus during the boom phase of the cycle will offset the deficit during the recession. On balance, over the entire cycle the budget will be balanced and there will be no systematic tendency for the public debt to build up.

This approach recognizes the fact that taxes are an endogenous variable: tax receipts depend on the level of income and profits. During a recession, tax receipts will fall automatically, and they will rise as the economy recovers and income and profits boom. However, these automatic variations, sometimes called *automatic stabilizers*, do not suffice to stabilize the economy on a full employment path. To provide sufficient fiscal stabilization, it may be necessary for the authorities to lower tax rates or increase spending in a recession and to increase tax rates or cut expenditures in the boom by discretionary fiscal decisions.

What are the practical difficulties connected with this approach? First, the business cycle is not symmetrical. Characteristically the boom part of the cycle lasts longer than the recession. But there have been times when economies have been depressed for many years, as in the 1930s, or when unemployment has persisted at a high level, as in contemporary Europe. Such a situation would lead to a persistent deficit and a buildup in national debt. That has been happening recently in Japan and represents a major concern to many observers. Political decision-making makes it less likely that surpluses will systematically offset deficits even when times are good. Politicians like to spend, since that will benefit their constituents, but they are reluctant to increase taxes. The result is that deficits may persist during periods of booming economic conditions, systematically increasing the national debt burden. This is what has happened in the US in the 1980s, despite repeated efforts by Congress to balance the budget. The US budget surpluses of the late 1990s reflect the booming performance of the US economy. It is not certain that these surpluses will persist once the US enters a slower phase of economic activity. At that point, legislators of both parties will quickly expand spending — at a time when revenues are declining! — to provide additional demand and jobs.

The discussion above has been largely in terms of the aggregate demand implications of fiscal policy. But the specific fiscal tools, expenditures and taxes, also have other effects that must be taken into account.

On the expenditure side, government spending involves budget allocations, a decision about what public money is to be spent on. That means, for example, whether additional spending is to go for investment in public facilities or for welfare and other social uses. This is a decision that depends on one's values and on one's view about the ability of governments to direct resources. One might argue, for example, that government investment in education, research and infrastructure will contribute to more rapid economic growth. On the other hand, spending simply to create employment, "make work," is wasteful and will do little more than create additional demand.

On the tax side, the issue is that taxes have incentive effects that cannot be ignored. Income taxes have been seen as reducing incentives to work and to invest. Tax reductions are said not only to have income and demand effects but also to stimulate work effort and investment. How big these effects are is the subject of much debate. (For a discussion of the effects of "Supply Side" tax reductions, see Case 10.1.)

Case 10.1
Supply-Side Tax Cutting Policies

Supply-side economics, the idea that cuts in tax rates would stimulate economic activity by providing supply-side incentives was the big idea of the Reagan years. Recently, the notion of stimulus through tax cuts was revived as part of the 2000 Presidential campaign.

During the 1970s, there was concern about the failure of the US economy to achieve rapid growth of productivity and to maintain international competitiveness. There was, and still is, considerable uncertainty about the cause of the productivity lag. The consensus was that the US needed to provide incentives for investment to modernize its industries. From that perspective, we are all supply-siders!

Responding to the dissatisfaction of the American middle class, increasingly burdened by rising tax rates, President Reagan proposed large reductions in *personal* income taxes. Many people were led to support the idea that marginal tax rates were too high and that tax rate reductions, particularly at the upper end of the income scale would significantly increase work effort, savings and investment. Thus reductions in personal, rather than corporate, income tax rates became the keynote of Reagan's supply-side policy.

Personal income tax rates were cut by approximately one-third in the early 1980s. A large deficit resulted, corresponding in magnitude approximately to the tax cuts. The economy expanded greatly but it is not clear the improvement was the result of changes on the economy's supply-side. Much effort to verify the supply-side hypotheses — that lower tax rates would produce more saving and investment and more work effort with little or no cost in revenue — showed little, if any, effect. Looking back, it is apparent that much of the stimulus in the mid-1980s originated on the demand-side as a result of old-fashioned deficit spending. Considering the high level of unemployment and unused capacity at that time, such policies may have been appropriate, no matter what they were called. On the other hand, in a full employment economy, precipitous personal income tax cuts might just bring about inflation.

Monetary Policy

Management of aggregate monetary policy is among the most important of the tasks assigned to central banks. The monetary authority is responsible for ensuring the smooth and secure operation of the banking system and for providing a money supply adequate for needs of business activity. In most countries, this is not simply supervision of an automatic monetary mechanism.[1]

Active intervention in the financial system, influencing the money supply and interest rates, seeks to bring the economy closer to its objectives of growth, full employment, price stability, and balance of payments equilibrium. If there is division of labor between the ministry of finance and the central bank, the latter will generally take greater responsibility for price stability and balance of payments whereas fiscal authorities will use their power of spending and taxes largely to combat unemployment. In this section, we outline the principal tools of monetary control available to the central bank.

Traditionally, it would appear that central banks have focused on controlling interest rates *or* controlling money supply. The strongest example is a *monetarist* policy, which advocates strict control of the money supply without regard to interest rates as the principal means of economic stabilization. But theory and real world evidence suggests that, if financial markets are allowed to work, central banks must recognize that money and interest rates are interrelated. It is not possible to deal with one without influencing the other. Given the economy's demand for liquidity, control of the money supply will influence interest rates. Similarly, except for possibilities for explicit market intervention like credit rationing, control of interest rates involves influencing the liquidity of the banking system. Central banks have only limited control either of money supply or of interest rates. With respect to the money supply, here seen as largely in the form of commercial demand deposits, central banks control bank reserves. The banking system determines to what extent these bank reserves are translated to deposits. With respect to interest rates, central banks have limited direct control, though they may set the discount rate or, in some cases, they may intervene by setting interest rate ceilings or floors. Generally, interest rates respond to market forces, the supply and demand for credit. As we note in

---

[1]After some difficult experiences, some countries like Hong Kong and Argentina have switched to "automatic." They have set up a "currency board" where all money issue is backed one for one by holdings of foreign exchange.

more detail in Chapters 11 to 13, the ability of a central bank to control the financial sector is very limited when financial markets are open to international capital flows.

Money and reserves

A central bank like the Federal Reserve has only indirect control of the supply of money. As we have noted above, the bulk of the money supply takes the form of demand deposits in the commercial banking system. The banks must hold reserves behind their demand deposit obligations, usually in the form of deposits at the central bank. Reserve requirements represent a way for the central bank to assure bank safety. But the more important function of reserves today is to limit the expansion of demand deposits. The total level of outstanding demand deposits is limited by the following identity:

$$M = 1/rr \times R \qquad (10.2)$$

where M represents the amount of demand deposit money (bank deposits), R represents the reserves of the banking system, and rr represents the required reserve ratio. If the reserve ratio required (rr) is 10% (.10) and reserves (R) are $1000, total demand deposit money (M) cannot exceed $10,000.

To reduce the money supply, the central bank would drain reserves from the system usually by selling bonds to the banks who would pay for them by drawing on their reserve accounts. The central bank could also increase the reserve ratio but that is done infrequently.

Turning now to expansion policy, the central bank could allow banks to expand money supply beyond $10,000 by feeding them additional reserves. That is most easily accomplished by buying short term Treasury bills or bonds from the banks. We assume here that the commercial banks are fully "loaned up," that they have extended loans and demand deposits as much as they are able, $10,000 in our example. In that case, an increase in their reserves will allow them to make additional loans, presumably at lower interest charges. But banks may have excess reserves. In that case, adding reserves may not affect the availability of credit and may not have much, if any, impact on the money supply. This is likely to occur in a recession, when opportunities to make sound loans are limited. A reduction of reserve requirements would only create excess reserves. Hence, we think of monetary policy in a recession as not being very effective, sort of like "pushing on a string."

Monetary policy tools

The tools of monetary policy can be summarized as follows:

Open market operations

As we have noted, identity (10.2) suggests that central banks can influence money supply by increasing or reducing available bank reserves. As we have shown, by increasing R, central banks can provide the banking system with additional reserves allowing banks to increase outstanding demand deposits beyond $10,000 without changing the required reserve ratio. Such an increase in the reserves will increase the availability of credit and tend to reduce interest rates. In the opposite direction, central banks may drain reserves from the banking system and thus tighten credit and raise interest rates.

How does a central bank influence the volume of outstanding reserves? Why do we refer to this process as *open market operations*? In the US, there is a huge market for short term government debt — Treasury bills. Billions of dollars are traded every day on the open market. When the Federal Reserve Open Market committee decides that the banking system should have additional reserves to stimulate credit expansion, it orders its open market manager to buy T-bills on the open market. A phone call to the leading brokers is enough to accomplish this task. Similarly when the Open Market committee wants to contract credit and raise interest rates, its manager is instructed to sell T-bills. The sale will influence the banking system's supply of reserves since the purchasers' payment for the T-bills is subtracted from bank reserves. Thus, to tighten financial markets, i.e. to reduce outstanding credit, the central banks use sales of securities to "drain" reserves from the banking system, forcing banks to pull in some outstanding loans and to reduce the outstanding deposits. Since these transactions take place in a large active market, we used to think that the Federal Reserve could act subtly, and that nobody would notice. In fact, in today's financial markets the *Wall Street Journal* will report, "Today, the Federal Reserve drained reserves from the banking system until the Federal Funds rate rose to 4 1/4 percent." Fed watchers are very aware of any action taken by the central bank to tighten or ease financial availability. Markets react very quickly to any actual or anticipated action by the monetary authorities.

Many other countries do not have large organized "open markets" like the US. But the process is similar. The central bank will make direct contact with the major banks to buy or sell government bonds as a way of easing or tightening financial markets.

Discount rate

The discount rate is the interest rate at which banks may borrow reserves from the central bank. In most cases, when banks run short of reserves they borrow reserves from each other in order to meet central bank requirements. They do so at the interbank rate, in the US called the federal funds rate, the very sensitive interest rate for overnight borrowing. But when the banking system as a whole is short of reserves, the central bank provides a discount window, the possibility for borrowing reserves from the central bank itself. The discount rate is the interest rate charged by the central bank to the banks for borrowing reserves. We might visualize it as a cost of obtaining reserves, hence it should influence the rates charged by banks on loans to their customers. But in most cases, borrowing from the central bank is very limited. The role of the discount rate is more as a benchmark, indicating to the banking system what the central banks thinks interest rates should be. If the discount rate is raised or lowered, all interest rates are likely to follow though not always by the same amount. Central bank policy is, consequently to raise (or lower) the discount rate depending on whether the central bank wants to reduce (or to expand) the money supply and, correspondingly, to raise (or to lower) interest rates. Frequently, changes in the discount rates serve as a signal to financial markets. Sometimes, though, the discount rate is adjusted simply to keep it in line with other rates of interest which have gone up or down as a result of market forces.

Reserve requirements

The central bank sets reserve requirements behind the banks' outstanding demand deposit liabilities. Originally such reserves were held only to assure that banks would always be able to meet their depositors' demands for cash. After all, deposits represent a liability of the bank; that liability must be met on demand when depositors write checks against their accounts or appear at the bank to withdraw their funds. But, this important function is a rather unusual one in a world where people have confidence in the banks — though it is exceedingly important at times when depositors are afraid of a bank failure. In principle, the central bank may lower reserve requirements, leaving banks with excess reserves that can be translated into additional credit extension. In the contrary direction, the central bank may raise reserve requirements in order to tighten credit conditions. In practice, reserve requirements changes are unusual. Because such changes are so clearly visible, they are viewed as a radical change in monetary policy. Central banks tend to keep reserve requirements fixed and to turn to other policy tools. However, reserve requirements are occasionally raised to soak up excess liquidity of the banks that might eventually be turned into excessive monetary growth. Over the long run, reserve requirements are lowered when it is clear that the banking system does not need so many reserves, for example, when banking system operation and safety have improved over time.

Market intervention

There are numerous other possibilities for intervention in financial markets. In many countries, the central bank intervenes in markets directly. For example, in countries where the banking system is not very competitive, the central bank may set interest rates directly, setting maximum rates that banks can charge on loans. In turn, that often also involves fixing the maximum that banks can offer to their savings depositors. Such direct intervention often implies that the market does not clear, that interest rates are lower than the market equilibrium. Some other mechanism must be found to allocate credit. Since the demand for credit exceeds the credit available, the banks will choose to allocate loans only to the most credit-worthy businesses. Small enterprises in risky industries like construction may find that credit is simply not available to them, a so-called "credit crunch." Alternatively, if banks are prevented from charging a market equilibrium interest rate, they may put their assets into bonds or other financial instruments whose rate of return is not controlled by the central bank. The result is that credit is shifted from its customary channels to business loans to other uses, a process called "disintermediation."

The central bank may also intervene directly in other ways. For example, some central banks, set a target figure for total credit extensions; new loans must not grow by more than a specified percent. Others set special reserve requirements for certain types of loans. Some mandate preferential interest rates for credit to agriculture or exports. Most central banks also specify the capital requirements of the banking system and frequently set specific limitations on the activities of commercial banks.

Moral suasion

Central banks also use their influence in more informal ways by using the power of persuasion. How seriously bankers take the broad messages from the central bank, to limit credit or to expand it, for example, is not at all clear. In countries where banks depend greatly on specific bank controls and regulations, "suggestions" from the central bank may almost have the force of law. In other countries, the central bank's pronouncements may make little difference unless they are tied to specific regulations or incentives. In both cases, however, the central bank may use its influence to form expectations about financial markets — whether its fight against inflation will be continued leading to the maintenance of high interest rates, or whether it will ease money supplies. In the US, the Federal Reserve governors have recently taken to announcing their "bias," whether they are inclined to tighten or loosen credit in view of the current economic situation. The attempt to influence expectations is a fine art that does not always succeed.

Bank supervision

Fiduciary supervision of the banking system is one of the most important tasks usually assigned to the central bank. While we leave the decisions about assets and liabilities of ordinary business to their management without much public sector supervision, the banking system has traditionally been supervised by the central bank. The banking system usually has far greater liquid liabilities than assets, so that the risk of a liquidity crisis if depositors lose confidence is considerable.

Until the advent of the Federal Reserve in the US and central banks elsewhere to supervise the risks taken by banks and to provide credit as a "lender of last resort," financial crises were a frequent event. These had far-reaching repercussions, affecting healthy financial institutions as well as "sick" ones and driving the economy into recession. Central banks have taken on the task of supervising the banks and of imposing minimum reserve standards. Internationally, the Bank for International Settlements (BIS) in Basle, Switzerland has proposed standards, for example, requiring banks to hold at least 8% of their net worth in high quality assets. Many economists have argued that even the Basle standard would be insufficient to meet liquidity needs if banks were in serious trouble.

Unfortunately, in many countries bank supervision has been lax. Moreover, many aspects of banking practice, and, particularly, the actions of non-bank institutions like finance companies remained unsupervised. The best bank examiners frequently cannot tell whether banks are taking unreasonable risks by extending credit to firms that may not be able to repay their loans. An example of these difficulties in Japan is summarized in Case 10.2.

The East Asian crisis of 1997 has frequently been considered a failure of bank regulation. Some, argue that "crony capitalism" persuaded financial institutions to make unsound loans. There is no doubt that lax lending standards, sometimes reflecting implicit government guarantees to bail out the borrower, contributed to the Asian crisis.

Case 10.2
The Japanese Policy Conundrum

The Japanese economy has been more or less in recession since the collapse of the "bubble economy" in the late 1980s. On one hand, the issue is one of monetary policy, on the other it is one of bank supervision and restructuring.

When the boom in stock and land prices collapsed at the end of the 1990s, financial institutions found themselves with mountains of non-performing loans. One way to deal with these would be recognize them as bad loans and to make appropriate writeoffs. This would have driven many of Japan's major banking institutions into bankruptcy or merger with healthier institutions. But it might ultimately have produced a healthy banking system. Instead, Japanese regulators permitted the banks to try to "ride out the storm," pretending that nothing was wrong in the hope that eventually profitable business would allow them to recoup. The attempt in the mid-1990s to meet the BIS standards only worsened the situation. Banks and others were holding "eligible assets," cash and government bonds, in an effort to redress their balance sheets, while commercial loans were not being made. At the same time, the Bank of Japan fed money into the system reducing interest rates to unprecedented low levels, less than 1% in some cases. Interest rates were low, but credit for investments was not being made available. Japan ran into a classic case of the Keynesian liquidity trap. Feeding additional bank reserves into the system would do little good.

Japan chose to respond to its crisis by using fiscal policy, in the form of expenditures and tax cuts. Large deficit-financed spending programs on infrastructure and urban amenities have helped the construction industry and have generated a stream of income. Modest tax cuts have had only limited impact on consumer spending. While this policy has temporarily stimulated the Japanese economy on several occasions in the 1990s, rising government debt has made the bureaucrats in the Ministry of Finance very uncomfortable. In 1997 for example, at their insistence the government raised the consumption tax back up to its old 5% level, provoking another dip of recession. Another period of deficit spending rekindled the economy in 1999–2000 but, once again, the effort quickly petered out and the large national debt rose further.

Today, Japan's quandary is that it cannot much longer bear the burden of expanding public debt, but private spending unsupported by deficits is not yet sufficient to maintain a prosperous economy.

Monetarism: A Key to Stability?

In the 1970s and 1980s, many economists promoted monetarism as a way to stabilize the economy. The idea was that the central bank would simply keep money supply on a steady upward path, at a rate corresponding closely to the normal real growth of the economy. It was thought that a policy of slow and steady money supply growth would lead to stable non-inflationary economic growth without inflation. The monetarist approach turned out to have merit as a way of beating down inflation in the early 1980s, but it did so at considerable economic pain. More recently, economists from central banks have reluctantly reached the conclusion that monetarism is not a wonder drug, after all.

What are the essentials of monetarism? We begin with a simple identity, the so-called *equation of exchange.*

$$M \times V \quad = \quad P \times Y \qquad (10.3)$$

Total Final Expenditure   Total Final Purchasing

where M stands for money supply, here currency and bank deposits.

V represents velocity, a measure of the turnover use of the average dollar,

P is the price level, a price index, and

Y is real GDP.

The equation is a truism. The number of dollars multiplied by the number of times each dollar is spent on final product, on the left side, equals the amount of total final purchasing, on the right side. (Since there are no independent measures of velocity, the calculation usually computes velocity as total purchasing ($P \times Y$) divided by money supply (M)). The identity must hold since we are measuring the same value of purchasing on both

Table 10.1 Alternative Approaches to Monetarism.

	Constant Parameters	Variables Controlled
Weak Monetarism	V	P × Y
Strict Monetarism	V, Y	P

sides. As the equation of exchange stands, it tells us nothing about behavior or appropriate policy.

An identity like this can be used as a sort of behavioral equation by making assumptions about certain of its parameters. In this case, monetarists assume that velocity (V) is fixed, determined by habits of consumers or financial institutions. If the identity holds, increases in M would then translate into increases in nominal GDP (P × Y). In addition, if we assume that Y, output of the economy is also fixed, for example, at full employment, then increases in M translate directly into increases in the price level (P). We will refer to these assumptions as *weak* and *strong* monetarism, respectively (Table 10.1).

These approaches offer a seductive policy prescription. The weak monetarist would control the growth of total expenditure (P × Y) simply by controlling the growth of the money supply. Picture a lively small dog with an upright tail marked "Money." If you can hold on to the tail tightly, directing its path, you can control the path of the dog. Or can you? Strict monetarists would go further. They would add the notion that in classical economics the economy is at full employment. In that case, control of the money supply should impact only on the price level. If we sufficiently limit the growth of money, we can prevent inflation.

In practice, it has proved more difficult to apply monetarism than its proponents had imagined. The Federal Reserve found it extraordinarily difficult to target on the money supply which does not always move the way the Federal Reserve intended. Moreover, while the formula M × V = P × Y is simple and seemingly painless, its implications are not. Many dimensions of the economy are involved in the relationship between M and Y. Interest rates depend on money supply and income as we have noted. It is not possible to manage M without impact on the interest rate. In turn, that will influence investment, GDP, employment, etc.

In recent years, the Federal Reserve has done many statistical studies to establish whether there is a link between money supply and nominal GDP. Attempts have been made to establish firm correlations between GDP and variously defined concepts of money supply. The Federal Reserve has concluded that the relationship between money supply and nominal GDP is not stable after all. This is not a surprising finding since there are varying "asset" demands for money as well as "transaction" requirements. The implication is that in formulating policy the Federal Reserve continues to look both at interest rates and money supply.

Case 10.3
Monetarism and the Federal Reserve in 1979–82

A classic case in the US was the Federal Reserve experiment with monetarism to combat the inflation resulting from the "oil shocks" in the 1970s. Federal Reserve Chairman Paul Volcker, not by conviction a monetarist, was determined to wipe out inflation, once and for all. For a period of three years, the Federal Reserve tried to keep the nominal money supply fixed, in the face of rising prices. In real terms, the money supply declined. The result was a spiking of interest rates, to levels as high as 15%. Not surprisingly, residential construction and other business investment dropped drastically, and the economy went into a sharp recession. The policy succeeded. Inflation was licked but at significant cost in real output and unemployment. In 1982, the Federal Reserve relaxed its strict monetarist stance. That policy shift along with the Reagan Administration's income tax cuts and provided the stimulus that was the basis for renewed economic growth.

Inflation targeting is a more recent scheme to shackle the hands of the central bank. The idea is to enact a law that would force the Fed to adopt a specific target for inflation. Then monetary policy would be used mechanically to achieve the target, come what may! One expert was quoted: "Inflation targeting is like... putting sunglasses on Greenspan, propping him up and keeping him going forever." (Frederic Mishkin quoted in *Fortune*, 21 February 2000). Many countries worldwide have tried such a scheme as a way of wiping out runaway, politically inspired, inflation. While the approach has had some notable successes, it is unlikely to take the place of flexible, wisely-administered, monetary policy.

Case 10.4
Hyperinflation

There is evidence that monetary excesses translate into high rates of inflation. There have been numerous instances of hyperinflation, with inflation rates higher than 1000% in a single year, for example, in Germany after World War I, in Israel, and more recently in Russia. When the government issues vast quantities of new money to offset the deficit, the public loses confidence in money, expecting prices to rise rapidly. Unwilling to hold money balances, people spend their receipts as quickly as possible. This means not only that money supply (M) increases rapidly but also that velocity (V) goes sky high, resulting in runaway inflation. Such high rates of inflation are very destructive. They destroy the assets of the middle class, many of which are denominated in the prevailing currency. They distort economic decisions, to take advantage of inflation. It is wise for policy authorities to avoid excess monetary expansion.

Many countries used to run large deficits consistently and monetized their outstanding public debts. Rapid systematic expansion of the money supply caused inflation. The ensuing inflationary pressures can be attributed not only to demand pressure but also to systematic loss of confidence in the nation's currency. People knew that more and more money would be created and that money was losing value. Better to spend it than to hold it. The result was hyperinflation. In some periods in Russia and in Brazil, for example, inflation rates reached 1000%.

Fortunately, the record of fiscal responsibility and price stability has been much better in recent years. Most countries have realized the folly of uncontrolled money creation and have reined in inflationary pressures.

Fiscal and Monetary Policy in Developing Countries

Are the tasks of fiscal and monetary policy different in developing countries from the challenges encountered in the advanced world? While many of the same issues are considered, in developing countries there is necessarily greater emphasis on growth. Building and controlling the financial system is an important objective. Public sector investment in infrastructure, recently with private financing, represents another important task.

Developing economies face political and economic challenges that greatly complicate the job of the central bank. Financial institutions are often not well developed and, typically, lack competitiveness. They are often owned by wealthy families that have powerful political connections. It is difficult to regulate the banking system and to influence the economy as a whole in the face of political pressures. Moreover, these banking systems often practice what has been termed *relationship banking*. Loans are extended not so much on the basis of sound collateral but on the basis of trust or family relationships. These loans may be sound, if the optimistic hopes of the borrowers are fulfilled. But what to do when the borrower is unable to make the payment, what is termed a *non-performing loan* (NPL)? In a developed mature economy, arrangements are made to take over the asset or the borrower is forced into bankruptcy. In a developing economy, the requisite laws may not be on the books, and, in any case, you don't take your "brother" to court.

Domestic stabilization in the developing economy is also challenging. Pressures to expand government spending are great in a world where there are overwhelming needs for infrastructure, education and social services. On the other hand, the tax base is very limited, particularly since much of the population lives near subsistence in a non-money economy. Finally, the task of the central bank is considerably complicated in a developing economy that is exposed to international flows of trade and capital. Appropriate exchange rate policy is another important challenge for the central bank. We note here simply that the policy options available in a closed economy are considerably circumscribed and the challenges considerably greater in a "globalized" world. We will turn to this topic at greater length in Chapters 11 to 13 below.

Case 10.5
The Functions of the Bank of Thailand

The case of the Bank of Thailand is a good vehicle for discussing fiscal and monetary policy making in developing countries. To a far greater extent than in developed economies, the central bank of Thailand is involved in many dimensions of development strategy and its implementation. It is, of course, charged with domestic and international monetary stabilization. In addition to the usual range of monetary policies, for many years the Bank intervened closely by setting ceiling and floor interest rates, by suggesting lending quotas — how much lending the banks should do during the current year — by controlling the issuance of banking licenses, and by closely supervising the range of activities in which domestic banks and their foreign competitors can engage. An important point is that the banking system is not as developed or, for that matter, as competitive as in industrial countries. As a result, the Bank must impose more regulations. It seeks also to encourage the development of a financial sector and increased flows of saving, a process referred to as "financial deepening."

With regard to development policy, the Bank is represented on the National Economic and Social Development Board (NESDB) which elaborates the plans and strategies for Thai economic development. The Bank consults with the NESDB and the government on its policies, lending its staff and their high level analysis for many different purposes. It plays a consultative role for major government expenditures. And, of course, it aids the government in required borrowing. The Bank seeks to provide specialized financing for agriculture and export industries.

Finally, the Bank is deeply involved in questions of exchange rate stabilization and holds the country's reserves of foreign exchange. The objective was to stabilize the exchange rate. After a devaluation in the early 1980s, the baht was kept in a narrow band relative to the US dollar and other currencies of countries with which Thailand trades. But the central bank proved unable to support the baht and it crashed in 1997. We will consider the reasons for this collapse further below. Here we should note that exchange rate depreciation has profound implications for the domestic economy for example by making imported goods more expensive and causing inflation.

In practice, the Bank of Thailand has had substantial independence from the political influence of the government. At least, that was the case until the mid-1990s, when political influences were at least partially responsible for the failure of the Bank's economic policy.

The Relationship Between Fiscal and Monetary Policy

We have already noted above that fiscal policy may have monetary policy implications. Unless the central bank takes deliberate neutralizing actions, a deficit will tend to increase money supply. When the deficit is a deliberate attempt to stimulate economic activity in a recession, a corresponding monetary expansion and likely decline in interest rates are a good thing. Lower interest rates will tend to stimulate investment and cause more rapid growth. But when the deficit is the result of "fiscal irresponsibility," the story is altogether different. Large uncontrolled deficits and money creation are an invitation to uncontrolled inflation.

A similar story can be told with regard to fiscal stimulus. In a recession, an increase in government spending or a tax cut will increase economic activity and advance the economy. But wasteful spending or excessive deficits when the economy is approaching full employment cause inflation, raise interest rates, and slow down the growth of the economy. Appropriate policies by the fiscal and monetary authorities call for flexibility and balance — a difficult challenge.

Policy and the "New Economy"

Does the "new economy" make a difference for public policy? As our discussion of current policy-making puzzles in the US suggests, the "new economy" poses some special challenges to policy management. What is needed is not so much a revolution in theory and policy-making practice, as a review of how the changes wrought by the IT revolution affect the situation of the economy and the appropriate policy mix.

The "new economy" changes some of the fundamental guidelines that policy makers have used. The productivity trend, once thought to be slow and mature has changed. If the economy has entered a "new era" of rapid technical change and productivity growth, the concepts of full employment and industrial capacity are called into question. Policy makers are no longer certain whether the economy's full production potential has been reached and when inflationary pressures will begin to mount. Wide open international markets and free international capital flows expand sources of supply for goods and services and capital. Can additional demand be satisfied, even though the economy is near full employment as measured by traditional standards? Will increased productivity or imports from abroad ease inflationary pressures? Can costs be kept down by new technology? Can additional demand for product be met within existing, but increasingly elastic, capacity constraints?

New information technology may make it easier to keep up to date, to do surveys and censuses, and to record and disseminate the most recent statistics. In principle, more and better data should improve the rationality and speed of decision-making. On the other hand, modern communications may amplify speculative bubbles.

As we have noted, a modern service economy with rapid technological changes challenges the ability of experts to understand the data. An additional billion dollars spent on Internet services or new software has very different implications for employment from a billion dollars spent on manufactures like automobiles or appliances. While the aggregate supply and demand framework we have outlined above does not change in a "new economy," the job of the policy maker becomes more difficult and more risky.

Implications for Business

Business people often have strong views about policy. These may reflect their political views. They are also likely to reflect what is best for their business. While one might not go as far as one former auto executive: "What is good for General Motors, is good for the country," one might be able to say: "What is good for the country is good for General Motors." This is particularly true of macroeconomic stabilization and growth policy. A healthy economy, with sufficient demand to maintain full employment and growth is a good setting for business. Consequently, one would anticipate that the business community would support macroeconomic stabilization and growth policies.

Business people should consider what alternative policies may mean for the economy. Forecasts of the economic outlook are conditional on the assumptions with regard to policy on which the prediction is based. At the time of an election, the forecaster may have to make two forecasts: one for a Democratic victory and another for a Republican victory. In practice, business economic forecasters must be fully aware of impending macroeconomic policy developments.

Questions for Discussion

* Contrast the role of fiscal and monetary policy in stabilizing the economy over the business cycle. Is one of the policies better suited to deal with recession and the other with inflation?
* Is the central bank in a developing economy likely to encounter contradictions in carrying out its various mandates?
* Evaluate the alternatives for controlling interest rates.
* What do we mean by a *liquidity trap*? How has it impacted on the Japanese economy?
* How might the "new economy" cause policy makers to change their approach to the economy?

PART IV

International Considerations

In this part, we open the domestic country model to the global world economy. We consider the implications for economic performance and policy making of the recent trends toward opening of international markets for goods, services and finance. Globalization is an important aspect of the "new economy." Chapter 11 covers international interactions, the balance of payments and the exchange rate. Chapter 12 deals with the theory of income determination in economies open to trade. Then, we consider the effect of opening to capital movements. We trace how the adjustment process operates to restore international equilibrium. Chapter 13 deals with policy in the global environment.

Chapter 11

Trade, the Balance of Payments and the Exchange Rate

In this chapter, we begin the discussion of international inter-relationships. Increasing globalization, rapidly growing international flows of trade and capital are a feature of the "new economy." The content of trade and the comparative advantage of trading countries are significantly affected by new technology. We show how trade links the world's economies and causes their economic performance to be interrelated. We present the balance of payments statement. We then examine the determination of the exchange rate. How is it influenced by trade imbalances and by capital flows? Finally, we ask how exchange rate and balance of payments considerations are tied together and their effects. The theory of income determination and adjustment in open economies and questions of international economic policy are discussed in the next two chapters.

Introduction

In today's world of global interchange, even a very large economy must pay attention to international economic forces. A smaller country, particularly one that is heavily involved in international trade and finance, is likely to be buffeted by international developments. Its policy makers must closely consider international considerations. The external world is a particular concern for developing countries like those of East Asia that must find markets for exports and whose competitiveness depends greatly on the exchange rate. Their economies are often influenced by foreign capital and technology inflows.

The "New Economy" and International Interactions

New high technology has drastically changed the comparative advantage of many countries. Advanced technology calls for high-tech education and expertise and "networks" in microelectronics and computer programming.

These are available in the mature economies of North America and Europe where most of the new technological developments are taking place. Only isolated developing regions have been able to leapfrog into the new age, among them, Israel, and the state of Bangalore in India that have become centers of computer programming. Some East Asian countries like Japan, Taiwan, Singapore and Korea have taken advantage of their skills in manufacturing to become users of the new technology and manufacturers of chips, computers, cellular telephones and disk drives. But many countries lack comparative advantage in the new technologies and may face serious barriers to participation in the new high-tech world.

Distance has become less important in some regards and more important in others. As the cost of transportation declines, as it has for many years, distance from the market is much less important. The world has become smaller and more interrelated. Where once it took a three months' steamship voyage to ship goods from China to European and American markets, today air transport and container shipping accelerate the process to a few days or weeks. For manufactures, transport cost is much less important than it used to be. For intellectual products, some of which can be sent as electronic signals, transport cost is practically non-existent. On the other hand, distance can be a significant barrier. High-tech products often call for consultation with highly trained technical consultants and suppliers. Such relationships are provided conveniently in special technology zones, growth poles, or networks like those in Silicon Valley. Many developing countries have provided special zones for high-tech production. But high-tech services and linkages may not be available in far away areas. This represents a serious barrier to the creation of "new" industries in many countries.

Financial flows are as much a part of the "new economy" as shipments of goods and transmission of messages. Globalization has resulted in a vast increase in international financing taking many forms: short-term bank loans, bond issues, direct foreign investment, etc. The expansion and volatility of the financial relationships between countries has extended the supply of capital to many parts of the world that previously lacked the financial resources required by modern industry. But the volatility of these financial flows appears also to have increased the risks of international financial crises. This has become a serious challenge to policy makers in the developing countries and at the international financial institutions like the IMF and the World Bank.

We summarize the major dimensions of the international impacts of the "new economy" as follows:

1. Transport and communication costs are declining. The world is becoming smaller.
2. World trade is increasing at twice the rate of growth of GDP and financial flows are expanding even more rapidly.
3. New technologies like the Internet, e-commerce, e-banking and cellular telecom greatly improve the efficiency of management even over long distances.
4. The new technologies greatly change comparative advantage for many countries.
5. New technologies have been advantageous for the leading countries that have been able to utilize them.
6. On the other hand, new technologies pose a serious challenge to countries that lack the required levels of education and technical expertise.
7. The challenge to development will be to develop the educational and technical infrastructure that will allow countries to participate in the "new economy."
8. Financial flows are an important aspect of the new economy. Their volatility represents a challenge to policy makers in the countries themselves and in the international financial organization.

International Economic Linkages and GDP

Traditionally, linkages between countries have taken the form of imports and exports of goods. These flows, usually measured by customs agents at harbors or points of entry, are the basis for establishing data on the "balance of trade." Trade flows of goods represent, even today, the most important link between different countries.

From a long term growth perspective, trade has accounted for much of the growth in world productivity. In the post-World War II period, trade has grown twice as fast as GDP. Goods are increasingly being produced where production is most efficient, where there is comparative advantage. Thus, the production of high labor content manufactures has migrated increasingly to East Asia and these products are being imported into the United States and Europe. As we have noted above, even in East Asia, shifts have been occurring. As wages in some countries have risen, these countries have upgraded their product mix toward more high-tech products, leaving the production of labor-intensive products to other countries where labor costs are still low, like China and Vietnam.

From a business cycle perspective, international trade linkages are important in providing demand for a country's production. Imports represent a demand leakage for the destination country and an export stimulus for the country of origin. As we noted in Chapter 6, the basic demand identity contains exports (X) preceded by a positive sign and imports (M) negatively. Expanding the basic demand model to include trade (country 1 and country 2), we can write

Country 1   **Country 2**

$$Y_1 = C_1 + I_1 + G_1 + X_1 - M_1 \qquad Y_2 = C_2 + I_2 + G_2 + X_2 - M_2 \qquad (11.1)$$

$$C_1 = c \times C_1 \qquad\qquad\qquad C_2 = c \times Y_2 \qquad\qquad\qquad (11.2)$$

$$M_1 = m \times Y_1 \qquad\qquad\qquad M_2 = c \times Y_2 \qquad\qquad\qquad (11.3)$$

Assuming I, G and X are exogenous, without international interaction, the effect on Y_1 of a change in G_1 would be

$$dY_1 = 1/(1-c+m) \times dG_1. \qquad (11.4)$$

The first round change in the income of Country 2 (Y_2), as a result of its increased exports to Country 1, would be

$$dY_2 = 1/(1-c+m) \times dX_2 = 1/(1-c+m) \times m \times (dY_1) \qquad (11.5)$$

since imports of Country 1 (M_1) are the exports of Country 2 (X_2). If we wanted to do additional arithmetic, we could follow through further to see the effects in an equilibrium solution.

The effects of expansion in one country through trade on the income of other countries are called international transmission or repercussion effects. A good example is the impact of the recession in Japan during the mid-1990s. This recession was one of the important contributors to the East Asian crisis, since low import demand in Japan reduced exports and economic activity elsewhere in Asia. When the Japanese economy recovers, the market in Japan for the products of East Asia improves, helping these countries in their own recovery. To consider another example, in the post-World War II period, journalists often saw the US as the "leader" of the world economy, the demand "locomotive" that pulled along the "boxcars" consisting of the countries that traded with the US. This made a nice picture. In more recent years, the US remains a big player in world trade but, with 25–30% of world imports, the US is no longer quite as dominant as it once was.

From the perspective of the developing countries, trade has done more than simply offering new markets. It has also been one of the forces causing them to reduce their costs to become competitive and to upgrade products to meet world standards. We note that, in turn, freeing trade into these developing countries, that is, lowering protective tariffs and regulatory barriers, has been advantageous even though imports represent a leakage of demand. Trade liberalization has provided a degree of competition that was not available while local industries remained protected.

In the past, the service components of trade were thought of as largely transportation and tourism as well as income flows like returns on investment and immigrants' remittances. More recently, financial services, licenses for technology, consulting fees, and entertainment like movies and recordings have become important components of international business. For this reason, the liberalization of financial services and other international services has become a primary item on the agenda of the World Trade Organization (WTO).

Finally, we must consider capital flows. As we will see in our discussion of the balance of payments statement, below, capital flows may be seen as a balancing item, offsetting the current account deficit or surplus. But recent experiences with financial crisis reminds us that capital flows can have a life of their own. Inflows of foreign capital, attracted by high returns, can overwhelm the financial system and stimulate investment and asset booms.

Then, if investors lose confidence and a flight of currency occurs, we have the makings of financial crisis. We will need to look more closely at how opening an economy to trade and capital flows affects its long run prospects and its stability.

The Balance of Payments Statement

A nation's transactions with the rest of the world are measured by the balance of payments statement. This accounting statement reflects a fundamental identity:

$$\text{Net Current Transactions (exports (+) and imports (−))} \quad (11.6)$$

Plus   Net Capital Transactions (inflows (+) and outflows of capital (−))

Equals Balance of Payments Surplus (−) or Deficit (−)

The Balance of Payments deficit or surplus is sometimes referred to as the "Overall Balance." It must just equal (with an opposite sign) the Change in Foreign Exchange Reserve Holdings (and/or errors and omissions). Why? Because, to the extent that capital inflows exceed the current account deficit, foreign exchange reserve holdings build up. In the opposite direction, to the extent that capital inflows do not cover the current account deficit, the balance must come out of foreign exchange reserves. That depends on whether capital flows are sufficient to offset the current account deficit.

The national balance of payments account is more detailed but scarcely more complicated. Table 11.1, shows the balance of payments account for the US in 2000. Note that the current account entries include all current transactions, with those yielding foreign exchange, like exports, carrying a positive sign and those using foreign exchange, like imports with a negative sign. The balance of trade represents simply the difference between exports and imports of goods where the US ran a substantial deficit. The current account also includes entries for services (travel, transportation, communications, etc.). This account is positive, in the US, because lots of services like consulting and finance are sold abroad. Investment income and unilateral transfers (including foreign aid) are also part of the current account.

Table 11.1 The Balance of Payments Account — United States, 2000 (Est) (billions of US$).

	Receipts	Outlays	Balance
Current Account			
Exports of goods	773		
Imports of goods		−1223	
Balance of Trade			−450
Services exports	296		
Services imports		−215	
Net services			81
Balance on Goods and Services			−369
Investment income receipts	345		
Investment income outlays		−359	
Balance on Income			−14
Unilateral transfers			−52
Balance on Current Account			−435
Capital and Financial Account			
Inflows (increases in foreign holdings of US assets)			
Direct investment	316		
Securities	600		
Total capital inflows			916
Outflows (increases in US holding of foreign assets)			
Direct investment		−161	
Securities		−395	
Total capital outflows			−556
Balance on Private Financial and Capital Account			360
Balance of Payments (Overall Balance)			−75
Change in official and reserve holdings			
US holdings of reserve assets	−1		
Foreign holdings of US reserve assets		36	
Net Change in Official and Reserve Assets			35
Statistical Discrepancy (Errors and Omissions)			40

The current account, which includes all these items, was negative in the US. By 2000, the US current account deficit had worsened to almost 5% of GDP.

The capital and financial account measures the impact of asset and debt transactions with foreigners, i.e. foreign direct and portfolio investment and borrowing of various types. The transactions are shown as positive if there is a net inflow of foreign exchange, for example from the sale of equity or debt instruments to foreigners, and negative if there is net outflow or repayment of debt. The overall balance then represents the net of current and capital transactions. The overall balance should match the balance of changes in official holdings of foreign exchange, by the US Federal Reserve and foreign central banks. But, often, the statistics do not match, so that there is a statistical discrepancy. The discrepancy reflects misreporting of the underlying data, sometimes unrecorded capital flight.

Case 11.1
The Thai Balance of Payments

A negative current account balance may be more than offset by the positive impact of net capital inflow if a country is very attractive to foreign investors. But, if investors were suddenly to switch from optimism to pessimism, there would be the makings of a financial crisis.

This happened in Thailand. In the early 1990s, despite a trade deficit, capital inflows caused a surplus in the overall balance that threatened to appreciate the value of the baht. The Thai authorities were anxious not to let the baht appreciate against other currencies, fearing that Thai goods would lose competitiveness in world markets. The surplus was consequently absorbed by accumulating reserve assets, basically holdings of dollars, mark, yen, and other currencies. The foreign exchange holdings of the Bank of Thailand approached US$39 billion in 1996, enough to pay for 8 1/2 months of imports. The continued positive overall balance and these large holdings of foreign reserves eased fears that the baht would need to be devalued even if foreign investment were to fall significantly. But things changed rapidly in 1996 and 1997. Thai exports showed little if any increase, in part because Thai products were not competitive at the prevailing exchange rate; meanwhile Thai imports surged. The result was a sharp increase in the deficit. The crash of the exchange rate and the crisis that followed are described in Case 11.2.

The Exchange Rate

A country's exchange rate is simply the price one must pay to obtain foreign exchange, US dollars or yen, in terms of one's home country's currency. Frequently, we will refer to the US dollar as the base currency for comparison, for example 50 baht per US dollar. But in practice there are separate exchange rates between the home currency and all of the world's currencies, i.e. the baht and the yen, etc. The exchange rates for all currencies must be related consistently. If the yen and the dollar are related by an exchange rate of 125 yen to the dollar, and the baht is 50 to the US dollar, the baht and the yen must be valued at 2.5 yen to the baht (125/50), or one yen equal 0.4 baht. For purposes of simplicity, we will focus on the exchange rate of the baht relative to the dollar, rather than dealing with the many currencies that would be involved in the term "foreign exchange."

The exchange rate is essentially market determined by the interaction of supply and demand for dollars (foreign exchange). The exchange rate regime that applies depends on government policy.

Floating exchange rate

If market forces are allowed to determine the exchange rate without government intervention, the exchange rate is said to be *floating*. In that case, we may see considerable variations in the rate from day to day, particularly for the currencies of smaller countries where the foreign exchange market may be thin. There may be speculative movements that cause rates to go up and down sharply.

Managed float

In order to avoid too much variation that may be burdensome to exporters and importers, many governments intervene in foreign exchange markets in order to stabilize the exchange rate. Governments try to keep the rate between fairly narrow bounds but they may allow the average rate to change gradually in line with competitive conditions. If domestic prices are rising as compared to other countries, the exchange rate will be allowed to depreciate in accord with the relative rate of inflation.

Pegged rate or fixed exchange rate

Whether the rate is fixed, formally or informally, we are concerned here with situations where the exchange rate is being held fixed in terms of a foreign currency, most often the US dollar. A truly fixed exchange rate offers some considerable advantages for importers or exporters, who need not worry about exchange rate fluctuations. It is particularly useful for foreign borrowers and lenders who need not fear the implications of devaluation. It is also often intended to serve as an "anchor" against inflation, since currency depreciation would quickly raise prices of imported goods and cause inflationary pressure. On the other hand, fixed exchange rates often get out of line with underlying competitive conditions and then governments are often forced to devalue the exchange rate abruptly. Indeed, that has been the pattern. A fixed exchange rate will last for a number of years and then crumble suddenly in a balance of payments crisis. In that case, the central bank will quit intervening, close foreign exchange markets over the weekend, and reopen foreign exchange markets with a new depreciated exchange rate. The damage to business people who failed to hedge their foreign exchange obligations is frequently severe. The experience of most developing countries suggests that a foreign exchange crisis is usually followed by a serious recession or growth slowdown.

Case 11.2
The Thai Exchange Rate Experience

For many years, the exchange rate between the baht and the US dollar had been approximately 25 baht to the dollar, sometimes a little more or sometimes a little less. This was claimed to be a market determined exchange rate, but it is apparent that the Bank of Thailand engaged in substantial market intervention. The exchange rate was pegged largely with respect to the US dollar. Thai products may have been overpriced in world markets as a result of the appreciation of the US dollar, to which the baht was linked, during the 1995–6 period.

That the Bank of Thailand engaged in exchange rate intervention in 1994–6 is apparent, first, from the buildup of US dollar and other strong currency reserves in Thailand, and second, from the relative stability of the US dollar/Thai baht exchange rate over a long period. The Bank of Thailand quotes a daily US dollar exchange rate posting. Such a posting is convenient from the perspective of doing business but is not inconsistent with a market determined exchange rate. The Bank of Thailand has suggested that the baht exchange rate was floating as determined by a market basket of currencies. The precise composition of this market basket has never been released though it was clearly very heavily weighted with the US dollar. The stability of the rate moving by less than 4% over a ten-year period suggests that intervention was used to stabilize the exchange rate with respect to the US dollar at the desired level near 25 baht to the dollar. This was a reasonable policy in view of the importance of the US and other countries whose currencies are linked to the dollar as markets for Thai export products. But it may not have been a very realistic one in view of the fact that the price level in Thailand had risen much more rapidly than in the US. As a consequence, the baht had become considerably overvalued.

The situation changed abruptly in 1996. The Thai economy began to deteriorate. Significantly, Thai exports showed no increase, compared to the rapid growth that had supported the expansion of the Thai economy in previous years. The slowdown of exports was attributed to the fact that some important customer countries for Thai exports were in recession, Japan, in particular. It may also have reflected a lack of competitiveness with suppliers in China. But circumstances also tended to discourage foreign lenders. The Thai stock market and the market for real estate — condominiums, office buildings and hotels — were sagging, and Thai finance companies and banks were overloaded with doubtful loan assets. As a result, what had been a massive inflow of capital into Thailand turned into an outflow. Everyone ran for the exit, so to speak. The capital flow turned negative. The new equilibrium exchange rate for the baht was far below 25 baht/one dollar, probably close to 40. The Bank of Thailand was under pressure to maintain the 25 baht rate. Many people had borrowed heavily in dollars on the expectation that this exchange rate would be maintained. At a lower rate, they would have to pay far more baht to cover their dollar obligations than they had anticipated, indeed, than many of them were able to pay. So the Bank of Thailand engaged in large scale intervention, supplying dollars to the foreign exchange market or selling dollars short. When foreign exchange reserves ran out, on 2 July 1997, the Bank of Thailand announced that it could no longer hold the baht and allowed market forces to have their impact. The exchange rate immediately moved to a new equilibrium. (Interestingly, the Bank of Thailand did not admit until August that its foreign exchange reserve statistics did not record the fact that substantial short sales of dollars offset almost all the remaining balance.) The new equilibrium exchange rate proved to be somewhat unstable, as speculative expectations at one point drove the rate to 55 baht/dollar. Eventually, the rate settled down to between 40 and 50 baht to the dollar where the Bank of Thailand is apparently once again trying to stabilize the baht. At that rate, Thai products are once again competitive in the world market yielding a trade surplus approximately sufficient to offset the continued capital flow.

How is the exchange rate linked to a country's balance of payments?

In principle, the exchange rate is determined by the demand and supply of one's currency in terms of all other currencies, usually referred to as "foreign exchange." To simplify matters, we will take a two-country case, the exchange rate of the US dollar in terms of Thai baht, even though in the Thai case the cost of the Japanese yen, the German mark, the French franc, the Malaysian ringgit, etc. are also important. In Fig. 11.1, on the vertical axis we show the price of the US dollar in terms of baht. On the horizontal axis, we show the demand and supply of US dollars. The downward sloping curve, marked D for $ (imports of goods and services), shows the demand for dollars in terms of baht. Thais want US dollars in order to buy goods and services in the US, to import. Since the price of imports is higher in baht, the more costly the dollar, less is imported at a higher dollar exchange rate, so the line slopes upward to the left. The slope of the line depends on the elasticity of demand for imported goods from the US. Here, imports from the US are assumed to be relatively price inelastic. The line sloping upward to the right, marked S of $ (exports of goods and services), represents exports of goods and services. Effectively, these represent a supply of dollars to be translated into baht, since the Thai exporter needs his home currency to meet production costs in Thailand. These two lines account for the current account. In the absence of capital flows and/or changes in Thai holdings of dollar reserves, the equilibrium exchange rate is determined by the intersection of the two lines at A, an exchange rate of 35 baht to the US dollar. At that point, the current

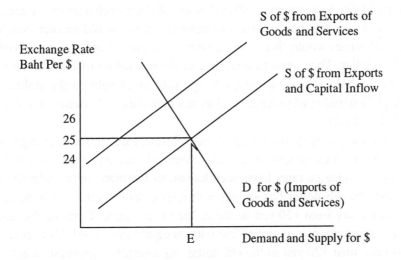

Fig. 11.1　Demand and Supply of Dollar Determine the Exchange Rate.

account would be in equilibrium: exports would just equal imports. But in addition to the supply of dollars arising out of goods and services trade, there are also capital movements. The capital flows from the US into Thailand and, presumably, also from other countries, represent dollar loans to Thai private citizens and to the public sector as well as acquisition by foreigners of equities in Thai businesses. Loans may take the form of long- or short-term loans. They may also represent changes in foreign holdings of deposit balances in Thai banks (note that these are demand deposit IOUs of the Thai banking system). The capital inflow is added to the supply of dollars from exports, yielding the line marked S of $ for exports and capital inflow, which represents the total supply of dollars available. In this case, the inflow of dollars strengthens the baht, i.e. reduces the price of the dollar, so that the equilibrium shown here is at point B with an exchange rate of 22 baht to the US dollar. This then represents the true market equilibrium. The baht could float up or down from this equilibrium value depending on exports, imports and capital flow developments.

If this exchange rate is acceptable to Thai authorities they need do nothing about it. On the other hand, suppose that an exchange rate of 25 baht to the dollar is thought to make American imports too cheap in Thailand and Thai exports too expensive in the American market. Developing countries frequently like to see some undervaluation of their exchange rate since that makes it easier for their products to compete in the world market. Suppose Thai authorities would like to see a somewhat lower baht, i.e. more baht to one US dollar. They need to intervene in the market by offering to buy US dollars for baht. To bring the exchange rate to 26 baht to the dollar, the Bank of Thailand must purchase dollars bringing the equilibrium to the desired level (Fig. 11.2).

Can we say more about the likely equilibrium value of the exchange rate? A figurative representation of the movement of exchange rates is shown on Fig. 11.3. Exchange rates have been known to fluctuate quite violently. For example, the US dollar has swung with respect to the yen by a wide range in recent years from 150 yen to the dollar to less than 80 yen to the dollar, by all considerations way out of line with its equilibrium level. More recently, it has been near 120 yen to the US dollar. As a result of speculative activity, exchange rates have a way of "overshooting," swinging more widely than

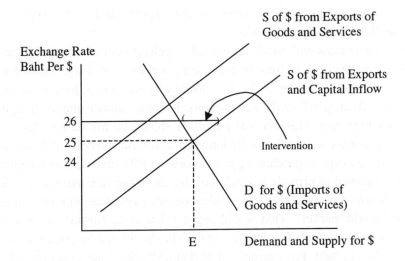

Fig. 11.2　Demand and Supply of Dollar Determine the Exchange Rate.

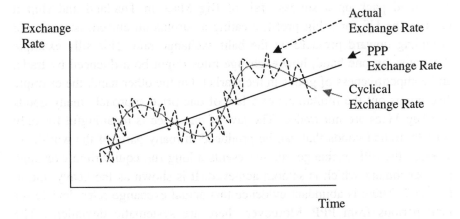

Fig. 11.3　Short- and Long-Run Exchange Rate Movements.

the underlying market forces would warrant. The short run speculative fluctuations of exchange rates are represented by the thin fluctuating line on Fig. 11.3. Such fluctuations pose difficult challenges for business people in the import and export business and for capital markets. It is best to leave speculation on currency markets to the experts and to "cover" one's outstanding exchange rate risks.

Exchange rates will also be affected by cyclical fluctuations since trade is sensitive to cyclical factors. In the boom, imports may surge leading to a trade deficit and a tendency for the currency to depreciate. In the recession, imports will drop off, tending to improve the trade balance and to strengthen the exchange rate. This cyclical pattern is shown by the dashed line.

We might ask then: what is the long run equilibrium level of the exchange rate? The concept of purchasing power parity (PPP), discussed in Chapter 3, has long served to provide a benchmark for exchange rate parities. The idea is as follows. In a world of free trade, countries compete with one another in the "world market." That would suggest that in equilibrium there would be a *law of one price*. The product in dollars should just be priced to match the product in baht. For example, if McDonald's Big Mac sold for US$2 in the US and for 80 baht in Thailand, the implied PPP exchange rate would be just 40 baht to the dollar. If the price were lower in Thailand, say 10 baht, one could pack up a suitcase full of Big Macs in Thailand and ship it back to the US for a big profit, creating a surplus on current account and providing upward pressure on the baht exchange rate. This silly example illustrates, on one hand, how exchange rates might be influenced by trade, and competitiveness of goods in the market. On the other hand, the example also points out the limitations of a law of one price approach, many goods like Big Macs are not traded. The law of one price is meaningful for only actively traded goods that can be produced in many parts of the world. As a result, the PPP exchange rate represents a long run equilibrium exchange rate benchmark which is seldom achieved. It is shown as the heavy line in Fig. 11.2. There is abundant evidence that actual exchange rates deviate for long periods from PPP. Moreover, there are systematic deviations. The exchange rates of developing countries are most often systematically below PPP, making their goods competitive in developed country markets. In the case of Thailand, for example, the 40 to 50 baht to the dollar exchange rate means that Thai goods like locally produced apparel and non-traded products like hotel and restaurant services are very cheap for foreigners, about half of what they would cost at home. On the other hand, imported products like cars and capital goods are very expensive in baht terms in Thailand. Comparing GDP per capita between different countries using a PPP exchange rate based on a market basket of commodities bought by consumers will give a picture of how well off consumers are. On the other hand, to compare the competitiveness of countries, we must compare prices of traded goods at the prevailing exchange rate. It is not straightforward consequently to establish what the true equilibrium exchange rate is likely to be over the long term.

We have seen a surprising amount of exchange rate volatility in recent years and many exchange rate movements have been in unexpected directions. There had been widespread expectations that the euro, introduced in the European Union as a medium of exchange in 1999, would be a strong currency, equal to US$1.17 when it was introduced. But this was not to happen. The euro fell systematically. By end 2001, one euro was worth only 90 US cents.

Implications for Business

The international implications of the "new economy" for business are substantial. The scope and scale of international competition has expanded. Businesses in the advanced countries have found wide new markets based on computer technology, microelectronics and bioengineering. These firms have spectacular competitive advantages which they have turned into rich and profitable markets. For more conventional firms, the "old" economy, competitive pressures from abroad have mounted as so many of our manufactured goods are, or could be, produced abroad.

As we have noted, financial markets are becoming far more international as instant communication and changes in financial regulations have opened financial markets across the world. Some people would argue that international diversification could be used to reduce risk, but recent experience with financial crises suggests otherwise.

The movements of floating exchange rates have important implications for business managers. For exporters, the exchange rate is a major determinant of price and competitiveness in foreign markets. Once domestic costs in Thailand are taken into account, the exchange rate will determine how much the product will cost at the destination, let's say in the US in US$ (allowing, of course, for shipping, tarriffs, handling costs and distribution). Not only must the product be competitive to goods produced in the US but it must also be able to compete with goods from other countries like China, making the exchange rates between the baht and the Chinese renminbi yuan an important consideration. (As we have noted, Thailand was at a disadvantage in 1996, a factor that figured importantly in the 1997 crisis.) Once we introduce capital flows, the exchange rate plays an even more critical role. Suppose a Thai firm takes out a loan in foreign currency, say one million US dollars. When the exchange rate was 25 baht equal one dollar, a million dollar loan represented a debt of 25 million baht. Now suppose the baht is devalued to 40 baht to the dollar. Since the intial loan was denominated in dollars, the borrower must repay 40 million baht. In cases like this, even the interest payments may be difficult to make. Loans quickly become "non-performing" and the borrowers and sometimes the lenders, too, go bankrupt.

In the developed countries, many transactions are denominated in the home currency, for example, the US dollar or the euro. Or else, firms will hedge their foreign currency exposure. That is much less customary in the developing countries. Hedging is expensive and may be technically difficult; hedging over the long term may not be possible. As a result, business managers in the developing countries often take on faith their government's promise to maintain a stable, read *fixed*, exchange rate. Borrowers and lenders have been burned many times. East Asia in 1997 is only the most recent example.

Questions for Discussion

* What do we mean when we say that if the US economy catches cold the rest of the world economy catches pneumonia. Is this likely to happen? Why?
* Consider the balance of payments statement. Is it possible for a country to run a capital account surplus that is greater than its current account deficit? What's going on?
* Discuss the fixed and floating exchange rate cases. Why is it frequently so difficult to maintain a fixed exchange rate?

* What are the principal determinants of the exchange rate?
* When a country runs a balance of current account deficit, it must run a surplus on its capital account or it must lose foreign exchange reserves. Explain.
* What is the meaning of "an overvalued exchange rate?" What are its implications?

Chapter 12

Income Determination and Adjustment in the Open Economy

In this chapter, we consider income determination and adjustment with particular emphasis on the open economy. The "new economy" represents a radical opening to trade and international financial movements. Opening the economy to trade and capital flows greatly complicates the nature of the system and creates new challenges for policy makers. First we consider a realistic case, not completely open to capital flows. Then, to better appreciate the consequences of market opening, we consider an economy that is fully integrated into the world financial system.

Globalization and the Open Economy

What are the characteristics that make for a truly open economy? Our concern here is with economies that are open with respect to capital flows as well as trade (current account). The integration of world financial markets is a central feature of the "new economy." The possibility of unrestricted capital flows greatly increases the risks of instability and the challenges to economic policy.

Until recently, only the mature economies have had internationally free capital markets. Most developing countries restricted capital flows, making it difficult for their citizens to exchange their currencies for dollars and/or to send capital abroad, and, frequently, limiting inflows of capital, as well. This meant that domestic financial markets were separated from financial markets in other countries and, as we will see in more detail in the next chapter, that central banks in each country had power to influence domestic interest rates. Typically, it also meant that domestic banks were able to charge high rates of interest, as compared to interest rates prevailing in mature economies. In the 1980s and 90s, the restrictions on foreign exchange transactions and capital flows were eased in many countries. At the same time, investors began to look for favorable opportunities across world markets, so that capital flows became responsive to interest rate differentials between countries. This has had profound consequences. There have been financial crises. Individual countries have had much less power to carry on independent monetary policy. As countries open to capital flows, we are coming closer to a "one world" capital market.

From a theoretical point of view, we can think of two extreme situations: one with restricted capital flows and the other with economies open to world capital. While neither of these extremes prevails in today's world economy, it is instructive to look at these situations to evaluate what will happen as the world comes closer to a unified world capital market. In the discussion below, we look first at financially closed economies and then we discuss the implications of opening to capital flows.

Opening and the Balance of Payments

Here, we extend the discussion of balance of payments and exchange rates from the previous chapter.

An economy that controls trade and capital movements, by imposing tariffs and/or other types of restrictions can maintain substantial control over its balance of payments and exchange rate. What are the consequences on the balance of payments of breaking down the barriers impeding imports and exports and capital movements?

We can think of a simple conceptual model of the balance of payments. This model, incorporating aspects of the mainstream view of open-economy macroeconomic equilibrium, is useful for understanding both medium term current account adjustment and the determination of the long run equilibrium path.

The forces operating on the current account can be viewed from two perspectives — the trade perspective and the capital flow perspective. Abstracting from unilateral transfers like foreign aid, the current account equals the goods and services balance (NX), as we have noted in the previous chapter:

$$NX = X - M \tag{12.1}$$

where X represents exports of goods and services and M stands for imports. Imports reflect demand in the domestic economy (Y), relative prices [foreign prices (P_f) and domestic prices (P)] and the exchange rate (XR).

$$M = f(Y, (P_f \times XR)/P). \tag{12.2}$$

That means that, given the effect of income, relative prices determine imports. The expression ($P_f \times XR$), represents the foreign price translated to domestic currency by the exchange rate. This is compared to the domestic price of the product (P). Note that, the higher foreign prices relative to domestic prices or the exchange cost of foreign currency, the lower the imports. The effect of the price term is negative.

A similar equation accounts for exports:

$$X - f(Y_f, (P_f \times XR)/P). \tag{12.3}$$

Here, the income effect is from foreign income (Y_f) since the exports of one country are the imports of others. The price effect is inverse of that for imports. The higher foreign prices adjusted by the exchange rate relative to domestic prices, the more we export.

The long term evolution of trade flows is driven by growth in incomes and changes in relative competitiveness, and perhaps in the long run, also by changes in propensities to import at home and abroad. Business cycle fluctuations in income and misalignments of the real exchange rate can exert strong influences on net exports in the medium run. In some cases, like that of Japan, import propensities have not been high, nor have trade flows been particularly sensitive to relative price or exchange rate movements. This may reflect the strength of Japanese brands in export markets and, until recently, the difficulties of foreign producers in selling imported products in the Japanese market.

Turning next to the international capital market, what determines capital flows? Net capital inflows (CF) represent net borrowing abroad or net additions to foreign holdings of domestic stocks and other assets. The demand for these assets depends on the relative rates of return at home and abroad adjusted for the exchange rate and expectations about future exchange rate change (i, i_f, XR, dXR^e):

$$CF = f(i, i_f, XR, dXR^e). \qquad (12.4)$$

Other factors that affect the desired asset mix may also affect net capital flows. Strong demand for foreign assets can produce a capital outflow. (This appears to be an important part of the story of the yen since 1995. Japanese investors have displayed a continuing desire to accumulate foreign assets, driving down the value of the home currency and helping to generate a rising net export surplus.

The current account then depends on the interplay of international trade and competitiveness with underlying determinants of saving and asset allocation. The balance of payments relationships are part of the broader macroeconomic system that includes domestic and foreign goods markets, financial relationships, and factor markets. Equilibrium for the complete economic system calls for all the relevant endogenous variables to be consistent, including income, interest rates, exchange rates and prices. If some of the underlying conditions or policies change, the economy will readjust with impacts on income and the price level. We discuss the adjustment process below.

Adjustment to Demand Change in an International Setting

How is equilibrium achieved? What happens when there is an exogenous change in demand in an open economy. One way of looking at these phenomena is to make use of the aggregate demand and supply diagram and the demand and supply of money diagram, we introduced in Chapters 7 to 10 and the demand and supply for foreign exchange graph introduced in Chapter 11.

In Fig. 12.1, Panel A (Aggregate Supply and Demand), on the vertical axis is price and on the horizontal axis is income. Equilibrium income and price are at Y_1 and P_1. In Panel B (Demand and Supply of Money), the interest rate is

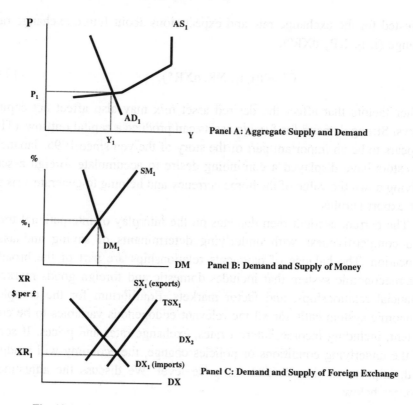

Fig. 12.1   International Adjustment: Equilibrium Starting Position.

on the vertical axis, and the demand for money and supply of money are measured on the horizontal axis. The equilibrium interest rate is at $\%_1$. In Panel C (Demand and Supply of Foreign Exchange), the exchange rate is determined by equilibrium in the supply and demand for foreign exchange from trade and capital flows. DX stands for the demand for foreign exchange, to purchase imports, for example. SX stands for the supply of foreign exchange from exports, and TSX stands for the total supply of foreign exchange from exports and from net capital inflows. The equilibrium foreign exchange rate is XR_1. Note that the vertical axis on this panel is scaled, dollar per pound Sterling, so that a move in the up direction means dollar depreciation and a move downward means appreciation. The dark solid lines stand for the initial equilibrium. The dashed and dotted lines in subsequent figures, indicate changes that are part of the adjustment to new conditions. In all the cases below, we will assume that there is an investment boom, sharply increasing aggregate demand. As a consequence of this disturbance, how and where does a country reach a new equilibrium? (This discussion is difficult. We present it verbally and graphically.)

Equilibrium with Floating or Fixed Exchange Rates

As we have noted, there are significant differences between the cases of fixed and floating exchange rates. As we will see, it also makes an important difference whether capital flows are restricted or free. First, we begin by contrasting floating exchange and fixed exchange rates. Here, we assume that international financial flows are restricted.

The floating exchange rate case

Suppose there is an investment boom. In Fig. 12.2, aggregate demand increases. Economic activity rises, income increases, imports increase, and because of rising prices and demand pressures, exports decline. In Panel A, this represents first a shift to the right of the aggregate demand curve to AD_2. In Panel B, higher income causes a shift of the money demand curve to DM_2. In the absence of monetary policy accommodation, the interest rate will go up to $\%_2$. As we have noted in Chapter 10, there is crowding out in the sense that interest sensitive expenditures are reduced; investment would have been still higher if the interest rate had not risen. Finally, the exchange rate effect is shown in Panel C. The increase of imports, as a result of higher Y, causes the demand for foreign exchange to shift right to DX_2. Since we have assumed that capital flows are restricted, there is no change in capital flows. The new exchange rate, XR_2, shows a depreciation of the exchange rate. That makes imported goods more expensive and exports cheaper so that imports and exports would change. These changes are also built into the change in aggregate demand. The principal international adjustment is through the

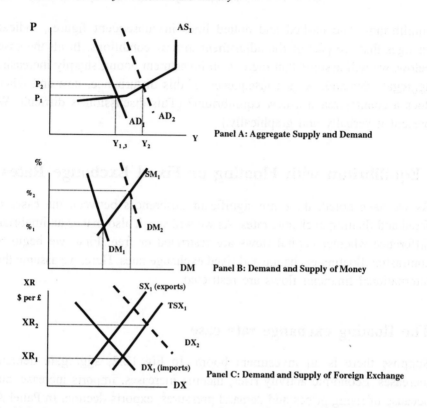

Fig. 12.2   International Adjustment: Floating Exchange Rate, Restricted Capital Markets.

change in the exchange rate and the impact on imports and exports, though, as we note, with restricted international capital flows, there is also an interest rate impact. Equilibrium is achieved simultaneously in all of the figures. In equilibrium, the values of Y, P, %, X and M, will be consistent. The domestic interest rate is higher than international interest rates since capital flows are controlled preventing additional capital inflow.

The fixed exchange rate case

We now turn to the case of fixed exchange rates. Beginning with equilibrium, we ask, as before, what changes occur if there is an exogenous boom in investment demand. While imports and exports change in response to higher income and prices, the exchange rate does not change. The central bank practices exchange rate intervention, using foreign exchange reserves to buy sufficient domestic currency in the foreign exchange market to prevent exchange rate depreciation. This means there will be an impact through the reduction in the money supply.

In Fig. 12.3, Panel A, there is an expansion of aggregate demand associated with the investment boom and changes in net export demand to AD_2. This change will reflect only the change in GDP and not, as above, a change in the exchange rate, since that remains pegged. In Panel B, there is a reduction in the money supply, as a result of the exchange rate intervention activities

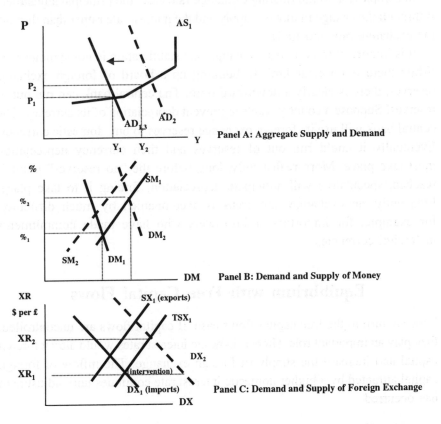

Panel A: Aggregate Supply and Demand

Panel B: Demand and Supply of Money

Panel C: Demand and Supply of Foreign Exchange

Fig. 12.3   International Adjustment: Fixed Exchange Rate, Restricted Capital Markets.

(purchase of international holdings of domestic currency) of the central bank, raising the domestic interest rate to $\%_3$. This rise of interest rates will tend to drive the aggregate demand curve, in Panel A, back toward $AD_{1,3}$ In Panel C, we see that central bank intervention has maintained the exchange rate at its original level (XR_1) despite the increase in demand for imports. Capital flows will not be affected in this example, even though the interest rate differential between domestic and foreign interest rates is bigger, because we have assumed that there are capital market restrictions. Maintaining fixed exchange rates and capital controls in the face of an investment boom requires continued foreign exchange intervention as long as there is a difference between domestic and foreign interest rates.

In comparison to the floating exchange rate case, the principal adjustment is through the change in money supply and the interest rate rather than through the exchange rate and trade.

It is important to note that exchange rate stabilization is not symmetrical. While there is no clear limit to building up a hoard of foreign exchange reserves, there is clearly a downward limit. The central bank can run out of reserves! Suppose a country wants to prevent depreciation of its currency. The central bank will use its foreign exchange reserves to buy domestic currency. Eventually it could run out of reserves and then currency depreciation must take place. More realistically, long before the "no reserves" point is reached, speculators will anticipate depreciation, forcing it to take place. Frequently, an exchange rate crisis is accompanied by much difficulty; for example, for importers or borrowers who have made commitments in foreign currencies.

Equilibrium with Free Capital Flows

Now we turn to the free capital flows case. If capital flows are uncontrolled, they play an important role. Higher domestic interest rates would attract foreign capital and increase the supply of foreign exchange. The inflow of foreign capital attracted by a higher domestic interest rate continues until adjustment has occurred.

The floating exchange rate case

In the floating exchange rate case, adjustment ultimately is determined by the exchange rate. An exogenous investment boom, will cause higher interest rates and will attract foreign capital. That will cause the exchange rate to appreciate, increasing imports and reducing exports. Aggregate demand and demand for money will shift back to their pre-investment boom levels and the domestic interest rate will again match world interest rates.

In Fig. 12.4, which corresponds in other aspects to Fig. 12.2, in Panel A, higher domestic demand appears in the shift of the AD curve to AD_2. This would lead to a higher domestic interest rate, $\%_2$, in Panel B. In Panel C, there are more imports and fewer exports, DX_2 and SX_2. The added inflow of

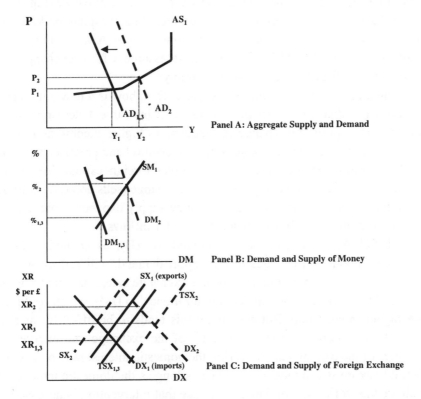

Fig. 12.4   International Adjustment: Floating Exchange Rate, Open Capital Markets.

capital shows up as a bigger difference between TSX_2 and SX_2 than between TSX_1 and SX_1. This capital inflow would cause the exchange rate to be higher (XR_3 is a higher exchange rate than XR_2 that would prevail in the absence of additional capital inflows). The resulting shift in trade, fewer exports and more imports, will cause the aggregate demand curve to shift back toward $AD_{1,3}$ — this will reduce the demand for money. This process will continue until the domestic interest rate is back down to the world interest rate level, $\%_{1,3}$. Importantly, the effect of open capital markets is that capital flows serve to eliminate differences between domestic and foreign interest rates.

The fixed exchange rate case

This case (Fig. 12.5) parallels the earlier fixed exchange rate case (Fig. 12.3), except that we assume an economy open to international capital markets. This case comes closest to the situation prevailing in East Asia, particularly in Thailand, prior to the 1997 crisis. Since we assume a fixed exchange rate, intervention will influence the money supply.

Beginning with equilibrium, we ask, as before, how is a new equilibrium established if there is an exogenous boom in investment demand? While imports and exports will change in response to higher income and prices, the exchange rate does not change, since the central bank practices exchange rate intervention. Higher interest rates attract foreign capital. To prevent appreciation, the central bank buys foreign exchange (sells domestic currency in foreign exchange markets) and the money supply expands. Note that this means the domestic boom is fueled by capital inflows.

In Panel A, the expansion of demand to AD_2, associated with the investment boom and changes in net export demand, will reflect only the change in GDP and not a change in the exchange rate, since that remains pegged. There is an increase in demand for money, to DM_2, which could lead to a higher interest rate. But eventually this tends to be offset by increase in the money supply to SM_2, as a result of the exchange rate intervention activities of the central bank, lowering the domestic interest rate to $\%_{1,2}$. The central bank must continue to intervene as long as the domestic interest rate is above the world rate. In Panel C, we see that intervention is necessary so

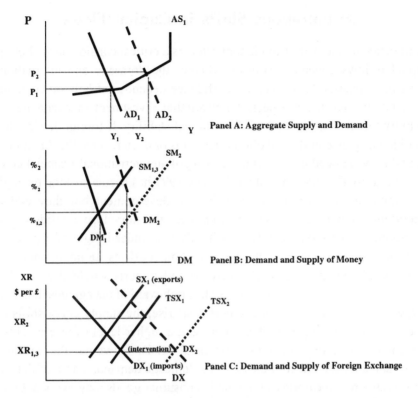

Fig. 12.5 International Adjustment: Fixed Exchange Rate, Open Capital Markets.

long as capital inflows are attracted by an interest rate differential and capital flows tend to appreciate the exchange rate. This suggests that maintaining fixed exchange rates in the face of an investment boom requires foreign exchange intervention and will feed additional money supply into the domestic system.

As we note earlier, potentially the problem would be different if the trade deficit is not offset by capital flows, since then the central bank must try to prevent depreciation. In this case, too there would be risk of unwanted currency depreciation if the central bank runs out of reserves but this risk is less since a conservative monetary policy and intervention to prevent currency depreciation would reduce money supply, raise interest rates, and attract foreign capital flows.

Autonomous Shifts in Capital Flows

Confidence on the part of foreign investors is a critical consideration. Foreign capital inflows depend greatly on whether the domestic and international economic situation looks secure. Confidence depends not only on economic expectations like the prospects for profitable investment or exchange rate stability but also on the outlook for political stability. If foreign lenders lose confidence, they could withhold further loans or even reverse the direction of capital flows altogether. This is the making of an international financial crisis. In this regard, the chaos in Indonesia since 1997 has been a striking example.

Capital inflows greatly help economic development but they add an important element of instability. Suppose investors lose confidence, as happened in East Asia. With less capital flow, or indeed flight of capital, the exchange rate depreciates. In the absence of other effects, an important caveat as we shall see, exports would increase and imports would decline. This translates into a stimulus to demand, a shift rightward of the aggregate demand curve. At the same time, since import costs rise, the supply curve shifts up. The result is likely to be higher output and a higher level of prices. This is the nature of readjustment to a financial crisis. However, the caveat is important since the effect of the crisis on domestic demand, a drop of demand for investment, inventories, and durable consumer goods may overwhelm the export demand shift, yielding an economy in recession. The movement of the curves and their slope are of critical importance. Much depends on how large a share of the economy is accounted for by imports and exports. The real sectors of a largely self-contained economy are little affected by financial crisis or currency depreciation. But if imports and exports account for a large part of GDP, currency depreciation may have big inflationary impacts.

Strong Export Performance — The Dutch Disease

Another interesting case is an economy that is highly successful in selling its primary resources, such as gas or oil in the world market. The potential surplus on current account can only be reconciled with capital flows with an appreciation of the exchange rate. This makes foreign goods cheaper and reduces the competitiveness of exports. This is a case that is often referred to as the

"Dutch disease," since it was what happened in the 1970s and 80s when the Netherlands developed its natural gas reserves for export and reduced the competitiveness of its manufacturing industry as a consequence. Fortunately, adjustment finally occurred and today the Netherlands is one of the most dynamic economies of Europe. But for some countries, like Venezuela, an important oil producer, the foreign exchange earnings from oil exports have resulted in a high exchange rate making it difficult for manufacturing industries to be competitive in world markets.

Real World of Exchange Rates and Capital Flows

As we have noted earlier, the distinction between floating exchange rates and fixed exchange rates are not as solid in the real world as in theory. Even a country that professes that it will keep its exchange rate solidly fixed can be forced to devalue when it runs out of foreign exchange. Indeed, history suggests that fixed exchange rate regimes are often subject to speculative attack when the underlying conditions suggest that the existing exchange rate cannot be maintained. As we have noted, this has often led to domestic and international financial crises, sometimes much worse than what would have occurred if exchange rates had been allowed to adjust gradually.

The distinction between the open and closed economy is also somewhat more clear in theory than in practice. Despite reductions in import restrictions worldwide, extensive regulations continue to affect trade in services. With respect to financial flows, the tendency for liberalization has been quite recent in the developing world. As a result of the misadventures resulting from the volatility of short term capital flows and capital flight, some countries like Malaysia reimposed restrictions on capital movements and others (Chile) have used taxes to "throw sand in the wheels" of excessively mobile capital.

The policy considerations will be considered in the next chapter.

International Adjustment and the "New Economy"

Globalization is an important aspect of the "new economy." It has had powerful impacts on business in developed and developing countries alike.

From the perspective of goods and services, markets have become larger and more competitive. For leading businesses, this has been tremendously advantageous. High-tech computer firms, financial services businesses, and entertainment giants have seen the entire world market as the field for competition. Vast new markets have been opened. The large scale of operation possible and the quick widespread introduction of new technology has offered enormous possibilities. E-commerce over the Internet and the worldwide cellular communications network offer further promise. Many of the firms taking advantage of these new horizons have been American, like Dell, GE and Citicorp, but many European ones, Nokia and Ericsson, or Japanese, Fuji and Hitachi, have also been successful in the global market.

From the point of view of more traditional heavy industries and for their workers in the mature industrial countries, the results have not always been so favorable. The US steel industry took a severe drubbing at the hands of foreign competitors. The consequences of free global trade for workers in the traditional industries have not been favorable. Wages have not grown as much as elsewhere in the economy and many jobs have been lost, hence the labor unions' traditional opposition to free trade. The US has gradually shifted from being the world primary manufacturing economy into a high level service and technology economy, as we have noted above.

For the developing world, the opportunities of trade have had multiple advantages. Exports are not only an opportunity to employ a large underutilized, often unskilled, labor force. Exports are typically an occasion for sharpening the quality of the product and updating production methods to make a country's goods competitive in the world market. Often, the prospective importers help the exporters set up their plants, sometimes they are subsidiaries or joint ventures of the multinational companies. As we have noted in Chapter 5, export trade has been the principal engine for economic development in East Asia.

The opening of the world economy to capital movements has been a more recent phenomenon. (Technically speaking, that is not quite true since the nineteenth century was a time of huge capital movements from Britain to the rest of the world. But capital movements were highly restricted during the Great Depression and after World War II. Large scale short term capital flows through banks and finance companies are a relatively recent phenomenon.) In recent years, many countries have lifted their capital controls. With increasing globalization, capital flows have flooded across the world to wherever there were opportunities to make returns, from developed countries to developing countries, and perhaps surprisingly, from Europe and Japan into the US. These flows consist of short- as well as long-term capital. Long term loans or bond issues have always been a way of drawing on foreign capital. (Note that foreign direct investment (FDI) which involved management as well as financial backing is an entirely different matter. The foreign direct investor often brings new technology as well as capital. Moreover, FDI is usually patient capital, in the sense that the foreign direct investor will stay with his investment through good times and bad. In recent years, a great deal of international capital movements has taken the form of short term capital movements — short term bank loans, purchases of equity on stock markets and bank deposits. These are short term in the sense that there is no prearranged holding period. Short term bank loans may be for six months at a time. The presumption is that they will be renewed, but, if times change or a devaluation is in the wind, the lenders may not be willing to roll over the outstanding loan. Often, as in East Asia in 1997, there are mismatches. Short term foreign capital serves to finance domestic investment that can only be realized in the long term. This means that the international financial system becomes very precarious.

Implications for Business

The volatility of exchange rates poses important risks to business and finance. Small short term fluctuations in exchange rates do not cause serious problems for importers or exporters. The costs of exchange are not large and, in most cases, the exposure can be hedged. Contracts can be written to allow for exchange rate changes, especially if they are small and more or less predictable. The difficulty is if there are sudden unpredicted variations. For over ten years, the exchange rate of the Thai baht was approximately 25 to the US dollar. Suppose a firm in Thailand had made commitments to purchase machinery in the US. The commitment was probably made on the assumption that the exchange rate would not swing far. A sudden devaluation carrying the baht to 50 to the dollar would double the cost. Similarly, a loan denominated in dollars would now take twice as many baht to repay. Difficulties with exchange rate fluctuations may also be serious with respect to foreign direct investments. The return on the investment and its capital value depends on the exchange rate. A devaluation abroad means that earnings are reduced when they are translated to home currency, indeed that the value of the foreign investment is less than had been anticipated. This explains the preference by many businesses for fixed exchange rates. Alas, fixed exchange rates do not seem to be guaranteed, as market forces often force devaluation even when a stable exchange rate had been promised.

Questions for Discussion

* Describe the cases of:
  1. floating and fixed exchange rates,
  2. restricted and open capital markets.

* How do GDP, interest rates and exchange rates respond to an investment boom? What are the differences between the various cases we have considered?

* Use the graphical AD/AS, DM/SM and SX/DX framework discussed above to look at the consequences of:
  1. a loss of confidence by foreign investors,
  2. the success of an export promotion drive,
  3. an increase in government spending.

* Suppose there is political turmoil and confidence in the economy collapses. What might be the impact on the exchange rate?

* Suppose a huge new oil supply that can be exported is discovered. What might be the effect on the exchange rate and on the international competitiveness of other domestically produced products?

* What might be the priority objectives of business managers with regard to international economic conditions?

Chapter 13

Policies in the Open Economy

The tasks of stabilization and development policy are considerably different and more challenging when one takes into account international trade and capital flows. In this chapter, we consider policy and policy-making international institutions in an open international economic system.

Introduction

As we noted at the close of the last chapter, an important feature of world economic development has been the gradual opening of many countries to foreign trade, investment and capital flows. Many economists, particularly from the United States, have looked to the static optimization properties of free competitive markets to argue that free trade and capital movements would ultimately be beneficial to all. For many countries, the dynamic effects relating to international competition may be even more important. However, some developing country economists have expressed reservations, arguing, for example, that liberalization of trade and capital movements may be of greater benefit to the rich mature world than to the LDCs. The experience of East Asia has supported the liberalization position, not so much for its static as for its dynamic effects. The East Asian countries have shown dramatic progress as a result of trade, foreign competition, technology transfers and foreign direct investment. There is little doubt that integration into the world economy is helpful in fostering economic development.

On the other hand, as we have noted above, inflows of short term foreign capital may have fueled investment and asset booms that were not warranted by underlying economic conditions, causing serious economic problems. The collapse and financial crisis in the East Asian countries that followed such a boom had widespread repercussions throughout their economies. For this reason, some economists are now urging caution with regard to financial opening, suggesting that restrictions be maintained, at least, on short term foreign borrowing and lending.

Regardless of one's view about international opening and liberalization, the globalization of the world economy appears to be an inevitable and logical trend. Consequently, policy questions should be considered from the perspective of open economies or at least from the perspective of economies that are in the process of opening. The important point is that policy makers in an economy exposed to free trade and capital flows have more limited room for independent policy and far more need for international cooperation than those in a closed economy.

In this chapter, we will first discuss the nature of the open economy. Then we will pose policy questions in an economy open to capital flows, the so-called Mundell-Fleming case. And then we will return to the more realistic view of how some degree of regulation of trade and capital movements would alter the picture. In connection with international policy cooperation, we will consider the role of the principal international institutions and monetary-trade unions, the International Monetary Fund (IMF), the World Bank, the Organization for Economic Cooperation and Development (OECD), the World Trade Organization (WTO), and the European Union (EU), Finally, we will ask about the potential effects of the "new economy" in today's global economic setting.

Making Policy in an Open Economy

In earlier parts of this volume, we have not explicitly considered the implications for policy that an economy is likely to be open to capital flows as well as international trade in goods and services. We have recognized in Chapters 11 and 12 that the exchange rate is influenced by the trade and other current account flows, and that it is also affected by capital flows. We continue to assume a fairly liberal trade regime, so that imports and exports can adjust to the exchange rate. If the exchange rate appreciates, there will be more imports and fewer exports. Exchange rate depreciation, in turn, will cause exports to increase and imports to fall, reducing the trade deficit.

Inflows of capital offset the current account, except for changes in foreign exchange reserves. In a world of fluctuating exchange rates, if capital inflows tend to fall short of the current account deficit, the exchange rate will depreciate until a new equilibrium is reached. And, similarly, if a current account surplus does not tend to be offset by capital outflows, there will be a tendency for the exchange rate to appreciate until a new equilibrium which matches the current and capital account balances is reached. In a fixed exchange rate case, central bank intervention in the foreign exchange market to maintain a fixed exchange rate affects the domestic money supply and interest rates. If there is a balance of payments surplus, the central bank will buy foreign exchange increasing the domestic money supply. If there is a deficit, it will sell foreign exchange for domestic currency. If foreign exchange reserves run out, the exchange rate may depreciate after all, usually in a financial crisis.

The issue posed here is: What does financial "opening" imply for a country's ability to manage its domestic policy? As we have seen, there are important differences between the situation where the exchange rate is allowed to float and the case where intervention is used to maintain a fixed exchange rate.

Policy in the Floating Exchange Rate Situation

We visualize an open economy that allows free inflows and outflows of capital. These flows may take the form of accumulation of bank deposits, loans, or financial investments (purchases of shares) by foreigners. Foreign capital is attracted by the opportunity to earn a high return, either interest or dividends, higher than can be earned at home or as a result of anticipated exchange rate appreciation. In other words, Japanese investors are willing to put their funds into US dollar securities because the interest rate in the US is higher than in Japan and/or because the US dollar is expected to appreciate relative to the yen. In equilibrium, with fully open capital markets and a freely floating exchange rate, a country's interest rate will match that of other countries (except for risk premia).

Suppose, now that the country is in a recession. The authorities want to stimulate aggregate demand. What is the appropriate policy, monetary or fiscal?

Monetary policy would call for a reduction in interest rates, usually through open market operations, to increase money supply and credit in the hope of stimulating investment. The reduced interest rate will cause capital to flow out until interest rates are back at the international level. An attempt to stimulate the economy with monetary policy would not ultimately lower the interest rate. But the attempt to lower interest rates will depreciate the exchange rate. This is the important step. It will improve international competitiveness and provide stimulus through an increase in exports (and a reduction in imports). Care must be taken since exchange rate depreciation may also have unwanted impacts on confidence or inflation.

What about fiscal policy? In a recession, this would mean a fiscal stimulus through increases in government spending, increases in transfer payments, or reductions in tax rates. The exact composition of a fiscal stimulus package may vary depending on the particular targets and conditions. A fiscal stimulus will shift the aggregate demand curve to the right and, given the money supply, it will tend to raise interest rates. In the open economy case, higher interest rates will attract foreign capital and bring the interest rate back down to the prevailing international level. The inflow of capital will cause the exchange rate to appreciate and will reduce export competitiveness. The gain in domestic demand as a result of fiscal policy stimulus is likely to be offset by a reduction in exports. Fiscal policy is not likely to be effective. The results are summarized in the first row of Table 13.1.

Table 13.1   Open Economy Stimulus Policy Options Under Alternative Assumptions.

	Monetary Policy	Fiscal Policy
Floating Exchange Rate	**yes**, lower %, lower cap inflow, lower x rate, more exports	**no**, more expenditure, higher %, higher x rate, less exports
Fixed Exchange Rate	**no**, more money, lower % rate, x rate intervention reduces money supply and raises interest rate back up	**yes**, expenditure stimulus causes increase in % rate, attracts capital inflow and increase in money supply, to old % rate

Policy in the Fixed Exchange Rate Case

As we have noted earlier, maintaining a fixed exchange rate assumes that the central bank will intervene in foreign exchange markets. When the exchange rate tends to depreciate from the central bank's target rate, the central bank must use its foreign exchange reserves to buy domestic currency. Domestic money supply shrinks! In the opposite direction, if the exchange rate strengthens, the central bank intervenes by buying foreign currency for domestic currency. The supply of domestic currency expands.

We ask again about the effectiveness of fiscal and monetary policies under these conditions (Table 13.1, second row). Monetary policy does not work in this case. A monetary stimulus would tend to reduce interest rates. But in order to stabilize the exchange rate, the central bank must intervene by buying domestic currency (and selling foreign exchange). The original increase in money supply is offset by the reduction of money supply as a result of the intervention needed to offset currency depreciation. Therefore, monetary expansion has no impact.

Fiscal policy does work effectively in this case. An increase in government expenditures (or a tax cut) will cause aggregate demand to rise. If the money supply is fixed, interest rates would go up and private investment would decline. Remember that earlier we have discussed this as "crowding out." But in the open capital flows case, this would not be for long. An inflow of foreign capital would be attracted by higher interest rates. To prevent this from appreciating the exchange rate, intervention by the central bank will mean purchases of foreign exchange for domestic currency. With more domestic currency, interest rates will come back down. There will be no *crowding out*! In other words, the fiscal stimulus will not cause higher interest rates and will not crowd out private investment, making it all the more effective. In other words, in the open capital market case with fixed exchange rates, monetary policy will not work, but — surprise! — fiscal policy will.

Policy in the Partially Open Economy

In the real world, we seldom encounter a fully open economy. There are many institutional and legal barriers to capital flows between countries. Smaller countries often have extensive regulations but a few, like Hong Kong (China), have a tradition of wide open trade and capital flows. Large countries have always been more insulated from the world economy. Even when there is not much intervention in international trade and finance, simply the fact that a country is large and self-contained means that it has substantial power to determine its internal economic policy. Trade and capital flows in large countries have significant influence, but are not so dominant that the open economy case applies. An important study by Feldstein and Horioka shows that investment and domestic saving within most countries are highly related and that the relationship is persistent. This study has been taken as evidence that international flows are not sufficient to cause full equilibrium adjustment as in the theoretical open economy case. The persistence of interest rate differentials between countries points in the same direction. However, in recent years, globalization has surely increased the influence of international flows in many parts of the world.

Most economies are not fully open, so that the domestic economy policy discussion in Chapter 10 still has substantial validity. As the US economy slowed in 2001, the Bush administration could argue that a reduction in income taxes would stimulate economic activity without greatly affecting interest rates, capital flows and the exchange rate.

International Policy Cooperation and Coordination

Management of policy faces considerable challenges in a world where economies are relatively open and where countries interact through capital flows as well as trade. Much international economic policy is effected through formal and informal cooperation between the monetary and trade authorities in many countries. Some international cooperation represents long term relationships, but often it is a response to an emergency situation.

Policy coordination is carried out formally through a number of international agencies, in particular, the IMF, the World Bank, the WTO and the OECD. In this section, we consider the roles of these organizations.

The International Financial and Trade Institutions

The major international economic institutions grew out of the 1944 Bretton Woods conference. The aim was to set up institutions that would prevent a repetition of the competitive devaluations and "beggar thy neighbor" trade policies that helped to make the pre-World War II period a time of worldwide depression. At the same time, there was also clearly a need to provide capital for countries that had been devastated by war or that had fallen behind in development. The idea was to create three institutions:

1. The International Monetary Fund (IMF) to promote international exchange rate stability and monetary cooperation.
2. The International Bank for Reconstruction and Development (now the World Bank) to provide capital for rebuilding and for economic development.
3. The World Trade Organization to oversee trade relationships among countries and to facilitate setting up an open multilateral trading system.

In addition, the Organization for Economic Cooperation and Development (OECD), the body facilitating policy coordination among the developed countries, dates from the immediate post-World War II years.

While, today, some economists are questioning how these organizations operate, they have undoubtedly had a good deal of success in making possible a more stable world economy. In this section, we provide a brief summary of how these institutions operate.

The International Monetary Fund (IMF)

The original aim at Bretton Woods was to set up a system of stable exchange rates linked to the US dollar as the reserve currency. Fixed exchange rates would be maintained, hopefully, for long periods of time and would be changed only if there was so-called "fundamental disequilibrium." The role of the IMF was to provide needed reserves when countries ran short of foreign exchange, to avoid depreciating the exchange rate, and to help make a transition when changes in exchange rates were required. After the floating of the US dollar in 1971 and the worldwide shift to floating (though often managed) exchange rates, the role of the IMF changed considerably. More recently, the countries running into balance of payments difficulty were mostly developing countries. The IMF provided them with emergency assistance and guided their economic policy toward more conservative, less inflationary directions. The typical IMF loan agreement contained conditionality clauses, calling for reductions in government spending, conservative monetary policy, and in recent years, structural reform of the banking system and corporate governance. Relating to the 1997 East Asian crisis, the IMF stepped in and provided necessary loans to Thailand, Indonesia and Korea. As the world economy becomes more interrelated, particularly with respect to capital flows, the IMF may play an increasingly important role. After all, the IMF's task is not just facilitating adjustment in an individual country. It is preventing the collapse of a closely interrelated worldwide financial system.

The World Bank

Responding to the perceived need of many countries for capital, the World Bank makes or underwrites loans for long term projects as well as for short term adjustment. These loans are usually at terms that are more favorable, with respect to interest rate and duration, than what would ordinarily be available from commercial enterprises.

As the advanced countries have reduced their needs for such special funding, most of the World Bank's lending has gone to developing countries and to the transitional economies. Many of the World Bank's loans come with conditionality clauses like the IMF's to make sure that macro- and micro-economic policies are consistent with the aims of the World Bank-supported projects. Over time, the World Bank has extended its activities into many areas outside of traditional infrastructure investment, for example into agricultural development, health, environment, structural reform, etc. In recent years, the World Bank has worked closely with the IMF providing added support, particularly for required structural changes, for IMF adjustment programs. The World Bank played a considerable role in dealing with the 1997 East Asian crisis.

The World Trade Organization (WTO)

The youngest of the international organizations (1995) grew out of the General Agreement on Tariffs and Trade (GATT). The WTO deals with the rules of trade between countries. In contrast to other organizations, it does not make decisions or provide loans. Rather, it administers the international agreements about trade like the 1986–94 Uruguay Round of tariff reductions. These negotiations are also creating rules for dealing with trade in services, intellectual property and dispute settlements. The aim is to establish a non-discriminatory trading system. Each country is assured that its exports will be treated fairly and consistently, and in turn, agrees to do the same for imports from other countries. In recent years, agreements have been reached on liberalization of telecommunications, and financial services. A new General Agreement on Trade in Services (GATS) will open some service sectors to non-discriminatory international trade. New talks have begun on agriculture and advanced services Many of the world's countries, both developed and developing, are members. Some special provisions in the trade agreements favor developing countries. China is striving to meet the WTO's rules on trade as it joins the organization.

The Organization for Economic Cooperation and Development (OECD)

The OECD started out as the institution that planned for and disbursed US and Canadian aid for reconstruction in Europe after World War II — the Marshall Plan. It evolved to become a setting in which governments could discuss and develop economic and social policy. The OECD Secretariat collects data, monitors trends, and analyzes and forecasts economic developments. The OECD makes policy recommendations but does not have the power to enforce them. The activities of the organization have spread broadly. Today, departments of the OECD consider social issues, trade, environment, agriculture, technology, taxation, etc. This work is done in close consultation with policy makers from the member countries who meet regularly in the committees of the OECD. The OECD has traditionally been a club of the well-to-do developed countries. How much the world has changed is illustrated by the fact that, in the mid-1990s, Korea and Mexico joined the OECD. They had achieved a level of development and industrialization equal to that of many OECD member countries when the organization was first established.

Case 13.1
Forecasting at the OECD

As we have noted above, macro forecasting and international policy coordination are one of the principal functions of the OECD. Some years ago, the author participated actively in this forecasting process. An interesting picture of the need for international cooperation arose in the forecasting meetings. Twice a year, the forecasters from the OECD countries would get together to present their country's forecasts. The OECD staff would then enter these separate country forecasts into their computer model to see whether they were consistent. After all, total exports have to be equal to total imports and each country's exports have to match the imports of its trade partners. At the end of the day, the OECD would report how far off forecasts were. Almost always, the sum total of exports would exceed the sum total of imports. The country forecasters had been optimistic about exports. The OECD would then provide revised consistent forecasts for each of the member countries. For the large countries, the forecast would generally change very little. But smaller countries, very dependent on trade with their neighbors, frequently found large changes between their original forecast and the OECD's consistent version. I remember the discomfort of a very eminent older economist from the Netherlands presented with a drastic revision of his country's projection. "This is not my forecast!"

International Trade Areas and Currency Unions

The creation of broad international free trade areas and currency unions has important implications for the development of international trade and financial flows. We are learning that it has important implications as well for stabilization policy.

Since World War II, international free trade areas have been created in Europe (EU), in North America (NAFTA), in Latin America (Mercosur), in East Asia (AFTA), etc. While the direct motives for establishing these trading zones have varied, some political and some economic, they have generally sought to increase the scale of markets and the extent of competition beyond that of the relatively small member countries. In this section, we will focus our discussion on the most important of these areas, the EU, that has carried the process of international integration the furthest and that may ultimately encompass almost all of the countries of Western, Central and Eastern Europe.

The European Union (EU)

The EU had its beginnings with six continental European countries in the Treaty of Rome (1957). The objectives, to create a common market without trade barriers or tariffs, were not only economic but also political. From an economic perspective, the European countries were trying to establish a common market in which it would be possible to achieve large scale production and competition. From a political perspective, this represented an effort to reconcile the differences between Germany and France, dating from before World War I, and to make a place for Germany as part of an integrated European community. Today's EU has its beginnings with the Single European Act (1987) which was intended to gradually remove all barriers to trade in goods and services, and movements of capital and people. This will provide a framework towards an ultimate political union. The EU has grown to 15 members including Great Britain and Ireland.

Since 1979, Europe sought to maintain internal exchange rate stability, permitting its currencies only small exchange rate variations relative to one another, while allowing all its currencies to float together against outside currencies. This arrangement, the European Monetary System (EMS), was known as the "snake" because all the member country currencies were kept in a narrow band with respect to each other and the band was allowed to fluctuate against the rest of the world. It worked well enough until the early 1990s when Britain was forced to devalue the pound Sterling, leaving the EMS. Under the Treaty of Maastrich (1993), the European countries (this time without Britain) committed themselves to giving up their separate currencies for the *Euro* which was introduced commercially in 1999 and will be distributed as currency at the beginning of 2002.

A monetary union can only work when most of the countries are on a similar monetary/fiscal policy track and when the macroeconomic performance of their respective economies is not way out of line. To join the European Monetary Union (EMU), each country committed itself to so-called convergence criteria. Their inflation rates and interest rates had to be within a narrow range of the region's average. They were not permitted to run large budget deficits nor to have huge debts relative to their GDPs. Twelve countries joined the EMU, some after some creative accounting permitted them to meet the requirements.

All member countries gave up not only their ability to issue currency and maintain their independent exchange rate but also gave up all control of monetary policy to the region's European Central Bank (ECB). As part of their Stability and Growth Pact, member countries are supposed to keep their budget deficits to less than 3% of GDP except in case of a drastic recession. The European Commission has the power to impose fines on countries that exceed the deficit target.

The EMU represents a radical realignment of economic policy-making in continental Europe. Member governments no longer control monetary policy. That is the responsibility of the ECB, and they have only limited authority to develop counter cyclical fiscal policy. We have yet to face up to a serious challenge to these constraints. Economists have worried about the "one size fits all" character of these regulations. Suppose, for example, that a country developed a high rate of unemployment. There can be no local monetary policy, since that is all handled by the ECB. Fiscal policy is also limited. Since member countries are still separate politically, one wonders what the political response to such a situation would be. Alternatively, in case there is inflationary pressure, what action could a country take to fight inflation? How might it respond to the loss of competitiveness as a result of rising local prices?

The "optimal currency area" perspective is suggestive. This idea was Prof. Mundell's response to the question of how large optimally a common market/common currency area should be. He argued that it was essential that within a currency area there is significant mobility of capital and labor. If a region became non-competitive, its shipments, i.e. exports to other regions in the currency area will fall short of its receipts. How does adjustment take place, since the exchange rate is fixed and there is no local monetary or fiscal policy? Adjustment would take place through a decline in income, with labor moving to other parts of the currency area where real wages are higher. If there is not much labor mobility, these adjustments can be impeded and may cause for long periods of hardship.

At this time, the EU/EMU faces some important challenges. It is still not clear whether or when the three countries that did not join EMU — Britain, Denmark and Sweden — will eventually join. Even more of a challenge is the desire by many other countries in Eastern Europe, most of them "transition" countries, to become part of Europe. Many of their economies are still in disarray and most are not yet ready to meet EU requirements. When all of them were to join — Bulgaria, Hungary, Poland, Romania, Czech Republic, Slovakia, Latvia, Lithuania, Estonia, Slovenia, Cyprus and Malta (others like Turkey are waiting in the wings) — the EU would encompass almost 30 countries, a very unwieldy organization. Finally, there are the questions of macro policy management. Already, the EU has complained to Ireland about excessive inflation and budgetary ease. Deterioration of economic conditions in some of the member countries could pose some serious problems for the EU.

The international organizations maintain very informative websites at:

http://www.oecd.org
http://www.IMF.org
http://www.worldbank.org
http://www.wto.org
http://europa.eu.int

Policy in a "New World Economy"

Information technology has crossed international boundaries. It has changed the nature of internationally traded goods and services. It has become a facilitator for trade. It has also greatly eased and speeded up the process of international financial transactions.

The "new world economy" is highly interactive. The links between countries involve more dimensions: trade, tourism, financial flows, intellectual products and services, etc. A generation ago, many countries were still protected and isolated. Today's growing international interaction has brought new challenges to policy-making. In open economies, policy makers must take into account the actions of the neighbors and trade partners. Particularly if international financial markets are free, policy makers are very limited in the independent actions they are able to take. International policy coordination is at a premium. On occasion, that may mean that the interest of a particular country must be sacrificed for the well-being of the broader regional group.

This places a heavy burden on political considerations. It would be naive to claim that economic decisions can be made independently of national and international politics. An open world economy calls for rational collaboration that may represent a difficult challenge to political leaders in various countries.

Implications for Business

An open non-discriminatory world trading and financial system offers great advantages for international business but it also exposes firms to new complex risks. It is possible to extend manufacturing and trading activity into many new regions, making use of their competitive advantages and increasing the scale of production. For example, products that require lots of labor will be produced in countries where labor is cheap and will be imported into countries where labor is expensive. An interesting example is the encapsulating of computer chips. Each chip, though a very high-tech product, must be properly packaged and connected to a large number of electrical leads. This labor-intensive effort is most economically done in a developing country, like the Philippines, where labor is inexpensive even though technology is not sufficiently advanced to produce the chips themselves.

The risks of operating in an open world system involve not only the typical risks of setting up businesses in foreign lands. They add the very substantial risk of unanticipated swings in the exchange rate. Even if many of the domestic forces in the country in which a firm is operating have been taken into account, external developments may influence the results of business in many ways. For example, in 2000, a modest appreciation of the US dollar caused IBM to explain that a decline of its earnings in Europe as a result of translation into US dollars would significantly affect is profit performance.

Legal, political and cultural considerations are often serious issues as well. International business managers and investors must be aware of the special legal/political/social circumstances that prevail in their industry and in the countries in which they plan to operate.

Questions for Discussion

* How does an open financial system limit a country's domestic policy actions? Suppose the country is allowing its exchange rate to float. Suppose, alternatively, that it is trying to maintain a fixed exchange rate.
* What do we mean by international policy coordination? What are the risks of not coordinating economic policies internationally?
* How do we distinguish the functions of the principal international economic institutions? Do their functions overlap? Should they be cooperating with one another?
* What political, legal and social considerations may have impact on your industry?

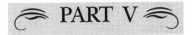

PART V

The Challenges of Stabilization, Growth and Development in the "New Economy"

In this part, we summarize the lessons of the previous chapters and of real world experience. What are the perspectives of the "new economy?" How do developed countries deal with the new opportunities and challenges? How do developing countries, with rather different policy priorities, succeed with the task of economic development? What are the lessons for business in the "new economy?"

Chapter 14

The Lessons for Growth
and Development

What are the lessons of historical experience for continued growth and development in the developed and developing countries? How does the "new economy" change macroeconomics? In this chapter, we summarize the prospects for a new era of rapid technology change and productivity growth, and we consider the challenges they pose to developed and developing countries.

Macroeconomics and the "New Economy"

The developments to which we have given the name "new economy" represent important changes, a new industrial revolution, so to speak. But they do not drastically re-structure the theory of macroeconomics. The basic framework of economic theory remains, though we may want to adapt some of it to new realities. The changing structure of the economy poses new challenges for the developed world and for the developing countries.

How is the basic framework of the macroeconomy affected? Looking closely at the structure of demand and supply, there are some important issues.

On the demand side, it is apparent that the emphasis of traditional macroeconomics on production of goods, with important capital plant requirements and inventories, is not entirely appropriate in a world where much activity is in high-tech services. Engineering, software production and operation, research, etc. call for very different inputs. Primary emphasis in these fields is on intellectual capital and highly educated and trained workers. Much depends on the interrelationships between these factors. There are important implications for growth of the "new economy." Moreover, over the business cycle, the behavior of "new economy" activities is likely to be very different from "old economy" hard goods industries. The traditional business cycle of hard industry may be replaced by more gradual adjustments in the knowledge-based fields.

On the supply side, the development of "new" industries has called into question the definition of capacity and full employment. We are no longer sure when capacity constraints begin to bite, since it is not so much a matter of physical capacity but of the ability of intellectual workers to meet output schedules. We are no longer sure about the significance of unemployment numbers, since intellectual workers are not laid off like production workers. Employers have much invested in their workers and make every effort to keep them. On the other hand, highly skilled workers move readily for higher wages and better working conditions. When unemployment is low, there is little loyalty to employers.

As yet unresolved is the question of whether integrated markets on the Internet will have the effect of bringing the economy more rapidly to equilibrium than in the past. Perhaps, wage and price flexibility is enhanced in the "new economy" but the impact on the macroeconomy is not certain. In any case, the integration of the economy on the electronic network still has a long way to go, so that the effects on the efficiency of the operation of the economy are not yet widely apparent.

Policy makers have found it difficult to deal with economic change. In the United States, the debate about the "new economy" has obscured stabilization targets. Should the Federal Reserve have acted more quickly to slow the pace of economic expansion in the face of rapid productivity growth and relatively stable wages? In Europe, should labor markets have been liberalized and social benefits reduced sooner to improve market flexibility and the pace of economic change? In Japan, can large firms be allowed to go bankrupt and government deficits be reduced so that resources can be steered to "new economy" industries? In East Asia, can infrastructure and education be developed rapidly enough to meet the needs of competing in an increasingly integrated and technically advanced world economy? In many poor countries, can anything be done to join the "new economy" development process?

Policy Lessons for Industrial Economies

Policy priorities in the industrial countries have been rather different than in the developing world. The emphasis on employment and, often to a lesser extent, on price stability has outweighed the pressure for growth. But in recent years, concerns about economic stagnation have caused the European countries to put greater emphasis on the growth objective. This has not meant a swing toward greater government planning and active directive policy. On the contrary, it has been part of a conservative movement toward privatization and deregulation based on the motto: "Let markets operate."

Moves toward freer trade in goods, services and capital have broadened the scope for international interaction. The development of common markets and free trade areas and the creation of institutions to facilitate trading relationships have expanded the scope for globalization into capital flows, intellectual products, financial markets, and mergers and acquisitions across international boundaries.

The technical developments associated with the "new economy" have come at a time when intranational and international integration is growing apace. Computer networks are putting the transactions related to trade and finance into an electronic universe where they can take place instantaneously at minimal cost. Advanced scientific developments are increasing the pace of progress in communications, electronics, medicine, bioengineering, etc.

For the mature countries, this has meant a revival of growth potential. The US has been a "new economy" leader but other advanced countries are catching up. Where once, we might have been content with the modest growth and stability of a mature service economy, now we see more dynamic growth. But there are also important challenges. These involve:

With Respect to Growth:-

- Growing intellectual capital. As the advanced countries turn increasingly to high-tech employment, the level of intellectual capital required is growing rapidly. Workers must be able to deal with computer hardware and software and scientific processes. This calls for an ever more widespread advanced education and for lifetime learning as the knowledge required at an early point in workers' careers later becomes obsolete and must be updated.
- Ever-increasing scale of operation. Economies of scale are an important aspect of the "new economy." Many of the intellectual products used

have high initial cost but little marginal cost as the scale of operations is expanded. Within countries, this has led to consolidations and mergers. The move to greater scale has also encouraged cross border mergers and vast multinational corporations that scour the world in search of investment opportunities and acquisitions.

- Common standards. The need for large scale also calls for agreement on common technical and quality standards. Many of the debates between countries, on issues of intellectual property and food quality involve different perceptions of the appropriate standards. Sometimes these represent a barrier to the spread of "new" technology.

With Respect to Stability:

- Maintenance of internal macroeconomic stability. Rapid change is making the challenge of maintaining economic stability more difficult than in the past. As we have noted above, the issues involve appropriate forecasts and macro policies. Increasingly, we find that policies must be concerned with the supply side as well as with aggregate demand.
- The maintenance of external stability. While external stability does not mean fixed exchange rates, it is important to avoid international crises that disrupt the world economic system. For this reason, it is important to maintain a degree of stability with flexibility in the balance of payments and the exchange rate. International policy coordination is another important mechanism for assuring a stable international economy.
- Reconciliation of policies at the regional and at the local level. From a policy perspective, as the world economy becomes more integrated, there will be increasing need to coordinate policies between regional organizations and local governments. For example, in the European Union, macroeconomic policy for Euroland as a whole must take into account the special needs of the countries that are part of the broader region.

How to Succeed with Economic Development

The development issues and priorities for the developing countries are somewhat different from those faced by the advanced world. Moreover, not all developing countries are alike. We have noted the success of the East Asian countries in climbing up the development ladder (Chapter 5). Clearly, some countries like Korea, Taiwan and Singapore are much more advanced and closer to the "new economy" than others like Indonesia and Vietnam. In Latin America, Mexico is an example of the group of countries that are making rapid steps toward development. Most of these countries have been able to meet the challenges of developing manufacturing industries, producing products, often sophisticated ones, for export. Few of them are yet leaders in the "new economy." Turning to the rest of the world, some countries are making significant strides forward. Big countries like India and China are examples. But there are still traditional Third World economies that have a surplus of unskilled labor and little else. Some have other important resources — land, minerals, forests, water, and natural gas and oil that are being developed with capital from the advanced world. The poor countries lack capital — machinery, transportation equipment, communications and infrastructure. Most importantly, they lack the technical and managerial skills that are necessary for participating directly in the "new economy."

What lessons have we learned to succeed with economic development?

Lesson 1: A developing country must build up its capital stock through high rates of savings and investments.

Few developing countries have pulled themselves up entirely by their own bootstraps. But some, particularly in East Asia, have accumulated capital through extraordinarily high rates of savings, gross savings rates as high as 41% in Singapore and 33% in Korea. Economists do not agree on how to explain these high savings rates. They are not just a cultural phenomenon. It is important to make sure that domestic savings, both private and public remain at a high level to support rapid growth.

Most countries are understandably reluctant to become dependent on foreign capital, but direct foreign investment has made an important contribution to growth. In recent years, direct investment from Japan, Taiwan and, surprisingly, to a smaller extent, from the US and other countries has been a mainstay of economic expansion in East Asia. These investments have had a special payoff in that they usually come with foreign management expertise and advanced technology.

Lesson 2: To attract direct foreign investment, a country must provide a favorable environment for foreign capital.

Foreign investors are attracted by profitable and secure business opportunities, by a suitable economic environment, by favorable, transparent and stable legal regulations, and particularly, by freedom to repatriate profits. Foreign capital also requires a stable political climate, though not necessarily one based on a democratic consensus. In some developing countries, like India, political instability has had an unfavorable impact on foreign investment in the past. Today, inflows of capital are responding to a more favorable climate. Private investment typically goes into manufacturing plants, mining and farming ventures, and commercial real estate and hotels.

Lesson 3: Investments in infrastructure make important contributions to economic development.

Investments in roads, harbors, sewers and water supply, electrical power, etc. have traditionally been the responsibility of the public sector. Inadequate infrastructure threatens to become a barrier to growth in many developing countries where traffic jams, shipping delays, pollution and insufficient water and power supplies already hinder some business operations. Resources must be set aside to build public facilities. Recently, there has also been a surge of private capital into mega-projects formerly reserved for the public sector, like communications, power plants, rapid transit systems and toll roads.

Lesson 4: Modern industry and commerce require a highly educated labor force.

A trained labor force is a critical necessity for economic progress. Both Taiwan and Korea began their industrialization drives with massive investments in education. They have continued investments in human capital by expanding secondary and technical training and their university systems on a large scale. Education is costly and takes time. It is necessary to look far ahead to build a labor force with appropriate literacy, computer skills and engineering and management education at all levels. This represents a serious challenge for many developing countries.

The successful countries of East Asia have acquired modern technology that, once upon a time, was available only in Europe and North America. They have learned the "hard" technology associated with mass production manufacturing and also the "softer" skills required to design high quality products and to manage modern business.

Lesson 5: Technology transfer must be encouraged by providing an appropriate legal and economic environment.

Relationships with foreign businesses and universities are useful. Many enterprises in Taiwan and Korea have close links — contracts, minority share ownership, licensing agreements — with firms in the US and Japan. Technology transfer is frequently associated with foreign direct investment particularly by multinational companies. Transfers of "knowledge" hinge significantly on the protection of patents and copyrights.

The next three lessons turn to the appropriate policy background, first considering development policy, next microeconomic policy, and last macroeconomics.

Lesson 6: Export promotion should displace import substitution as a development strategy.

The export drive of some countries, particularly in East Asia, has been unprecedented. This expansion was not just a matter of growing demand, or of America's prodigious appetite for foreign goods. It was more a matter of conscious export development and promotion, an expansion of supply. As the production potentials of the East Asian Tigers increased, they established secure markets for their highly competitive products in the industrial world. They took part in a "product cycle," first selling textiles, footwear, apparel and simple electronics, then turning to more sophisticated products like personal computers and consumer electronics. More recently, they have gone into auto parts, auto assembly, and even, machinery. Because they are competing in a worldwide market, their industries have been able to operate at a large and efficient scale.

Infant industry protection of import substituting industries may still be appropriate at early stages of industrialization. But it is best to dismantle protective barriers as early as possible and to build the development process on export promotion with industries honed by exposure to world competition.

Lesson 7: Prices and exchange rates should reflect market-based values.

Unrealistic prices and exchange rates have been a barrier to growth in many countries of Latin America and Africa. Too low agricultural prices and too high urban prices reduce incentives for farm production; unrealistic interest rates distort resource allocation.

There is still debate among economists about the virtues of the free market as compared to an organized industrial policy. But there is little disagreement on the proposition that prices are vital guides to production and investment. Public sector interventions in the form of price and interest rate ceilings and artificial exchange rates often distort incentives away from development objectives and tend to slow growth.

A realistic exchange rate is particularly important. If the exchange rates is overvalued, imports will be cheap and exports will not be competitive. Countries using a high exchange rate "anchor" as a means to hold down inflation, have found their domestic industries overwhelmed by cheap imports. Many developing countries have tried to undervalue their currencies to make their goods more competitive in world markets. But, in the long run, an undervalued exchange rate makes essential imports too expensive and encounters opposition from the industrial countries who see it as unfair competition. Successful development has usually been based on prices and exchange rates that reflect world market conditions realistically.

Lesson 8: Stick to conservative fiscal and monetary policies.

What are appropriate fiscal and monetary policies for the developing world? One of the striking contrasts between Latin American economic development and that of East Asia was with respect to macroeconomic policy. Latin American countries, like Argentina and Brazil, ran huge budget deficits.

These deficits were financed by borrowing, and ultimately by "printing" money, leading to hyperinflation and vast foreign debts. The "debt crisis" in turn caused the 1980s to represent a "lost decade" with little or no growth in that part of the world. Only recently, after a turn toward conservative macroeconomics, has the outlook in Latin America improved.

In contrast, the successful East Asian countries were notable for many years for their conservative fiscal and monetary policies. They kept public sector deficits to a minimum; they closely controlled the money supply and the expansion of foreign debts. The East Asian financial crisis in 1997, that followed the abandonment of conservative fiscal and monetary policies, represents the exception that proves the rule. Conservative macroeconomic strategies appear to be the *sine qua non* of sustained growth and development.

Lesson 9: Participate closely in an integrated world economy.

Increasing linkages to the world economy have greatly benefited many of the world's developing economies. This is not simply a matter of increased trade. It involves flows of capital, technology and knowledge, all of which contribute to the growth of productivity. The linkages to other countries — markets for domestic products, sources of advanced capital goods and technology, and sources of competitive pressures — are most important. These dynamics are clearly more important for growth than traditional concerns with static optimization. Participation in the world economy is one of the keys to economic progress.

Is there only one way to successful economic development? There is much agreement on the lessons that we have considered above. They are drawn from the experience of the advanced countries and the most highly successful East Asian economies. They contain important guidelines for other countries that are not yet as far along the development path. But, they may not contain all the ingredients of successful development. Nor may they be the only way to development success.

It is interesting to note that there have been important differences even among the most successful East Asian countries, Taiwan and Korea, for example. Korea followed the Japanese model closely by adopting a highly structured industrial policy environment, with much government intervention, a small number of large, locally owned conglomerates (chaebols) aiming to build large scale heavy manufacturing industry. In contrast, Taiwan built a much smaller scale entrepreneurial environment on the basis of many independent companies, some with foreign backing.

We have noted above that East Asian development has been based on export orientation to developed country markets, particularly the US. There is still room for products of the developing countries in the mature world, particularly for the many products where the developing countries have a comparative advantage. The ability to upgrade technology and enter markets for more sophisticated products will be an important consideration. Since, there will be increasing competition in the production of mass-produced manufactures as more populous countries, like China, India, Indonesia, and Vietnam in Asia, and Mexico in North America, pursue an industrialization development strategy. Fortunately, living standards are rising in the countries that are now developing successfully. As they become high mass consumption economies, they will in turn provide markets for the upcoming developing countries.

Economic Development Policy and the "New Economy"

The impact of information technology in the developed world is quite apparent but the impact on many developing countries is not so clear. The question is: What does the "New Economy" contribute to economic progress in the developing countries? While some of the rapidly growing countries of East Asia have jumped, one might even say leapfrogged, into the "new economy," others are a long way from an information technology revolution. To give some examples, Singapore prides itself in establishing a "wired" island and a highly educated labor force. Malaysia is developing Cyberjaya, an Internet corridor, and Korea has a high rate of Internet and cellular phone penetration. On the other hand, the principal participation of these countries in information technology is not so much in the development of software as in the manufacture of important hardware components like chips and PCs. Other developing countries, even in East Asia still have a long way to go in business and consumer applications of information technology. As we note earlier, they lack the knowledge base, infrastructure and networks that support widespread applications of the new approaches. This represents at once a serious challenge and an opportunity. Integration into world markets will call for greatly improved technology and knowledge. Countries that can develop the requisite skill will play an important role in the "new economy."

Implications for Business

Are there also some lessons for business managers? How does our discussion of growth and stabilization in developed and developing countries provide guidelines for business decision-making? Much depends on the nature of business with which we are concerned — manufacturing or services, old economy or new economy, domestic or international.

Lesson 1: There are many business opportunities in developed and developing countries.

The information technology revolution has created a gamut of new opportunities in the developed world. Where once we thought that the limits of technology had been reached in the developed world, now we find numerous new options. These are not only in high-tech sectors. Many of the applications of the new economy are in traditional industrial and service sectors where new means of networking and communication offer possibilities for improved efficiency. There are also many similar opportunities in developing countries. But in these regions technology is not as far advanced. As a result, there will be more traditional industrial investments drawing on capital and technology from the developed world and taking advantage of cheaper labor and resources in the developing countries.

Lesson 2: The macroeconomic and political setting can have important implications for the success of a venture.

The macroeconomic situation can have important implications for whether a new investment succeeds or fails. Business decision makers track the economy closely. An unanticipated decline in demand and the resulting run-up of inventories can seriously affect the firm's profitability. A sudden burst of inflation, perhaps beginning with a rise in oil prices can be damaging. Business managers must be aware of the relationship between their organization and the broader economy. Many dimensions of macroeconomic activity must be taken into account. Political issues are also of great importance. In many cases, the economic situation is closely linked with political elements; Indonesia is a good example. Political considerations have more than just economic impact. They may determine the degree to which foreigners can participate, e.g. in what organizational form, in what industries, etc. They may greatly influence the legal setting for carrying on business, the ability of businesses to make independent profit maximizing decisions, for example. One need only look at the turmoil of business in Russia to recognize the potential difficulties.

Lesson 3: The risks of international integration must be recognized and measures must be taken to deal with them.

There is increasing evidence that international integration is not without risk. These risks apply in the domestic economy, subject to the vagaries of a rapidly changing world, and to an even greater extent, to businesses operating outside their home environment. Business managers must be aware of these risks and must be prepared to deal with them, preferably before the crisis rather than afterwards. For example, this means that contractual arrangements must deal with all eventualities; that foreign exchange risks must be covered; that local consultants must be employed, etc. Understanding the risks and dealing with them, where possible, are important aspects of business management in the "new economy."

Questions for Discussion

* What are the most important lessons for the management of macroeconomic policy in the developed world?
* Are the prescriptions for managing a developing country very different from those that are required to run a developed economy?

* What kind of opportunities does the "new economy" offer?
* How does the operation of the macroeconomy affect business? Discuss the different nature of macroeconomic impacts on different kinds of business.
* In what principal ways are international ventures more risky, more complex, and more difficult than domestic investments?

Index

303